Lecture Notes in Computer Science 12518

More information about this series at http://www.springer.com/series/7407

Külli Kori · Mart Laanpere (Eds.)

Informatics in Schools

Engaging Learners in Computational Thinking

13th International Conference, ISSEP 2020
Tallinn, Estonia, November 16–18, 2020
Proceedings

Springer

Editors
Külli Kori
Tallinn University
Tallinn, Estonia

Mart Laanpere
Tallinn University
Tallinn, Estonia

ISSN 0302-9743 ISSN 1611-3349 (electronic)
Lecture Notes in Computer Science
ISBN 978-3-030-63211-3 ISBN 978-3-030-63212-0 (eBook)
https://doi.org/10.1007/978-3-030-63212-0

LNCS Sublibrary: SL1 – Theoretical Computer Science and General Issues

This Springer imprint is published by the registered company Springer Nature Switzerland AG
The registered company address is: Gewerbestrasse 11, 6330 Cham, Switzerland

Preface

This volume contains papers presented at the 13th International Conference on Informatics in Schools: Situation, Evolution, and Perspectives (ISSEP 2020). The conference was held at Tallinn University, Estonia, during November 16–18, 2020. Due to COVID-19 related traveling restrictions for the majority of participants, the conference had to be switched to a partly online format.

ISSEP is a forum for researchers and practitioners in the area of informatics education, in both primary and secondary schools. The conference provides an opportunity for educators and researchers to reflect upon the goals and objectives of this subject matter, its curricula, various teaching and learning paradigms and topics, as well as the connections to everyday life, including the various ways of developing informatics education in schools.

This conference also focuses on teaching/learning materials, various forms of assessment, traditional and innovative educational research designs, the contribution of informatics to the preparation of individuals for the 21st century, motivating competitions, and projects and activities supporting informatics education in schools. The ISSEP series started in 2005 in Klagenfurt, Austria, with subsequent meetings held in Vilnius, Lithuania (2006), Torun, Poland (2008), Zurich, Switzerland (2010), Bratislava, Slovakia (2011), Oldenburg, Germany (2013), Istanbul, Turkey (2014), Ljubljana, Slovenia (2015), Münster, Germany (2016), Helsinki, Finland (2017), St. Petersburg, Russia (2018), and Larnaca, Cyprus (2019). The 13th ISSEP conference was hosted by Tallinn University in Estonia.

The conference received 53 submissions. Each submission was reviewed by up to four Program Committee members who evaluated the quality, originality, and relevance to the conference of all the submissions. Overall, the Program Committee wrote 132 reviews. The committee selected 18 papers for inclusion in the LNCS proceedings, leading to an acceptance rate of 34%. The decision process was made electronically using the EasyChair conference management system.

The previous ISSEP conferences attracted contributions in various topics ranging from informatics teacher education to methods of teaching informatics. While these topics were also present in ISSEP 2020, this time the main focus was on informatics competitions and computational thinking.

We would like to thank all the authors who responded to the call for papers and all the members of the Program Committee.

October 2020

Külli Kori
Mart Laanpere

Organization

General Chair

Mart Laanpere	Tallinn University, Estonia

Program Chair

Külli Kori	Tallinn University, Estonia

Local Organizers

Maia Lust	Tallinn University, Estonia
Katrin Kuus	Tallinn University, Estonia

Steering Committee

Erik Barendsen	Radboud University and Open University, The Netherlands
Andreas Bollin	University of Klagenfurt, Austria
Valentina Dagiene	Vilnius University, Lithuania
Yasemin Gulbahar	Ankara University, Turkey
Juraj Hromkovič	ETH Zurich, Switzerland
Ivan Kalas	Comenius University, Slovakia
Sergei Pozdniakov	Saint Petersburg Electrotechnical University, Russia

Program Committee

Mikko Apiola	University of Helsinki, Finland
Erik Barendsen	Radboud University and Open University, The Netherlands
Andrej Brodnik	University of Ljubljana, Slovenia
Špela Cerar	University of Ljubljana, Slovenia
Valentina Dagiene	Vilnius University, Lithuania
Christian Datzko	Wirtschaftsgymnasium und Wirtschaftsmittelschule Basel, Switzerland
Vladimiras Dolgopolovas	VU MIF, Lithuania
Gerald Futschek	Vienna University of Technology, Austria
Juraj Hromkovič	ETH Zurich, Switzerland
Mile Jovanov	Ss. Cyril and Methodius University, North Macedonia
Kaido Kikkas	Tallinn University of Technology, Estonia
Kati Mäkitalo	University of Oulu, Finland
Dennis Komm	ETH Zurich, Switzerland

Külli Kori	Tallinn University, Estonia
Marge Kusmin	Tallinn University, Estonia
Mart Laanpere	Tallinn University, Estonia
Peter Larsson	University of Turku, Finland
Marina Lepp	University of Tartu, Estonia
Inggriani Liem	Sekolah Teknik Elektro dan Informatika, Indonesia
Michael Lodi	University of Bologna, Italy, and Inria, France
Birgy Lorenz	Tallinn University of Technology, Estonia
Piret Luik	University of Tartu, Estonia
Maia Lust	Tallinn University, Estonia
Mattia Monga	Università degli Studi di Milano, Italy
Tauno Palts	University of Tartu, Estonia
Arnold Pears	KTH Royal Institute of Technology, Sweden
Hans Põldoja	Tallinn University, Estonia
Sergei Pozdniakov	Saint Petersburg Electrotechnical University, Russia
Andrus Rinde	Tallinn University, Estonia
Ralf Romeike	Freie Universität Berlin, Germany
Joze Rugelj	University of Ljubljana, Slovenia
Giovanni Serafini	ETH Zurich, Switzerland
Tomas Šiaulys	Vilnius University, Lithuania
Gabrielė Stupurienė	Vilnius University, Lithuania
Reelika Suviste	University of Tartu, Estonia
Maciej M. Syslo	UMK Torun, Poland
Michael Weigend	Universität Münster, Germany

Contents

Informatics Teacher Education

Curriculum and Pedagogical Issues

Tasks for Informatics Competitions

Difficulty of Bebras Tasks for Lower Secondary Blind Students

Ľudmila Jašková(✉) and Natália Kostová

Comenius University, Bratislava, Slovakia
jaskova@fmph.uniba.sk, kostova17@uniba.sk

Abstract. A special category for blind lower secondary students has been in the Bebras challenge since 2013. During its existence we have adapted 63 tasks for blind students. But in many cases their difficulty was not correctly determined. We have analysed the influence of various factors on the real difficulty of tasks. We have discovered a significant influence of affiliation to the thematic area. It is also important what cognitive operations the competitor must perform to solve the task. We also observed a lower success rate of younger blind students. It has not been confirmed that the length of the assignment would have a significant effect on the difficulty.

Keywords: Contest · Difficulty · Blind · Tasks · Factors

1 Introduction

The main goal of the Bebras challenge is to motivate students to be interested in informatics topics and to promote thinking that is algorithmic, logical, operational, and based on informatics fundamentals [1]. The idea is to encourage children to learn informatics concepts, and to support development of computational thinking [2]. Carey [3] claims, that tests and quizzes are an effective way of learning if students in a relatively short time get feedback and have opportunity to learn the right solutions. The Bebras contest fulfils this condition. Contestants know their score immediately and sample solutions with explanations are ready in few weeks. The archive of tasks from previous years also contributes to effective preparation of participants.

The competition is not only a tool for learning, but it is also a tool for researching and evaluating students' competencies, as it allows data from large number of respondents be obtained.

In keeping with the UN Convention on the Rights of Persons with Disabilities [4], learning is a basic right of every individual. It is therefore important to enable blind pupils to participate in the Bebras contest as well. Suggested adaptations of rules and tasks for blind students were presented in several surveys [5, 6]. These adaptations we will describe in the following section.

In Sect. 3, we provide an overview of several studies aimed at analysing the difficulty of Bebras tasks for able-bodied students. Our research focused on the influence of various factors on the difficulty of tasks is described in Sects. 4 and 5. In the last section we compare our findings with the findings of other authors and present the conclusions.

K. Kori and M. Laanpere (Eds.): ISSEP 2020, LNCS 12518, pp. 3–14, 2020.
https://doi.org/10.1007/978-3-030-63212-0_1

2 Bebras Contest for Blind

Blind students work with computer using a screen reader and the only information they can work with is text and sound. They cannot use a mouse to control the computer, but they enter input only using the keyboard. As regards the Bebras contest for mainstream students, they cannot participate at all, despite of the fact that they achieve comparable results with intact students in computer science classes. Bebras tasks contain elements inaccessible to the blind, such as images, colours, interactive features, and so on. To enable blind students to enter the competition, it was necessary to make some changes of rules [7]. We created a separate category for lower secondary blind students (aged 11 to 15) and another one for upper secondary blind students (aged 15 to 18). As a rule, able-bodied students of the same age can solve 15 tasks (5 easy, 5 medium and 5 hard) within 45 min. An average time for solving one task is 3 min. When testing blind students, the time is usually increased according to their individual needs. RNIB [8] suggests increasing the time by 25% to 100%. According to the recommendations of RNIB, the time should be extended by 50%. Since a standard school lesson lasts 45 min, we decided to set this as a limit for solving 9 tasks (3 easy, 3 medium and 3 hard). An average time for solving one task is 5 min. This means that blind students were given 60% more time than the able-bodied students.

Further we will focus only on the category of lower secondary blind students. The competition for them was held for the first time in 2013. The tasks were presented in a text document on the computer because lower secondary students were able to use a text editor smoothly. This could not be said about their experience with a web browser. Since 2017, the tasks have been presented in a web browser, as students who have learned to use a web browser at primary level have reached lower secondary level. But they could also use a text editor to write notes and process steps to solve tasks. In addition, they could use a pencil and foil to draw relief pictures and a relief table (see Fig. 1).

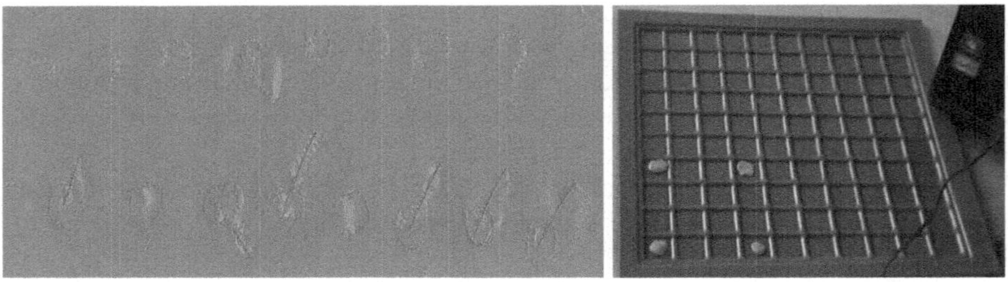

Fig. 1. Foil with relief image, drawn by blind student solving the task and relief table.

Tasks for these participants [9] were obtained by slight adapting the tasks originally intended for able-bodied students of the same age (Benjamin and Cadet category [10]). When modifying tasks, we tried to keep the essence of the tasks and make only the necessary adjustments. Some tasks could be used without any modification. But most tasks required minor or larger modifications of the following character.

- Replace images containing relevant information by text.

- Avoid colour references.
- Use tables with correct linear order or replace them with lists or text.
- Do not use interactive tasks that can be solved using the mouse only.
- Use shorter sequences of objects or elements because blind participants must remember the sequence.
- Change the level of difficulty if the students must remember a lot of information in the solution.

3 Related Work

As mentioned in the previous section, students solve tasks with different levels of difficulty - easy, medium, and hard. Tasks with different levels of difficulty are evaluated with different scores. It is therefore important that the authors of the tasks correctly estimate their difficulty. Many studies on the difficulty of the tasks for able-bodied students were carried out during the existence of the Bebras challenge. We will mention some of them in this section.

Degiene an Futschek [1] presented the list of criteria for good tasks. These are general criteria that are used by the International Bebras Organizing Committee. In terms of difficulty, it is required, that the tasks are adequate for the age of contestants. Authors emphasize that the tasks should be interesting and provoke some excitement. In some cases, a suitable story may make a presentation of a task much easier so that also younger participants may solve the problem.

Lonati and her colleagues [11] observed how a few changes in some computational thinking tasks proposed during the Bebras challenge 2016 affected the solvers' performance. A clear indication from their study warns about the use of examples and figures that must be chosen and designed with much care, since their effect can be distracting or distortionary instead of useful for understanding and addressing the question.

Five authors from five universities [2] collected and analysed performance data on Bebras tasks from 115 400 students in grades 3–12 in seven countries. Their study provides further insight into a range of questions addressed in smaller-scale inquiries about the possible impact of school's systems and gender on students' success rate. They realized that to estimate the difficulty of new tasks is an open issue. It is necessary to better understand and characterize the range of algorithmic strategies used in the challenge, and the factors that caused large task performance variations among countries. Authors claim that the computational thinking conceptual content does not seem to play a major role in assessing how difficult a task is.

Van der Wegt with his colleagues have analysed the real difficulty of the tasks in the Dutch Bebras challenge and published the results in several studies [12–14]. They used several tools to predict the difficulty level of tasks. Specifically, they mentioned two questionnaires, a rubric and a procedure. They also tried to analyse the ratio between content difficulty, stimulus difficulty and task difficulty. They concluded that content difficulty is the most unclear item in predicting difficulty. They further claim that more research is needed on the use of taxonomies, especially for questions that do not use any previous knowledge, or other systematic approaches to identify content difficulty. Another tool was the Dutch contest system Cuttle that has a new module for analysis.

Using quantitative methods, they were able to confirm a relation between answer types and difficulty and a tendency that tasks on data, data structures and representation are better answered than tasks on algorithms and programming.

Vaníček [15, 16] writes about factors, which demonstrably increase the difficulty of tasks for students. According to him, presence of formalised description, structuring, optimization and demands of assignment reading comprehension are substantial factors making a task more difficult. On the other hand, length of the text, use of technical terminology, algorithms, diagrams, negative questions did not prove to affect the difficulty of tasks.

Močarníková [17] found that the algorithmic tasks were most challenging. On the contrary, the tasks about principles of ICT and information society proved to be the simplest for students.

Tomcsányi [18] found that it is difficult for students to solve tasks that use a command sequence in an unconventional, fictional "programming language". Tasks related to everyday life and tasks in which students ought to find out the original information based on an encryption key proved to be the simplest.

Tomcsányi and Tomcsányiová [19] emphasize that students should read the assignment with understanding and be careful not to make mistakes when solving tasks.

Gujberová [20] found that the difficulty of the task can be influenced by several factors and even a small change in the assignment can affect the difficulty of the task [21]. She concluded that the form of the answer is also an important factor. It is more difficult for younger students to enter a specific answer without a choice or without an interactive tool than to enter one of four answers. She also examined the impact of the use of the image in the assignment, based on an analysis carried out by Tomcsányiová and Kabátová [22]. In addition, she examined the effect of text length on a task difficulty. However, she did not find any significant connection.

All the studies mentioned above are a valuable inspiration for us in finding factors influencing the difficulty of tasks for the blind.

4 Research Design

During the seven years of monitoring the results of blind students in the Bebras challenge, we observed that the real difficulty of the tasks was different as expected. On average more than 50% of the tasks (see Fig. 2, green dotted line) had a different difficulty than expected. We can also notice that the number of tasks that had a lower real difficulty than expected slightly increased (blue dotted line). On the contrary, the number of tasks that had a higher real difficulty than expected slightly decreased (red dotted line).

In order, to better estimate the difficulty of the tasks in the future, we decided to observe the influence of some factors on the difficulty of the tasks [23]. We were looking for answers to the following research questions.

Q1: What is the relationship between the length of the assignment and difficulty of the task?
Q2: What is the relationship between task's affiliation to the thematic area and the difficulty of the task?

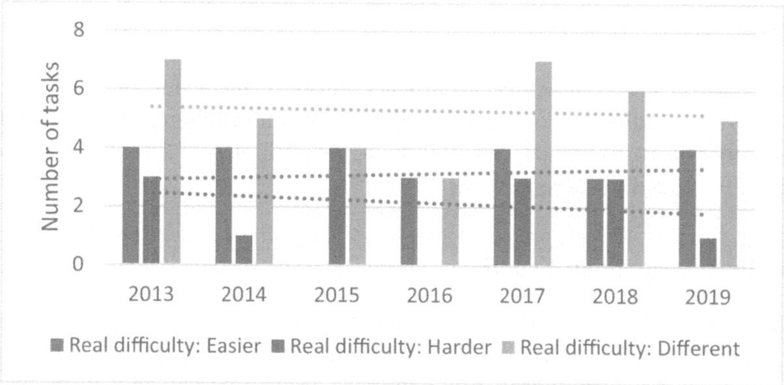

Fig. 2. Graph illustrating the number of tasks with different real difficulty as expected. (Color figure online)

Q3: What is the relationship between the required skills and difficulty of the task?
Q4: What is the relationship between the age of students and the difficulty of the tasks?

We used a case study research strategy. The 63 tasks used in the competition for the blind were observed cases. For each task, we found its real difficulty Q as a percentage of incorrect answers and all responses [18, 24]. Tasks with a Q value less than 30 were easy, tasks with difficulty of 30 to 70 were medium and tasks with difficulty over 70 were hard.

We observed the success rate of blind students of one school. In selected school we had the opportunity to directly observe the students while they were solving the tasks during the real Bebras challenge. We obtained valuable data in the form of field notes and interviews with students and computing teachers. We also knew that students in computer science classes covered all the thematic areas according to the valid curriculum. They also dealt with algorithms and problem solving, which is not common in all schools. The average number of blind students who took part in the competition each year ranged from 6 to 8 students (see Fig. 3) from fifth (age of 10 to 11) to nineth grade (age of 15 to 16).

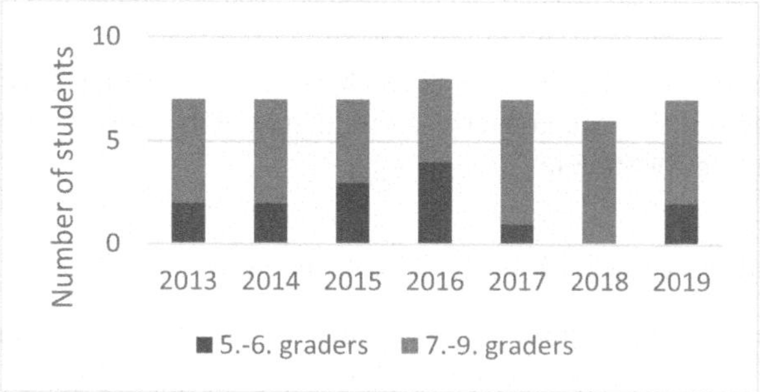

Fig. 3. Number of blind students solving the Bebras tasks.

5 Results

We divided all 63 tasks into three groups according to the value of Q. We obtained 26 easy tasks, 20 medium tasks and 17 hard tasks. Within each group we evaluated the average number of words in the task assignment, the affiliation of the task to the thematic area and skills needed to solve the task.

5.1 The Task Assignment Length

The number of words in the assignment could be a problem for blind students, as they use a screen reader. The reader does not read all texts clearly, such as a sequence of characters that do not form words. Students must read some passages more than once and or character by character. Blind students also cannot use the information represented by the image to understand the problem. We therefore considered it very important to thoroughly examine the relationship between the length of the task and its real difficulty.

The graph on Fig. 4 illustrates the number of words of each task. We see that the shortest task was 18 words and the longest was 130 words. Both belonged to a group of tasks with easy real difficulty. The average length of the assignment in the group of easy tasks was 70.8 words, in the group of medium-difficult tasks it was 65.6 words and in the group of difficult tasks it was 82.1 words. Although the trend line has a slightly increasing tendency, **it cannot be said that the length of the assignment has a significant effect on the real difficulty of task (answer to Q1)**.

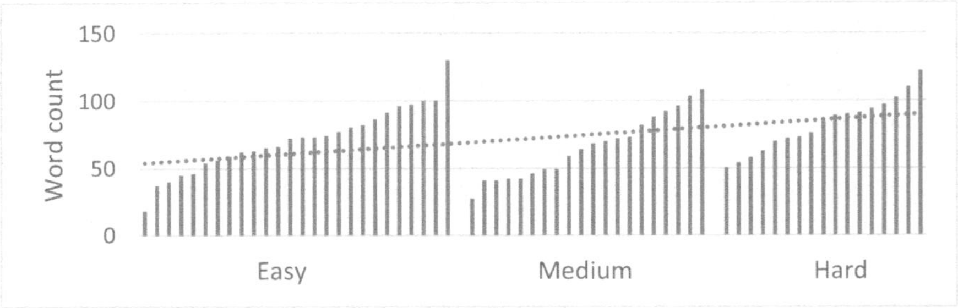

Fig. 4. Number of words in task assignments.

Based on interviews with students and teachers, we can say that students do not mind a longer assignment if the task concerns an issue they have already encountered and if the task is interesting for students.

5.2 The Affiliation of the Task to the Thematic Area

According to the valid curriculum in our country, informatics as a separate specialized subject includes five main thematic areas: (1) data structures and tools - DST, (2) algorithms and problem solving - APS, (3) communication via internet, (4) principles of hardware and software, (5) social aspects of using ICT.

We have assigned tasks to these thematic areas. Some tasks could be assigned to two thematic areas. As there were not many tasks from areas (3), (4) and (5), in this article we merged them into one group called Other. The most tasks in individual years (see Fig. 5) belonged to area (1) and (2), or both. Likewise, most of the tasks, up to 84%, used in the competition for 7 years belonged to area (1) and (2), or both (see Fig. 6). Each task is counted only once, either in a group for one area or for two areas.

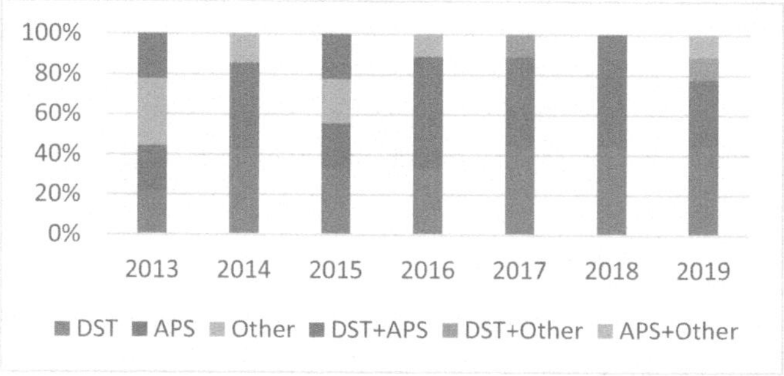

Fig. 5. Affiliation of tasks to thematic areas in individual years.

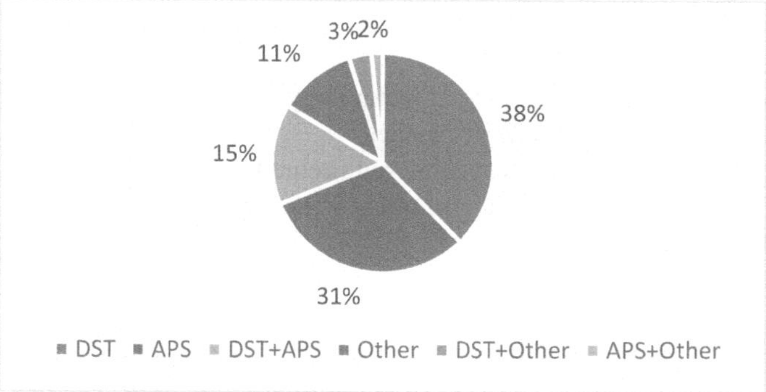

Fig. 6. Affiliation of all tasks to the thematic area.

For each level of real difficulty of the tasks, we analysed the affiliation of the tasks to thematic areas (see Fig. 7). We can conclude that easy tasks are mostly belonging to the thematic area of DST. It is up to 65% of the tasks. Only 19% of tasks belong to the APS area. Among the medium-difficult tasks, there is a higher percentage of tasks from the thematic area of APS than in the group of easy tasks. Even the most tasks are from this area. But the differences between the DST and APS areas are very small. Compared to easy tasks, the percentage of tasks included in the DST thematic area is 35% lower. The group of hard tasks is dominated by tasks from the thematic area of APS. Only 18% of the tasks belong to the thematic area of DST. Up to 29% of the tasks fall into both thematic areas. Tasks from other areas are not in the group of hard tasks. **It is therefore evident that belonging to a thematic area has an impact on the difficulty of the tasks (answer to Q2).**

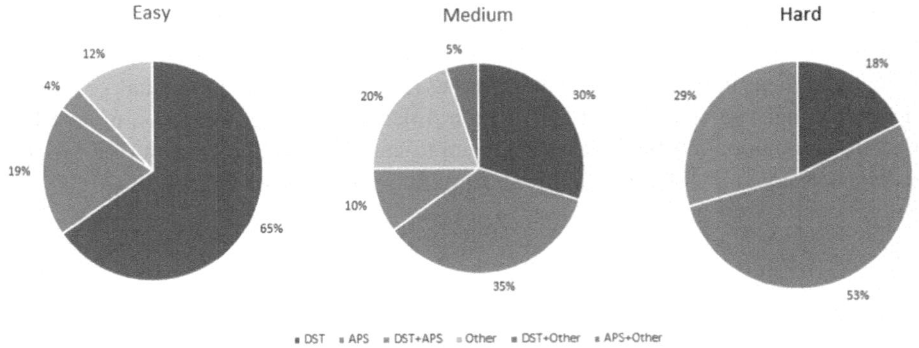

Fig. 7. Affiliation of tasks with different levels of difficulty to the thematic area.

5.3 Required Skills and Knowledge

Several authors (Van der Wegt, Vaníček) consider the knowledge and skills needed to solve the task to be an important factor influencing its difficulty. It is also important what information is given and what is the goal of the task. By analysing these assignment properties, we found several groups of tasks with common characteristics for each difficulty level.

The following knowledge and skills were required to solve easy tasks:

- knowledge of the rules for safe use of technology,
- knowledge of the use of peripheral devices,
- identifying an object that meets specific requirements,
- determining relationships in the hierarchical arrangement of objects (maximum three levels of the hierarchy),
- finding the shortest path (between linearly arranged objects with a maximum of five objects),
- repetition of a sequence of commands without parameters controlling the movement of an object over a small square grid (without rotating the object in place, grid is up to 3×3 fields),
- edit input text using key sequence (to fix one error),
- rearrange the elements of the input sequence as required (one exchange is required),
- create combinations of objects that meet the given requirements (maximum four values and the sum is up to fifteen).

The following knowledge and skills were required to solve medium-difficult tasks:

- determining relationships in the hierarchical arrangement of objects (more than three levels of the hierarchy),
- text encryption if given input text and modification procedure (the modification is backward rotation and a maximum of two modifications are required),
- arrange the elements of the linear input sequence according to the requirements (it is necessary to determine the number of pair exchanges),

- create combinations of objects that meet the given requirements (more than four values and the sum is greater than twenty).

The following knowledge and skills were required to solve hard tasks:

- text encryption if given input text and modification procedure (the modification is backward rotation and the shift of letters in the alphabet),
- repetition of a sequence of commands controlling the movement of an object over a square grid (with rotating the object in place),
- repetition of a sequence of commands with parameters controlling the movement of an object over a square grid (grid is more than 3×3 fields),
- arrange the elements of the linear input sequence according to the requirements (it is necessary to determine the number of moves to an empty space).

We can see that very similar skills are needed to solve tasks with different levels of difficulty. We could give many examples of tasks with different difficulty and similar skills needed to solve them. However, the scope of the article does not allow us to do it. These examples would illustrate that **not only required skills, but other factors also have an impact on the difficulty of the tasks (answer to Q3).** These are, for example, the following factors:

- the number of objects in the sequence,
- the number of levels in the object hierarchy,
- the number of steps to solve the task,
- the size of the grid along which the programmed object moves,
- the presence of a parameter in the command,
- whether the sequence of actions needs to be performed (easier) or their number needs to be determined (more difficult), or calculations need to be made when performing actions (the most difficult).

5.4 Age of Students

The category for blind lower secondary students is intended for students in the 5th to 9th grade. Age differences between students are relatively large. We therefore considered to find out whether the age of the students has an impact on the real difficulty of the tasks.

We determined the real difficulty of the tasks separately for the group of younger students - 5th to 6th graders and for older students - 7th to 9th graders. We found that only 46% of tasks had the same real difficulty for both groups (see Fig. 8). Almost half of the tasks (48%) were more difficult for younger students (in the sense that the category of the difficulty should be changed). Only 6% of tasks were easier for younger students (as mentioned above). It is therefore clear that **the age of students has an impact on the real difficulty of the tasks (answer to Q4).**

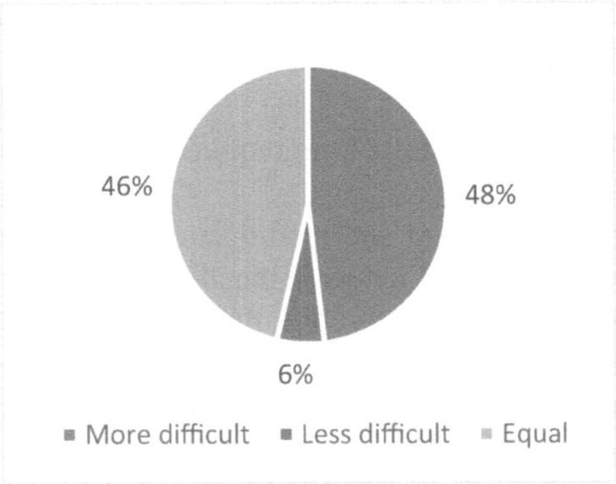

Fig. 8. Comparison of real difficulty of tasks for younger and older students.

6 Conclusions

In this article, we analysed the impact of some factors on the difficulty of Bebras tasks for blind lower secondary students. We determined the real difficulty of all 63 tasks used in Bebras challenge in the period 2013–2019. We divided the tasks into three groups according to the real difficulty (easy, medium, hard) and we analysed whether the difficulty is influenced by the length of the assignment, belonging to the thematic area, skills needed to solve the task and the age of the participants.

We found that the difficulty is influenced by the affiliation of the task to the thematic area. Tasks from the thematic area Data structures and tools are easier than tasks from the thematic area of Algorithms and problem solving. This result seems to be similar as what other authors have described about able-bodied students [14, 17].

Next we found that it is important not only what cognitive operations the competitor must perform to solve the task, but also the number of actions required, the number of objects in the sequence, the size of the grid when programming the movement of the object and the like.

It was not confirmed that the length of the assignment would have a significant effect on the difficulty of the task.

We also noticed clear difference in success rate between younger and older students. Therefore, we think that in the future it is necessary to divide the category for Blind lower secondary students into two separate categories, one for younger students and the other for older students.

We are aware of the fact, that our findings cannot be generalized, as we focused only on the results of students in one school. This was because we could observe the students during the Bebras challenge. We were also able to obtain detailed information about the students, as well as about their computing lessons.

The weakness of our research is the low number of monitored blind students. In future we consider using of item response functions to measure the overall performance of each contestant. We would also appreciate the opportunity to verify our findings with a larger group of blind students from other schools in our country and abroad.

Acknowledgment. This paper was created as part of a project funded by KEGA grant (Kega 018UK-4/2019). Special thanks to the teachers and students at the school for students with visual impairment where we conducted our research.

References

1. Dagienė, V., Futschek, G.: Bebras international contest on informatics and computer literacy: criteria for good tasks. In: Mittermeir, R.T., Sysło, M.M. (eds.) ISSEP 2008. LNCS, vol. 5090, pp. 19–30. Springer, Heidelberg (2008). https://doi.org/10.1007/978-3-540-69924-8_2
2. Izu, C., et al.: Exploring Bebras tasks content and performance: a multinational study. Inform. Educ. **16**(1), 39–59 (2017). Vilnius University
3. Carey, B.: How We Learn. Random House, New York (2014)
4. UN Convention on the Rights of Persons with Disabilities. United Nations. http://www.un.org/disabilities/documents/convention/convoptprot-e.pdf. Accessed 02 July 2020
5. Jašková, Ľ., Kováčová, N.: Bebras contest for blind pupils. In: Proceedings of the 9th Workshop in Primary and Secondary Computing Education, London, UK. ACM DL, New York (2015)
6. Jašková, Ľ., Kováčová, N.: Contest for blind pupils – universal design of tasks. In: Proceedings of the Conference Universal Learning Design, Linz, pp. 79–97. Masaryk University, Brno (2016)
7. Allman, C.B.: Test Access. Making Tests Accessible for Students with Visual Impairments: A Guide for Test Publishers, Test Developers, and State Assessment Personnel, 4th edn. American Printing House for the Blind, Louisville (2009)
8. Overview of exam access arrangements. http://www.rnib.org.uk/sites/default/files/Overview_of_exam_access_arrangements_May_2014.doc. Accessed 02 July 2020
9. Beaver contest for blind – local webpage. http://vin.edu.fmph.uniba.sk/iBobor.html. Accessed 02 July 2020
10. Bebras contest – local webpage. http://www.ibobor.sk. Accessed 02 July 2020
11. Lonati, V., et al.: How presentation affects the difficulty of computational thinking tasks: an IRT analysis. In: Koli Calling 2017: Proceedings of the 17th Koli Calling International Conference on Computing Education Research, November 2017, pp. 60–69 (2016)
12. Van der Vegt, W.: Predicting the difficulty level of a Bebras task. In: Olympiads in Informatics. Vilnius University, (2013). https://ioinformatics.org/journal/INFOL127.pdf. Accessed 02 July 2020
13. Van der Vegt, W.: How hard will this task be? Developments in analyzing and predicting question difficulty in the Bebras challenge. In: Olympiads in Informatics. Vilnius University (2018). https://ioinformatics.org/journal/v12_2018_119_132.pdf. Accessed 02 July 2020
14. Van der Vegt, W., et al.: Analysing task difficulty in a Bebras contest using cuttle. In: Olympiads in Informatics, pp. 145–165 (2019)
15. Vaníček, J.: Bebras informatics contest: criteria for good tasks revised. In: Gülbahar, Y., Karataş, E. (eds.) ISSEP 2014. LNCS, vol. 8730, pp. 17–28. Springer, Cham (2014). https://doi.org/10.1007/978-3-319-09958-3_3
16. Vaníček, J.: What makes situational informatics tasks difficult? In: Brodnik, A., Tort, F. (eds.) ISSEP 2016. LNCS, vol. 9973, pp. 90–101. Springer, Cham (2016). https://doi.org/10.1007/978-3-319-46747-4_8
17. Močarníková, K.: Difficulty of tasks in the Bebras challenge. Master theses. FMFI UK, Bratislava (2014). (in Slovak)
18. Tomcsányi, P.: Difficulty of tasks in the informatics Bebras contest. In: DidInfo 2009. Univerzita Mateja Bela, Banská Bystrica (2009). (in Slovak)

19. Tomcsányiová, M., Tomcsányi, P.: Analysis of solving the Bebras tasks in the Benjamin category in the school year 2012/13. In: DidInfo 2013. Univerzita Mateja Bela, Banská Bystrica (2013). (in Slovak)
20. Gujberová, M.: Development of algorithmic thinking of students in primary education. Doctoral theses. FMFI UK, Bratislava (2014). (in Slovak)
21. Gujberová, M., Kalaš, I.: Designing productive gradations of tasks in primary programming education. In: The 8th Workshop in Primary and Secondary Computing Education (2013)
22. Tomcsányiová, M., Kabátová, M.: Categorization of pictures in tasks of the Bebras contest. In: Diethelm, I., Mittermeir, Roland T. (eds.) ISSEP 2013. LNCS, vol. 7780, pp. 184–195. Springer, Heidelberg (2013). https://doi.org/10.1007/978-3-642-36617-8_16
23. Kostová, N.: Difficulty of tasks in the Bebras contest for the blind. Master theses. FMFI UK, Bratislava (2020). (in Slovak)
24. Chráska, M.: Methods of Pedagogical Research: Basics of Quantitative Research. Grada Publishing, Prague (2008). (in Czech)

Bebras Based Activities for Computer Science Education: Review and Perspectives

Sébastien Combéfis[1(✉)] and Gabrielė Stupurienė[2]

[1] Computer Science and IT in Education ASBL, 1348 Louvain-la-Neuve, Belgium
sebastien@combefis.be
[2] Vilnius University, DMSTI, 08412 Vilnius, Lithuania
gabriele.stupuriene@mif.vu.lt

Abstract. The Bebras international challenge on informatics and computational thinking (CT), targeted to pupils in primary and secondary schools, is being run in more than 50 countries yearly. Tasks used in this challenge are created by an international community that meets once a year to improve them. In addition to a large amount of work done on tasks, this community is also conducting research on different aspects of Bebras, from the study of good task criteria to analyses of the organisational structure of the community. This paper presents a review of research aiming at building activities based on Bebras material to serve computer science (CS) education. They include classroom activities, workshops, games development, and design of tests to evaluate CT skills. The paper also presents the results of a survey conducted among the Bebras community to identify existing activities using Bebras tasks and ideas for future ones. The results are summarised as a guideline with perspectives aiming at fostering teachers to spread CS and CT related competencies to their pupils. The paper concludes by proposing new research directions and experiments that may be led in schools.

Keywords: Computer science education · Informatics education · Computational thinking · Bebras challenge · Bebras based activities

1 Introduction

Bebras is an international informatics and CT challenge born in Lithuania in 2004. In 2019, it attracted about three million pupils (from primary and secondary education) from all over the world[1]. The challenge is based on tasks that pupils have to solve [17]. They are created by an international community made of Bebras enthusiasts from participating countries. They then improve and polish the proposed tasks once a year during an international workshop [14].

In addition to a large amount of work done on tasks, Bebras community members are also active in conducting research related to various aspects of the

[1] Based on the Bebras challenge website: https://www.bebras.org/?q=countries.

K. Kori and M. Laanpere (Eds.): ISSEP 2020, LNCS 12518, pp. 15–29, 2020.
https://doi.org/10.1007/978-3-030-63212-0_2

Bebras challenge. During the past five years, research about the design of activities based on Bebras materials and tasks to serve computer science education is being led. These activities include the development of classroom activities and workshops, the creation of games, and the design of tests to evaluate CT skills.

The research presented in this paper has two goals. The first one is to review the literature to find the existing research about activities based on Bebras materials and tasks, built for CS education. Based on the review, the second goal is to identify research directions for the development of relevant activities, thanks to a survey conducted among Bebras community members.

Instead of the term "computer science", many countries use other words such as computing or informatics, especially in multilingual Europe. The terms "informatics", "computing" and "computer science" are used interchangeably in this paper, to refer to the same subject, that is, the entire discipline.

The remainder of the paper is organised as follows. Section 2 reviews the literature on Bebras based activities design. Section 3 presents the research methodology. Section 4 draws up the detailed results of the survey. Section 5 discusses the results of the presented research and gives several recommendations. Section 6 concludes the paper with further work and future perspectives.

2 Literature Review

The literature review highlighted five main categories of activities, created based on Bebras tasks, and that are used to support CS education.

The first kind of activity is the creation of task books or textbooks to use in classrooms with pupils. Several countries do create annual books with tasks used in their national challenge. In addition to the task itself, they are typically enriched with detailed explanations about the correct answer and about what they have to do with informatics. The goal of these books is, in the end, to provide teachers materials to delve into computer science concepts with their pupils. No specific research has been carried out about the design of such books.

The second category is related to task creation activities. Teachers can learn about informatics concepts in two ways: by creating tasks and by analysing and solving them and explaining why it is informatics [10]. Therefore, creating tasks is an interesting activity for people willing to learn informatics concepts, should it be pupils or their teachers. One approach is to ask pupils to create Bebras-like problems during an activity in classrooms [19]. These problems are evaluated by teachers according to three criteria: quality, originality, and understandability. The materials used by teachers to help their pupils creating tasks are existing Bebras tasks and a booklet for beginners in informatics.

The third category is about the development of games based on Bebras tasks and materials. Games provide learners with the most interactive experience and increased motivation thanks to elements such as goals, scoreboards, competitions, etc. compared to other kinds of resources [7]. They are one important kind of resource to teach and learn CS concepts [8]. A quick search in the Google Play Store reveals several game apps, either made of a collection of tasks to solve or as standalone games built from a single Bebras task. In the literature review, two different kinds of game-related activities have been found: tangible games and game design process workshops.

The first kind of activity related to games is the creation of tangible ones, such as a card game for high school students to discover algorithms and CS concepts unplugged [9,12]. The content of the cards is inspired by Bebras tasks, shortened to only contain the task formulation and a short explanation about why it is informatics. They are used to start the problem-solving process leading to the learning of new computer science concepts [11].

Another approach involving games is the development of classroom activities where pupils are asked to imagine and design games based on Bebras tasks. For example, an experiment asked groups of pupils to think about and design a tangible game based on Bebras tasks they first solved and understood [3]. In this latter experiment, the 6th-grade pupils who created the games also had to train 3rd-grade pupils to play the games they designed. This activity is an example of situated learning whose content is built based on Bebras tasks.

The fourth category consists of tests to assess computational thinking (CT) skills. The goal is to measure CT abilities or skills using Bebras tasks, which is possible by analysing the answers given by pupils according to some research [1, 16]. These tests have also been shown to be complementary to others such as CTt and Dr. Scratch [20]. Based on these observations, tests used to assess acquired CT skills either targeted to pupils [5,6,18] or teachers [2] have been developed in different contexts. The goal of these various researches is to assess quantitatively whether the targeted public has acquired CT abilities.

The fifth category consists of activities developed to train pupils' CT skills [22] or to build pieces of training for teachers with workshops, for example [13]. The activities from the two last categories show the close relation between Bebras tasks and CT skills, even if it is not always clear whether some tasks do contribute to a better understanding of CT skills or not. Bebras tasks can surely be used as part of a larger activity meant to work on and train CT skills.

According to this literature review, there is an interest in building activities based on Bebras tasks to serve CS education. Although research in this direction is quite recent, five categories of developed activities have been identified. The four main characteristics of Bebras tasks, highlighted in the literature, that make them relevant to develop such activities are the following:

- The close relation between Bebras tasks and CT abilities make them suitable to design activities to acquire CT skills and to measure their mastery level.
- Bebras tasks typically having visual graphics and fun stories make them suitable to work with younger pupils, fostering soft skills such as their imagination and creativity and making these tasks relevant for game development.
- Both the task solving and task creation processes can be used to design activities related to CS education, either on their own or as part of larger activities, typically as workshops or other in-classroom activities.
- Metadata associated with Bebras tasks (answer explanation, '*It's Informatics*' section, category and difficulty level by age groups, etc.) make them useful for various kinds of activity that can be targeted to several age groups.

Finally, Bebras tasks are also used to teach some concepts of CS-related to other fields, such as mathematics. The literature review revealed research highlighting the fact that Bebras tasks can be used to teach the concept of graphs and their properties to younger pupils [4,15,21].

3 Research Methodology

This mixed-methods research uses qualitative and quantitative data collection methods. A literature review of designed Bebras based activities is used as a qualitative one. As a quantitative data collection instrument, a questionnaire survey has been designed based on the results of the literature review.

A web-based questionnaire has been used and data collection was performed from July 5 to July 18, 2020. Participants of this study consisted of 24 representatives from different countries belonging to the Bebras community (out of 67 countries). Countries are volunteers to do any additional activity in addition to run the annual Bebras challenge. Respondents were the only ones who volunteered to take part in the survey. The questionnaire consists of 23 questions: 18 open-ended questions, two five-level Likert-scale questions, and three multiple-choices questions. Data collected from both the literature review and the survey have been used to provide answers to the goals addressed in this paper.

4 Survey Results

Table 1 shows the list of participating countries, including 14 from the European region and ten non-European countries. They have been divided into three groups: (I) old-timer countries, (II) experienced countries, and (III) newcomers, depending on how long they are involved with the Bebras community.

Table 1. Period at which surveyed countries started to be involved with Bebras.

Period		Countries
(I)	2004–2010	Austria, Canada, Estonia, Latvia, Lithuania, The Netherlands, Switzerland, Ukraine
(II)	2011–2015	Australia, Belarus, Belgium, Hungary, Singapore, South Africa, Turkey
(III)	2016–2020	Croatia, India, Indonesia, Ireland, Portugal, Serbia, Syria, South Korea, Uzbekistan

The first set of questions of the survey is about annual brochures, with tasks and solutions, of national Bebras challenges. These brochures are sometimes used as the base to build textbooks. The vast majority of surveyed countries (22 of 24) prepare such brochures. They aim to provide more details on the Bebras challenge as a way to learn informatics and CT. As reported by the representatives, more attention is paid to teachers, mainly to explain the correct answer and the relation with CT, for them to explain it to their pupils. For some countries, brochures are dedicated to students to help them understand the task and the correct answer. They also are a resource for pupils that did not get the opportunity to participate in the challenge or want to train off-contest. To write the brochures, 71% of representatives need more information than what can be found in the original task. Almost 42% of countries create additional information: improvements (graphics, explanations), lesson ideas, or other technical information (authors and contributors). Some countries also add mappings to their schools' curriculum or educational goals (see Appendix A).

The next set of questions is about the use of eleven identified activities from the five main categories identified in the literature review, for different target groups. Table 2 shows the mapping between the activities and the categories.

Table 2. List of activities organised following the five main categories.

Category	Activities
1 – Textbooks	A1. Textbooks for schools
2 – Task creation	A8. Classroom workshops with pupils A10. Teacher training activities for higher CT/CS skills (in/pre-service)
3 – Games	A2. Games development (for unplugged activities) A3. Games development (for mobile/online activities)
4 – Tests	A4. Tests to evaluate pupils' CT skills A5. Tests to evaluate teachers' CT skills A6. Tests to evaluate high school students CT skills
5 – CT skills training	A7. Workshops for classrooms with pupils A9. Teacher training activities to train school teachers for higher CT/CS skills (in/pre-service) A11. Workshops for public targets (for parents, communities, sponsors, journalists, etc.)

Figure 1 summarises the relevance of the activities for their country and following their personal opinion. Data analysis reveals that the most relevant activities for countries are A7 and A9 (average score of 4.4) and the less relevant are A5 and A11 (average 3.7). According to personal opinions, the most relevant is A1 (average 4.1) and the less relevant is A11 (average 3.5). Figure 2 shows the activities' relevance grouped by countries' experience with the Bebras community. For old-timer countries, the most relevant is A7 (average 4.5) and the less relevant are A3 and A11 (average 3.4). For experienced ones, the most relevant is A10 (average 4.4) and the less relevant is A1 (average 3.6). For newcomers, the most relevant is A9 (average 4.6) and the less relevant is A8 (average 3.7).

Grouping the results according to the five main categories results in the following orders, starting with the most relevant one:

- CT skills training, games, task creation, textbooks, tests (for countries),
- textbooks, CT skills training, games, tests, task creation (personal opinion).

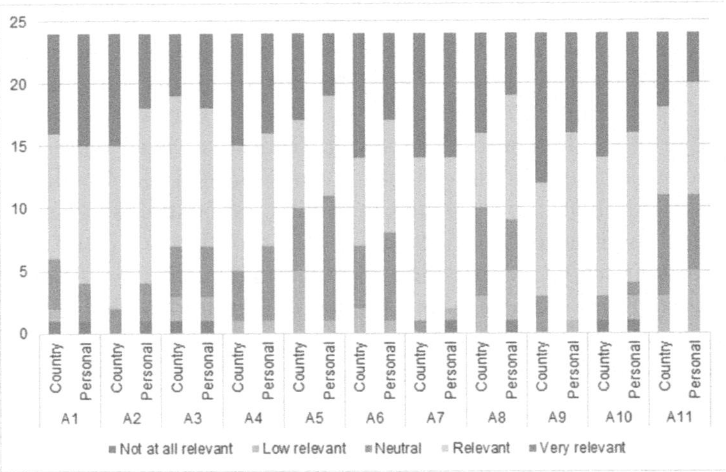

Fig. 1. Relevance of activities for the country and according to the personal opinion.

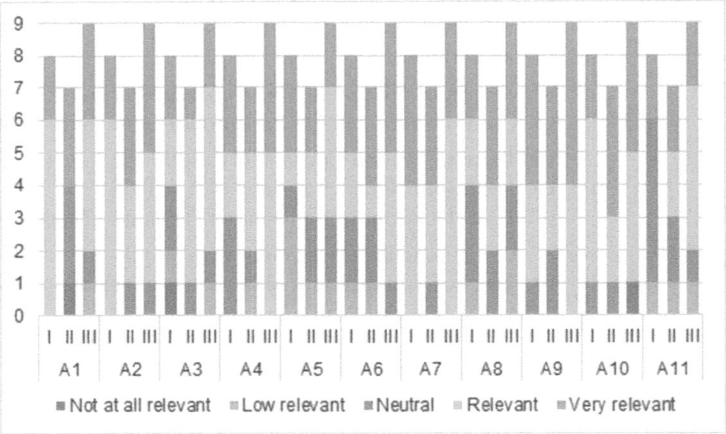

Fig. 2. Relevance of activities by country experience with Bebras.

Looking at the results from the countries' experience perspective gives the following relevance order for the five main categories:

- CT skills training, tests, games, textbooks, task creation (newcomers),
- task creation, games, CT skills training, tests, textbooks (experienced),
- textbooks, CT skills training, task creation, games, tests (old-timer).

The next questions of the survey are specific to the five activity categories. Respondents were asked to describe in detail the activities using Bebras tasks that are run in their country. They were asked to give the goal, continuity (one time or periodic), organiser (lecture, teacher, researcher, etc.), and whether the activity is an extra activity out of school or scheduled at school. The results are grouped following the five main categories and detailed in Appendix B:

Textbooks for schools based on Bebras tasks are written in 25% of countries. In South Korea, textbooks' content is aligned with the national curriculum. In Lithuania, Bebras-like tasks are included in textbooks for primary schools, but not for secondary schools because their textbooks are focused on special topics. Switzerland is a champion with 13 books, those for primary schools using the challenges approach to introduce/train a topic. Their annual brochures serve as a kind of textbook since they are designed to be used by pupils and their teachers. Turkey also wrote a book targeted to higher education students.

Task creation activities can be workshops for classrooms with pupils or teacher training activities. In Hungary, a CT course exists for university students where they create and solve Bebras-like tasks. Also, part of a teacher training university course is based on Bebras tasks and activities with robotics. In South Korea, they both focus on problem-solving and making, in the teaching training process. Lithuania started with in-service teacher workshops and is now working on pre-service ones, in particular for task creation. Switzerland also organises similar workshops, to prepare teachers to create Bebras tasks for their pupils.

Games for unplugged activities are developed in almost 16% of countries. In Australia, they are a resource for learning rather than explicit games. They created downloadable and printable cards to encourage pupils to develop CT skills as well as teamwork, collaboration, and critical thinking. Hungary provides two types of challenges. In the shorter version, pupils have to solve four Bebras tasks to obtain a code to open a treasure box. The longer version is a challenge game with ten stations where different activities with physical game-parts like board games, robots, etc. are organised. Lithuania created three different sets of "Bebras cards" for pupils from 7 to 13 years old, based on Bebras tasks. Switzerland designed postcard-sized descriptions of activities and riddles based on Bebras tasks, for primary school teachers. Ireland is preparing dynamic instances of Bebras tasks, with difficulty level based on player's ability and South Korea has a plan to realise an online game.

Assessment tools to evaluate pupils', teachers' or high school students' CT skills are in the beginning stage. Hungary created a test for first-year students and a course to improve CT skills. There are also some attempts from PhD students in Austria to do this. Turkey is also currently developing such an assessment tool, focused on the design of a self-efficacy perception scale for CT.

CT skills training is organised in classrooms for pupils in 29% of countries. India does this during school visits. South Korea ran an offline Bebras camp. In Indonesia, the training is conducted by universities collaborating with the National Bebras Organiser. In Canada, the Centre for Education in Mathematics and Computing runs workshops in classrooms, from grades 7 to 12.

Training targeted to teachers is organised in 50% of countries. South Korea organises teacher training sessions, introducing Bebras tasks in the pre-teacher training course. In Lithuania, there are workshops and seminars for teachers, in different places. They like hands-on activities when something to play and to discuss is provided. South Africa runs in-service two-hour workshops for teachers, especially in non-urban/rural communities. Turkey wrote two books and prepared online training for the Ministry of National Education. Ireland brings a "*Computational Thinking Obstacle Course*" to schools where pupils solve Bebras tasks in small groups. They then discuss their strategies and researchers explain alternative strategies if needed. They also host workshops for primary and secondary teachers, both in- and pre-service, to learn about CT using Bebras tasks and help them creating lesson plans. These activities take place at school if several teachers from the same school request it, or at university. Australia organises webinars to discuss CT skills, how relevant they are to the Australian Curriculum, and how Bebras can be used in the classroom to teach and learn these skills. Bebras unplugged and CT in Action activities, which draw on the CT skills but in contexts outside of Bebras, are also offered. These sessions are open to primary and secondary teachers, should they be pre-service or substitute teachers. In Switzerland, workshops were offered at the central CS teachers meetings once or twice a year, when asked for by the meeting offerers. In the context of pilot projects to introduce CS education in primary schools, they also organised a few workshops for teachers to make them discover the contest and other resources of Bebras, like the annual brochure.

The survey also revealed that task solving workshops are also organised for public targets (parents, communities, sponsors, journalists, etc.) Ireland contributes to a "pub quiz" for parents and teachers from a local school, supplying one round of questions using Bebras tasks, once a year. South Korea also has a future project for public targets.

The next question reveals that 54% of countries have events where Bebras-based tasks are used. In Ireland, they have summer camps for 13–18 years old, the "*DojoMor*" computer science event (Scratch, Raspberry Pi, Web, audio and video tutorials), and the "*Science Week*", a science and engineering showcase for the public. In Austria, Bebras tasks are used during the "*Abenteuer Informatik Workshops*" at TU Wien or Teacher Days. Some year, Belgium organises a second round of the Bebras challenge which takes place during a "*Computer Science Day*" where other activities are organised for the pupils (a CS Escape Game, unplugged activities workshops, conferences, robot programming activities, etc.). South Korea organises government-led online software coding parties, offline software festivals, and more. Participants solve tasks online and receive certificates, or participate in offline camps to collaborate and solve tasks. Lithuania has had a summer campus together with Kangaroo for many years, it means mathematics and informatics together. Bebras tasks are also used in national education exhibitions and for kids' TV shows (as part of a quiz). In Portugal, "*TreeTree2*" organises a Summer Academy for young and gifted students, where Bebras is part of their CS introduction. In South Africa, Bebras is introduced as part of the "*Programming and Application Olympiad*" workshops. Switzerland uses Bebras tasks in central CS teachers meetings and "*Schweizer Tag für Informatik Unterricht*", an annual half-day teacher training. Syria uses them in training sessions for the kids and adolescents' programming marathon.

Bebras based activities are not limited to CS and CT. Syria uses them for mathematics activities. Bebras unplugged in Australia is mostly marketed to Digital Technology/STEM teachers, but with an emphasis on Critical Thinking, which can be integrated by schools in other disciplines. They encourage teachers from a broad range of disciplines to attend.

5 Discussions and Recommendations

Following the purpose of the study, the literature about activities serving CS education and based on Bebras tasks has been reviewed. Five main categories of activities have been identified. Adding the results from the survey lead to several observations detailed below.

Textbooks for schools are created and used in 25% of the surveyed countries. This category is also very important to representatives according to their personal opinion about each activity. Also, this category is emphasised by old-timer countries, otherwise than for experienced countries. In Switzerland (involved in Bebras since 2010), there will be 20 available textbooks (for a spiral curriculum) based on Bebras tasks. Lithuania (involved since 2004) uses Bebras-like tasks in primary school textbooks.

Researchers and educators see Bebras tasks as a way of engagement in computer science and CT. Materials based on Bebras tasks could find a place in curriculums. But more data should be provided on curriculum issues, in the original Bebras tasks, such as the related CT concepts or in which other disciplines/contexts they can be integrated. Also, no research on the design of textbooks based on Bebras materials and tasks seems to exist.

Task creation activities were mainly highlighted by experienced countries of the Bebras community. The opinion of newcomers is on the opposite, with the lowest scores as well for the relevance for the country as for the personal opinion. Such activities are not easy to create and organise, because participants in workshops should first understand the principles of CS and CT. In countries, this kind of activity is more applicable for in- and pre-service teachers to help them acquire not only problem-solving but also problem making skills.

More methodology about how to create good Bebras tasks should be provided. Existing research about this is mainly targeted to the Bebras community members but should be extended to reach teachers. Such a methodology would also be useful for new countries that are interested in starting the Bebras challenge in their country. They have indeed to provide task proposals for the international workshop.

Games development is the second most relevant category of activities for countries. Games are indeed a good way to motivate people to learn, especially for younger ones. But in practice, there are very few examples of such activities developed. Only 16% of countries are involved in games creation (such as card games) for unplugged activities. Ireland and Hungary would find physical versions of selected Bebras tasks very engaging for young pupils, such as made of wood/plastic/magnets and using marbles/water or board games. Also, Ireland is preparing dynamic instances of Bebras tasks.

Bebras tasks being tightly related to CT skills, games targeted at learning these skills should be developed, should it be physical tangible ones or virtual ones. Then, studies about the effectiveness and efficiency of these games should be conducted. Of course, developing games takes time, so they may be designed to be easily translated so that to reach as many people as possible.

Assessment tools are the second most relevant category for newcomer countries while other countries do not pay attention to them. This is the most scientific research consuming activity. As found in the literature review, Bebras tasks can be a complementary part of other tests to evaluate CT abilities. More research should be done on how to design such assessment tools and how they can be linked to curriculums. Identifying which psychometric methods could be used to build such assessment tools would also be a promising research direction.

CT skills training activities are almost the most popular and relevant category for all countries, especially for newcomers. Workshops for classrooms with pupils are organised in 29% of countries and workshops for teacher training in 50% of them. Countries' representatives highlighted two concrete activities as the most relevant ones: workshops for pupils and teachers. This is probably because they are easy to directly organise from Bebras tasks and because they are perceived as the most effective kind of event to promote the Bebras challenge. Only part of in- and pre-service teachers are familiar with CS and CT, which may also explain the success of these workshops. They are very important, especially for primary school teachers. Solving Bebras tasks helps them understand more about CS and CT. Workshops targeted at the public were decided as least relevant. Although workshops are organised in many countries, very few research about how to design and structure them does exist. Another possible research direction would be to study how effective they are to make pupils and teachers learn CS and CT. This is of course related to the fourth category of activities.

Suggestions about what should be further developed were also asked in the survey. A first element raised by South Korea is the possibility to run tracks and sessions at academic conferences. They also think that Bebras could be linked to the International Olympiad in Informatics and, at a local scale, with the Korean Education Broadcasting. Singapore highlighted the fact that more online training materials based on Bebras tasks should be made available. Explaining to students how CT is helping them for programming would also be valuable. According to Lithuania, it would be good to systemise Bebras tasks that teachers can use to teach concrete topics. For example, it would be good to have a set of tasks to introduce algorithms on graphs. Switzerland thinks about how they could implement a database with all the necessary information in an easily usable form for teachers and educators. Making such a database free to use may help teachers to pick individual tasks or even to develop their own task sets. Of course, issues may arise concerning the maintenance and upgrade of such a database system.

6 Conclusion

Results from the qualitative research revealed that there are five main categories of activities based on international Bebras challenge tasks in the scientific literature (textbooks, task creation, games, assessments, task solving). Results from the quantitative study supplement the meaning of these categories and show that countries are developing concrete activities from them. Countries have been grouped into three groups according to their experience with Bebras. For old-timer countries, the most relevant activity is task-solving workshops for classrooms with pupils. For experienced countries, it is teacher training activities on task creation for higher CS/CT skills. For newcomers, it is teacher training activities on task solving. The survey also put in light that the Bebras community is very active, but there is still room for more collaboration and the production of easily shareable and translatable materials.

This paper also shows a gap between the number of organised activities and the percentage of them subject to objective research. This observation highlights a big potential for research about Bebras based activities serving CS education. Systemising Bebras tasks for wider use in CS/CT education also needs further investigation and is one of the directions for future work.

Acknowledgment. We acknowledge all the international representatives who took part in the survey on Bebras based activities for their active participation and collaboration.

A Detailed Results About Annual Brochures

The vast majority of surveyed countries regard the annual brochures as a resource mainly targeted to teachers:

- "We develop a solutions guide each year which is aimed at teachers. It includes how to get the correct answer as well as computational thinking explanations" (*Australia*)
- "For teachers: to develop children's logical thinking and increase their interest in CS" (*Belarus*)
- "The aim is to introduce for teachers and students how informatics tasks can look like. Also it is important for teachers especially primary school teachers to get explanations of each task that they can discuss with students and be sure about informatics content. Many teachers like tasks and use them to motivate students to start some informatics topics" (*Lithuania*)
- "For teachers to use as classroom resources. For students for their own understanding" (*Canada*)
- "Teachers who want to reuse this as additional teaching material or explain the past competition's task to the student" (*Switzerland*)
- "After the 1st part of the challenge we offer access to all the tasks (with answers) for teachers so they can use it to help prepare students for the final challenge and for the next year" (*Latvia*).

Some countries put the accent on the pupils when building their brochures:

- "To share tasks with those who did not participate in the challenge, did not achieve good results to pass to the 2nd round or a pupil had no opportunity to participate in the challenge (no responsible teacher at a school)" (*Estonia*)

- "Pupils who want to train more off-contest" (*Switzerland*).

Several countries need or produce additional information about tasks in order to write their annual brochures:

- "Sometimes images for the solutions or the solutions need to be reworded to improve the explanation for teachers" (*Australia*)
- "Sometimes we add more information about 'It's Informatics'especially for primary school teachers" (*Lithuania*)
- "We always had to hunt down information to complete the meta sections. Authors and contributors names as well as comments were usually all over the place and had to be searched. This includes the **complete** data set of the authors and contributors: full name, email address and country" (*Switzerland*)
- "We map CT themes to those used by our program" (*India*)
- "Links to Ireland schools curriculum" (*Ireland*)
- "Educational goals related to Informatics, teaching and learning methods, etc." (*South Korea*)
- "Sometimes we give lesson ideas" (*The Netherlands*).

B Detailed Results About Activities Using Bebras Tasks

This appendix gives the detailed answers from respondents to the survey about the activities they are organising in their country, for the five main categories of activities identified from the literature review.

B.1 Textbooks for Schools

- There is in *Hungary* the CT course for university students where they create and solve such tasks and also they have a part of a university course in teacher training (based on bebras tasks and activities with robotics)
- "The national curriculum was analyzed so that informatics teachers can teach using Bebras tasks, and textbooks were developed and published based on this. For this, we conducted relevant educational researches" (*South Korea*)
- "There are some tasks similar for bebras tasks used in primary school textbooks. For secondary schools usually textbooks concentrate on special topics and not include small tasks (as bebras tasks are)" (*Lithuania*)
- "A spiral curriculum of textbooks is available in Switzerland comprising currently of 13 books, further are being written, so the total will be 20 books from Kindergarten to Maturity (University entrance). Books for primary schools - where not related to programming - are using the approach of challenges to introduce and/or train a topic. Also, our brochures serve as a kind of textbook. They can be used in class and are prepared to be used by students and teachers. In 2019/2020 we also prepared special A5 cards with a task on the front side and the explanation and ?It?s Informatics? part on the back side. They were received very well" (*Switzerland*)

- "We wrote a book named - from computational thinking to programming (for higher education students and graduates)" (*Turkey*)
- "We applied to be part of a new series of textbooks on Informatics in our country" (*Uzbekistan*).

B.2 Task Creation

- "When introducing tasks in our teacher training process, not only problem solving but also problem making is used as an important learning activity. This draws a lot of consent from teachers" (*South Korea*)
- "We did several times with in-service, it was great but it takes time. Now we are doing with pre-service teachers (teacher students), they like to create similar Bebras tasks" (*Lithuania*)
- "In the years before we had a national workshop in preparation of the submission of task proposals to the international workshop where every submitter was invited. In the context of professional development for future high school teachers, we organized some workshops to first make them discover the contest and the activities, then help them create Bebras tasks for their pupils. Also the online environment (which is free for anybody) allows to create new tasks and to publish them to anyone by assigning a small key, which can be sent to those who you wish to solve the tasks." (*Switzerland*).

B.3 Games

- "Bebras unplugged is a resource for learning, rather than an explicit game. It is a series of downloadable and printable cards that encourage students to develop CT skills as well as team work, collaboration and critical thinking. They are free to access on our website, and we have sets developed for each of the main age bands, except the oldest as it is least connected to the curriculum. While we provide guidance and additional worksheets to use these cards, it is up to the teachers as to how they want to implement them in a classroom" (*Australia*).
- *Hungary* provides two types of challenges. Shorter version (Treasure hunting) solving of 4 Bebras-tasks (handouts) - then with the code they can open a treasure box. Longer version: challenge game with 10 stations. In each station different activities - with physical game-parts (like board games, robots).
- "We created three different sets of "Bebras cards" for students from 7 to 13+ age. It is based on the idea of Bebras tasks. (*Lithuania*). "Bebras cards" are postcard-sized descriptions of activities and riddles based on Bebras tasks. They are meant for primary school teachers" (*Switzerland*).
- *Ireland* are preparing dynamic instances of Bebras tasks (multiple instances of the same task generated automatically, with difficulty level based on player's ability). Planned as periodic (weekly activity). Not running yet (under development) but the plan is for use at school with the teacher in charge.
- *South Korea* has not yet realized a game (online), but has a plan to do so.

B.4 Assessment Tools

- *Hungary* created a test for first year students, and a course for improving CT skills.
- Also there are some attempts from PhD students in *Austria* to do this.
- "We developed an assessment tool" (*Turkey*).

B.5 CT Skills Training

- *India* does this during school visits.
- *South Korea* ran an offline Bebras camp.
- In *Indonesia* the training is conducted by Bebras Biro (universities that collaborate with NBO).
- In *Canada* the Centre for Education in Mathematics and Computing runs workshops in classrooms, from grades 7 to 12.

References

1. Araujo, A.L.S.O., Andrade, W.L., Guerrero, D.D.S., Melo, M.R.A.: How many abilities can we measure in computational thinking? A study on Bebras challenge. In: Proceedings of the 50th ACM Technical Symposium on Computer Science Education (SIGCSE 2019), pp. 545–551 (2019)
2. Bavera, F., Quintero, T., Daniele, M., Buffarini, F.: Computational thinking skills in primary teachers: evaluation using Bebras. In: Pesado, P., Arroyo, M. (eds.) CACIC 2019. CCIS, vol. 1184, pp. 405–415. Springer, Cham (2020). https://doi.org/10.1007/978-3-030-48325-8_26
3. Bellettini, C., Lonati, V., Monga, M., Morpurgo, A., Palazzolo, M.: Situated learning with Bebras tasklets. In: Pozdniakov, S.N., Dagienė, V. (eds.) ISSEP 2019. LNCS, vol. 11913, pp. 225–239. Springer, Cham (2019). https://doi.org/10.1007/978-3-030-33759-9_18
4. Budinská, L., Mayerová, K.: From Bebras tasks to lesson plans – graph data structures. In: Pozdniakov, S.N., Dagienė, V. (eds.) ISSEP 2019. LNCS, vol. 11913, pp. 256–267. Springer, Cham (2019). https://doi.org/10.1007/978-3-030-33759-9_20
5. Chen, J.-M., Wu, T.-T., Sandnes, F.E.: Exploration of computational thinking based on Bebras performance in Webduino programming by high school students. In: Wu, T.-T., Huang, Y.-M., Shadieva, R., Lin, L., Starčič, A.I. (eds.) ICITL 2018. LNCS, vol. 11003, pp. 443–452. Springer, Cham (2018). https://doi.org/10.1007/978-3-319-99737-7_47
6. Chiazzese, G., Arrigo, M., Chifari, A., Lonati, V., Tosto, C.: Educational robotics in primary school: measuring the development of computational thinking skills with the Bebras tasks. Informatics **6**(4), 43 (2019)
7. Combéfis, S., Beresnevičius, G., Dagienė, V.: Learning programming through games and contests: overview, characterisation and discussion. Olympiads Inform. **10**, 39–60 (2016)
8. Combéfis, S., de Moffarts, G., Jovanov, M.: TLCS: a digital library with resources to teach and learn computer science. Olympiads Inform. **13**, 3–20 (2019)
9. Dagienė, V., Futschek, G., Koivisto, J., Stupurienė, G.: The card game of Bebras-like tasks for introducing informatics concepts. In: ISSEP 2017 Online Proceedings. Helsinki, 13–15 November 2017 (2017)

10. Dagienė, V., Futschek, G., Stupurienė, G.: Teachers' constructionist and deconstructionist learning by creating Bebras tasks. In: Proceedings of the 2016 Constructionism Conference, pp. 257–264 (2016)
11. Dagienė, V., Futschek, G., Stupurienė, G.: Creativity in solving short tasks for learning computational thinking. Constr. Found. **14**(3), 382–396 (2019)
12. Dagienė, V., Stupurienė, G.: Algorithms unplugged: a card game of the Bebras-like tasks for high schools students. In: Poster Presented at the 10th International Conference on Informatics in Schools: Situation, Evolution, and Perspectives (ISSEP 2017) (2017)
13. Dagienė, V., Vinikienė, L., Stupurienė, G.: Teaching informatics: activities-based model. In: Poster Presented at the 9th International Conference on Informatics in Schools: Situation, Evolution, and Perspectives (ISSEP 2016) (2016)
14. Datzko, C.: The genesis of a Bebras task. In: Pozdniakov, S.N., Dagienė, V. (eds.) ISSEP 2019. LNCS, vol. 11913, pp. 240–255. Springer, Cham (2019). https://doi.org/10.1007/978-3-030-33759-9_19
15. Erdősné Németh, A.: Teaching graphs for contestants in lower-secondary-school-age. Olympiads Inform. **11**, 41–53 (2017)
16. Hubwieser, P., Mühling, A.: Investigating the psychometric structure of Bebras contest: towards measuring computational thinking skills. In: Proceedings of the 2015 International Conference on Learning and Teaching in Computing and Engineering (LaTiCe 2015), pp. 62–69. IEEE (2015)
17. Izu, C., Mirolo, C., Settle, A., Mannila, L., Stupurienė, G.: Exploring Bebras tasks content and performance: a multinational study. Inform. Educ. **16**(1), 39–59 (2017)
18. Lockwood, J., Mooney, A.: Developing a computational thinking test using Bebras problems. In: Joint Proceedings of the 1st Co-Creation in the Design, Development and Implementation of Technology-Enhanced Learning Workshop (CC-TEL 2018) and Systems of Assessments for Computational Thinking Learning Workshop (TACKLE 2018), vol. 2190 (2018)
19. Manabe, H., Tani, S., Kanemune, S., Manabe, Y.: Creating the original Bebras tasks by high school students. Olympiads Inform. **12**, 99–110 (2018)
20. Román-González, M., Moreno-León, J., Robles, G.: Complementary tools for computational thinking assessment. In: Proceedings of the International Conference on Computational Thinking Education (CTE 2017), pp. 154–159 (2017)
21. Sysło, M.M., Kwiatkowska, A.B.: Playing with computing at a children's university. In: Proceedings of the 9th Workshop in Primary and Secondary Computing Education (WiPSCE 2014), pp. 104–107 (2014)
22. Zamzami, E.M., Tarigan, J.T., Zendrato, N., Muis, A., Yoga, A., Faisal, M.: Exercising the students computational thinking ability using Bebras challenge. J. Phys.: Conf. Ser. **1566**(1), 012113 (2020)

Assessing the Agreement in the Bebras Tasks Categorisation

Žan Ternik[1](✉), Ljupčo Todorovski[2,3], and Irena Nančovska Šerbec[4](✉)

[1] Gymnasium Ledina, Resljeva cesta 12, Ljubljana, Slovenia
zan.ternik@gmail.com
[2] Faculty of Public Administration, University of Ljubljana, Gosarjeva 5, Ljubljana, Slovenia
[3] Department of Knowledge Technologies, Jožef Stefan Institute, Jamova 39, Ljubljana, Slovenia
[4] Faculty of Education, University of Ljubljana, Kardeljeva ploščad 14, Ljubljana, Slovenia
irena.nancovska@pef.uni-lj.si

Abstract. The participants of the Bebras competitions solve tasks that involve informatics concepts and require computational thinking (CT) skills for general problem solving. The recent popularity of Bebras is closely related to the increasing interest in development of the CT skills among the school students of all ages. Despite the increase in interest, we still lack a consensual, unambiguous definition and/or categorization of CT skills. In this paper, we provide an empirical evidence for the ambiguity of the current categorization of CT skills by assessing the agreement among experts when annotating five tasks of the Slovene Bebras competition in 2019. The empirical data include the annotations of the selected tasks by six experts, where each of them was required to annotate a given task with one to three categories of CT skills required to solve it. The categorization of the CT skills used in the experiment include the five categories of the well-known categorization Dagiené, Sentance and Stupuriene: algorithmic thinking, decomposition, generalization, evaluation and abstract thinking. To narrow down the broad scope of the first category of algorithmic thinking, we introduced a new, sixth category of modelling and simulation. Despite this specialization of the categorization scheme, the measurement of the Fleiss' Kappa statistics on the empirical data, shows a weak agreement among the experts, especially for the general category of abstract thinking. This result confirms the lack of consensus among experts about the delineation between different categories of CT skills. A possible explanation of this results is that reaching a consensus about the definition and categorization of the CT skills within the heterogeneous group of experts involving teachers, programmers and computer scientists, is a challenging task. The result also calls for further effort in reaching such a consensus that would lead to deeper understanding and better teaching of the CT skills.

Keywords: Computational thinking skills · Bebras contest · Task categorization · Fleiss' kappa statistics · Reliability of agreement

K. Kori and M. Laanpere (Eds.): ISSEP 2020, LNCS 12518, pp. 30–41, 2020.
https://doi.org/10.1007/978-3-030-63212-0_3

1 Introduction

The Bebras (Beaver) competition promotes computing and computational thinking [1]. It is especially important in Slovenia and other countries, where computing is not a compulsory subject in the primary school curricula. Bebras competitions helps teachers of closely related subjects to present school students in various age groups with tasks that require skills and knowledge related to computing. Due to the popularity of the competition, they are one of the few resources that reflect the way students of different ages think when solving computational problems. These skills are commonly referred as computational thinking skills and are not only important for solving computational problems but are also considered crucial "21st century" skills.

Note that thinking about the "big ideas of computer science" follows the tradition of Seymour Papert and Marvin Minsky, established long before 2006, when the skills of computational thinking became popular. As part of the K-12 education, Papert in the 1980s pioneered the idea that children develop algorithmic thinking through LOGO programming [17]. The more recent "21st century" perspective on the topic is a logical starting point for our critical examination of the current interpretation of the computational thinking skills required by the Bebras tasks [10].

Computational thinking is a set of problem-solving methods in which problems and their solutions are expressed in a way that an information-processing agent (a computer) could be deployed [21]. It includes the mental skills and practices for designing calculations that make computers perform tasks for us as well as explaining and interpreting the world as a complex of information processes [9]. They include a wide range of basic, intermediate and advanced skills that allow educators to assemble tasks of varying difficulty targeting different age groups [19]. The Bebras challenge promotes problem-solving skills and computer science concepts in accordance to the definition by the International Society for Technology in Education (ISTE): the ability to break down complex tasks into simpler components, algorithm design, pattern recognition, pattern generalization and abstraction [1]. Note that the definition provides a categorization of the CT skills. However, various authors define CT skills in different ways and propose different categorization schemes [8, 15].

In this paper, we conjecture that the various definitions and categorizations of CT skills lack clarity and unambiguity that would allow for better planning appropriate competition tasks and teaching exercises. We empirically test the validity of this conjecture by assessing the degree of agreement among experts on the set of CT skills categories that are necessary to solve a given task. The empirical data include the annotations of five tasks included in the Slovene Bebras competition in 2019 by six experts, i.e., academics, members of the contest Program Council and participant mentors. We required each expert to follow a fixed, six-category scheme and annotate a given task with one to three categories of CT skills required to solve it. In turn, we use the collected data to calculate the Fleiss' Kappa statistics that measure the agreement among the annotations provided by different experts. Weak agreement among the annotations would confirm the validity of our conjecture.

The paper is organized as follows. Section 2 provides an overview of recent categorisations of CT skills used for different competition categories and in different countries and introduces the categorisation scheme to be used in the experiments. Section 3 introduces the experimental setup, the Fleiss' Kappa statistics for measuring the degree of agreement among the annotators, and, finally, reports and discusses the experimental results. Section 4 summarizes the contributions of the paper and outlines venues for further research.

2 Theoretical Background

2.1 Development of Categorization

Categorization is an activity that consists in placing tasks into categories based on their similarities or with regard to expected solutions. It allows us to organise tasks or analyse the skills needed to solve them, or to reflect on the concepts behind the tasks and facilitate their understanding. Through the history of the Bebras contest, we can find different ways to categorize tasks. While some authors of tasks from certain countries face the obstacle of specifying the difficulty of competition tasks or problems [20], others try to characterize the tasks and their solutions taking into account objective and subjective factors, e.g. national curricula and/or the age, gender and other personal characteristics of the participants etc. [3, 5, 6]. The identification of key characteristics of the tasks is essential for modelling and predicting the success of the participants and could also influence the curriculum content of a particular country.

At the beginning of the competition in 2006, Opmanis, Dagienė and Truu proposed a categorisation of the tasks: general logic, ICT in everyday life, practical and technical issues, information comprehension, algorithms and programming, mathematics underlying computer science and history and trivia [16]. In 2008, Dagiene and Futschek analysed the competition tasks and defined criteria for the selection of the tasks. They corresponded to the new categorisation, which was introduced by Bebras Organizing Committee: Information comprehension, INF–representation (symbolic, numerical, visual), coding, encryption; Algorithmic thinking, ALG–including programming aspects; Using computer systems, USE–e.g., search engines, email or spread sheets; Structures, patterns and arrangements, STRUC–combinatorics and discrete structures (such as graphs); Puzzles, PUZ–logical puzzles, games (e.g., mastermind and minesweeper); SOC ICT and Societ–social, ethical, cultural, international, legal issues [7].

Vaniček discusses indicators and their combinations that influence a contest task difficulty [20]. He considered the following indicators: length of the text, reading comprehension requirements, task formulation, formulation of the answer, use of an explanatory picture, use of an illustrative example; topic-specific factors: area, way of solution, situation, existence of a formal description, expertise in task assignment. He examined which of the indicators are correlated and concluded that the comparison of different indicators does not always match with other indicators and that the indicator "no answer" describes a task difficulty very well.

Kalaš and Tomcsanyiova characterised tasks for categories Benjamins (10–12 years old) and Cadets (12–14 years old) into four categories of informatics education: digital literacy, programming, problem solving and data handling. They emphasized the importance of the programming category and found that the students' interest in programming has been confirmed and that the attractiveness of education in lower secondary education is pleasingly high. It is of crucial importance to provide support for them through various strategies [12, 13]. Budinská, Mayerová and Veselovská proposed a new categorisation of tasks for the Little Beaver category: digital literacy tasks, logical tasks subdivided into graph tasks and statement tasks, algorithmic tasks and programming tasks [5]. They compared the results of competition with respect to the competitors' gender and country. The qualitative analysis revealed several factors among the tasks that may have led to very similar tasks differing in difficulty, such as: different wording of tasks, different distractors, different accompanying graphics and different ways of formulating answers.

The researchers conducted international research on difficulties, gender differences and CT skills reflected in Bebras problem solving. They use their own categorisation for the tasks. They analysed performance data on Bebras tasks of 115,400 students in grades 3–12, using categorization based on CSTA/ISTE categories: data collection DC, data analysis DA, data representation DR, problem decomposition PD, abstraction ABS, algorithms & procedures ALG, automation AU, parallelization PAR and simulation SIM. Algorithms and data representation dominated the challenge, and accounted for 75–90% of the tasks, while other categories such as abstraction, parallelization and problem decomposition were sometimes represented by one or two questions in different age groups. Overall, they found that students from different school systems had comparable CT skills. In particular, CT skills did not play a major role in assessing the difficulty of a task, but they were reflected in the students' willingness to solve tasks and understand the core concepts of computer science [11].

Broad international qualitative research conducted prior to the research described above, which focused on CT skills in Bebras challenge for K-9 students, also confirmed the predominance of ALG and DR tasks (Fig. 1). They suggested using CT skill tuples (pairs or triples) to classify certain tasks and defined subcategories in ALG categories such as: Constraint, Formula, Optimization, Procedures, Verification, Sequencing, Ordering and Identification. They used an inductive method (analytical coding) when looking at the structure of Bebras tasks that include pure algorithmic concepts. A member of the team read each task in the corresponding years and created a classification for the questions, including a description for the classification. The classification scheme was discussed with other team members. The classification of each relevant task was completed by one team member and then reviewed by at least one other team member. Conflicts were resolved during a discussion phase before the final classification for the task was established [4].

2.2 Categorization Used in Tagging Bebras Tasks

In the previous section we saw that there is no general categorization of concepts of CT skills. In our empirical research, we used a CT model that consists of concepts in cross section. As main categorization we used a categorization by Dagiene, Sentance and Stupuriene [8], which we modified according to the categorization of ACARA [15]. The new categorization consists of six CT skills - five skills from Dagiene's categorization, which are also in the cross section to ACARA categorization, and one additional skill, Modelling and Simulation. The new categorization includes six CT skills: Algorithmic thinking, Generalization, Decomposition, Evaluation, Abstraction and Modelling and

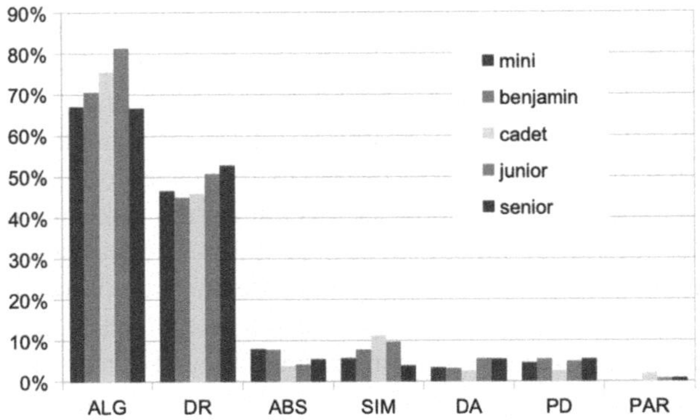

Fig. 1. Percentage of the seven categories of CT skills ALG, DR, ABS, SIM, DA, PD and PAR (see the text) assigned to the Bebras tasks over different age groups (colours). Source: [10].

Table 1. The categorization of CT skills used in this paper

CT skill name	Description
Algorithmic thinking	Thinking in terms of sequences and rules; Executing an algorithm; Creating an algorithm
Modelling and simulation	Making a model or system to illustrate a process in a computer; System testing; Algorithm-based modelling
Decomposition	Breaking down tasks → thinking about problems in terms of component parts; Making decisions about dividing into sub-tasks with integration in mind, e.g. deduction
Generalization	Pattern recognition, simulations and links from data collected; Solving new problems on the basis of already known solutions to similar problems; Inductive reasoning
Evaluation	Finding best solution; Making decisions about whether good use of resources; Fitting to purpose
Abstract thinking	Removing unnecessary details; Spotting key elements in problem; Choosing a representation of a system

Simulation. Skill of Modelling and Simulation allowed us to achieve a greater spread of CT skills between the Bebras tasks.

3 Empirical Research and Analysis

3.1 Examples of Task Categorization

In the empirical research we wanted to find out how high the degree of agreement is among the experts annotating the Bebras tasks with the categories of CT skills needed to solve them. The annotating questionnaire consisted of five tasks from Slovene Bebras competition in 2019 [18]. The tasks were selected from different competition and age groups from 6th grade to 9th grade of elementary school and 1st to 2nd year of high school. The results from the questionnaire were compared with the categorization of the Bebras tasks we had undertaken. Each annotator selected one to three of the most important CT skills that we believe the child should know when solving a certain task. To better understand our way of annotating the Bebras tasks with categories, let us consider a few examples.

First, let us analyse the example task of Roundabout city, depicted in Fig. 2. To solve the task, we think the child should have knowledge in modelling and simulation. We have chosen modelling and simulation because the task illustrates the sequence of command execution. Just as the computer executes commands sequentially, the child had to execute the sequence of exports in a roundabout to find a solution to the task. There may be some other CT skills, but the skill of Modelling and Simulation takes precedence over the others.

In Roundabout City, the navigation software does not give instructions like

- At the next roundabout, take the 4th exit.
- At the next roundabout, take the 1st exit.
- At the next roundabout, take the 2nd exit.

Instead, it gives you a sequence of numbers, like "4 1 2" which would make you go this way:

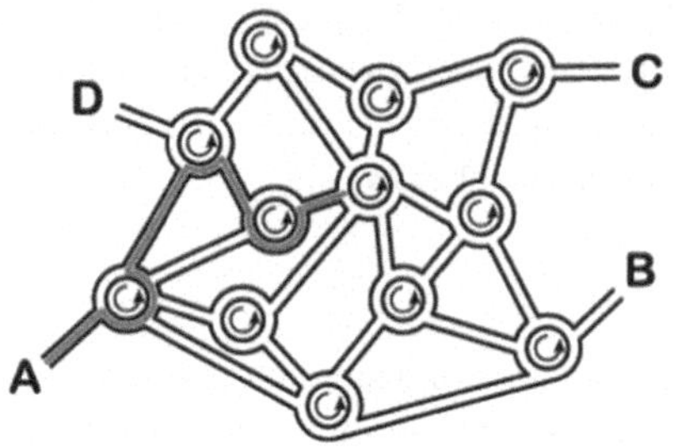

Question:
If we start from A and follow the sequence 3 1 3 2 3, where will we end up?

A B C or D

Fig. 2. Bebras task roundabout city

In the Bebras task of Colouring inn, depicted in Fig. 3, the competitors are asked to colour the pattern with as few colours as possible. One of the characteristics of the evaluation skill is to find the best solution. Since the pupils should find as few colours as possible, knowledge for evaluation is necessary. However, another skill that is important for the solution of this task is the skill of Modelling and simulation. We can present the task as a system test if the system is looking for the best solution. Another skill is a skill of Abstract thinking. In order to solve the task, the students have to identify key elements in the problem and remove unnecessary details.

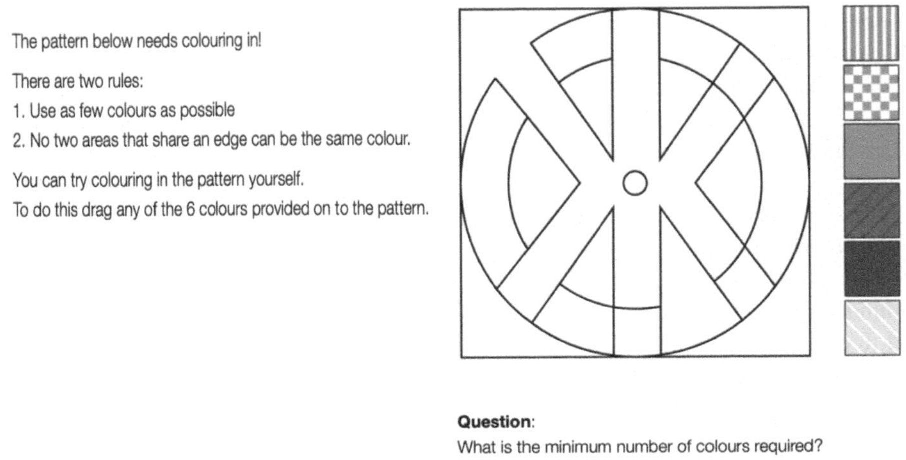

Fig. 3. Bebras task colouring inn

We have to be aware that despite clear definitions, the annotation of a given Bebras tasks with CT skills necessary to solve it can be very subjective. That is why we wanted to assess the validity of the CT skills categorization scheme. We checked this with a questionnaire in which 5 university employees, mentors of the Bebras competition and members of the competition's program council participated. The questionnaire contained more detailed descriptions of individual CT skills. Participants were given five tasks from the Bebras contest, each task being categorized according to CT skills. To perform this analysis, we used the Fleiss' Kappa statistics introduced below.

3.2 Fleiss' Kappa Statistics

In many research areas, the analysis of the agreement among annotators often provides a useful tool for assessing the reliability of an annotating (in our case, categorization) scheme. A typical example would include physicians (annotators) that categorize patients to those who need and those who do not need a therapy. To assess the reliability of the diagnostic procedure followed by the physicians, we can examine the degree of agreement between the physicians' categorizations of the fixed set of patients [2].

Commonly used method for measuring the inter-annotator agreement is Scott's Pi statistics, which was later generalized by Cohen kappa. Both are based on the basic idea of the kappa statistics (also kappa coefficient), which assumes that some of the actually observed cases of inter-annotator agreement ($\overline{P}$) are due to pure chance ($\overline{P_e}$), i.e.,

$$\kappa = \frac{\overline{P} - \overline{P_e}}{1 - \overline{P_e}}.$$

While Scott's Pi statistic assumes that the responses of the annotators have the same distribution, this assumption is reversed in Cohen's Kappa. Both statistics are limited on measuring the degree of agreement among two annotators. Since our experiment involve six annotators, we use Fleiss' kappa statistics, a generalization of Scott's Pi that can be used to assess the agreement among an arbitrary number of annotators.

The proportions of the agreement $\overline{P}$ *observed* in the experiment and the *expected* random agreement $\overline{P_e}$ are estimated using the contingency table (see the example in Table 2). Each column in the contingency table corresponds to one of the N subjects (patients in the example in the first paragraph or Bebras tasks in our case), while the k rows correspond to the subject categories (the same example includes two categories of antibiotic and non-antibiotic patients, in our case, we have two possible decisions of the annotator). Each cell in the table, n_{ij}, takes into account the number of annotators that assign the j-th subject (Bebras task) to the i-th category (of CT skills).

Table 2. Example of the contingency table used to calculate the Fleiss' Kappa statistics for the inter-annotator agreement when categorizing five Bebras tasks into the category of Algorithmic thinking.

	Task (1)	Task (2)	Task (3)	Task (4)	Task (5)	$\sum_{i=1}^{5} Task(i)$	p_i
Algorithmic thinking (YES)	4	2	0	4	1	11	0.44
Algorithmic thinking (NO)	1	3	5	1	4	14	0.56
P_j	0.60	0.40	1.00	0.60	0.60		

Furthermore, for each subject (column in the contingency table), we first calculate P_j, the extent to which the annotators agree for j-th subject as $P_j = \frac{1}{n(n-1)}\left[\left(\sum_{i=1}^{k} n_{ij}^2\right) - n\right]$, where $n = \sum_{i=1}^{k} n_{ij}$ is the total number of ratings per subject. Next, we calculate p_i, the proportion of all assignments to the i-th category as $p_i = \frac{1}{N \cdot n} \sum_{j=1}^{N} n_{ij}$. Finally, the values of $\overline{P}$ and $\overline{P_e}$ are calculated as:

$$\overline{P} = \frac{1}{N} \cdot \sum_{j=1}^{N} P_j$$

and

$$\overline{P_e} = \sum_{i=1}^{k} (p_i)^2.$$

Note that both values are in the range between 0 and 1, which means that the extreme values of kappa are -1 and 1. The kappa value of -1 corresponds to the case of total disagreement between the annotators (note that in that case $\overline{P} = 0$ and $\overline{P_e} = 1$), while the value of 1 indicates perfect agreement among them (i.e., $\overline{P} = 1$ and $\overline{P_e} = 0$). In light of the running example, the value of $\kappa = 1$ would mean that all the experts agree on the annotation of the Bebras tasks with a certain category of CT skills. Landis and Koch [14] have proposed a guide for interpreting the intermediate Fleiss' kappa values, summarized in Table 3.

Table 3. A guide for interpretation of the values of the Fleiss' kappa statistics

κ value	Interpretation
<0	Poor agreement
0.01–0.20	Slight agreement
0.21–0.40	Fair agreement
0.41–0.60	Moderate agreement
0.61–0.80	Substantial agreement
0.81–1.00	Almost perfect agreement

3.3 Results

When determining the categorical designations according to the skills, the participants in the questionnaire were asked to annotate each task with one to three categories of CT skills. Thus, we calculate the Fleiss' Kappa statistics for each CT skill separately, the results being shown in Table 4. The mid column in the table reports the values of the statistics for the five participants in the experiment, while the right-most column reports the values of Fleiss' Kappa when our own annotation was added to the experimental data as a categorization provided by a sixth annotator.

Table 4. Fleiss' kappa statistics for the six categories of CT skills from Table 1.

Category of CT skills	Five annotators	Six annotators
Algorithmic thinking	$\kappa = 0.27$	$\kappa = 0.29$
Modelling and simulation	$\kappa = 0.19$	$\kappa = 0.21$
Decomposition	$\kappa = 0.17$	$\kappa = 0.23$
Generalization	$\kappa = 0.03$	$\kappa = 0.03$
Evaluation	$\kappa = 0.17$	$\kappa = 0.27$
Abstract thinking	$\kappa = -0.14$	$\kappa = -0.06$

Firstly, if we look at the values for each skill, we can see that by adding our categorization, the value of Fleiss' Kappa increases consistently for all categories of CT skills. For example, the value of Fleiss' Kappa for the five annotators is $\kappa = 0.19$, indicating a slight agreement between them. By adding our own categorization, the Fleiss'

Kappa value increases to $\kappa = 0.21$. The increased value of κ tells us that our categorization bears more similarities than differences when compared to the categorizations (annotations) of the five participants in the experiment.

Furthermore, it is obvious that the degree of agreement among the five annotators is mostly poor or slight at reach a fair level only for the category of algorithmic thinking. On the other hand, the agreement among the annotators becomes poor for the category of abstract thinking, where the value of Fleiss' Kappa is $\kappa = -0, 14$. The weak agreement for the same category is observed also when we add our own categorization as the sixth annotator. The result shows that there are many different perceptions of the category abstract thinking, which means that we should reconsider its definition.

The highest value of agreement was achieved by the CT skill of algorithmic thinking, which was expected because it is tangible, clearly defined, easy to understand, not only for experts but also for laymen. An important observation is also the higher degree of agreement for the category of Modelling and simulation. The result might be due our decision to separate the latter category from the (formerly too general) category of algorithmic thinking skills.

Finally, let us note that the results confirm our central conjecture that the various definitions and categorizations of CT skills lack clarity and unambiguity that would allow for better planning appropriate competition tasks and teaching exercises. Overall, the results show that we should consider reformulating the definitions for most of the categories of CT skills. Especially those where the level of agreement among the annotators is poor or slight, i.e., have the values under 0.20. Most critical categories include generalization and abstract thinking, while the categories of decomposition and evaluation might be considered close to critical.

4 Conclusions

In Slovenia, as in other countries without compulsory computing curricula at the primary level, the results of Bebras competition present important source of evidence of the development of the computational thinking of students. In order to gain substantial insight, we need a valid and reliable categorization of Bebras tasks based on CT skills.

Based on the empirical analysis of the reliability of the current schemes for annotating Bebras tasks with categories of skills necessary to solve them, we can conclude that we still lack valid, consensual and generally accepted categorization scheme. Our attempt to separate the category modelling and simulation from the previously too general category of algorithmic thinking seem to be a step in a right direction towards more complex, but clearer categorization scheme. Our results suggest that abstract thinking is another too general and vaguely defined category of CT skills.

While the empirical results show clear need for improvement of the categorization schemes, they do not reveal the reasons for disagreement among the annotators. The origin of the observed disagreements might be due to different understanding of the problem-solving processes between the two types of annotators participating our study: teachers and academics. We hypothesise that mentors (primary and secondary school teachers) categorize the tasks based on their own practical experience, while academics probably categorised the tasks according to learning theories, knowledge and skills from the field of problem-solving CS or by simulating the problem-solving process. Checking the validity of this hypothesis is out of scope of the experiment performed in this paper. In further studies, one would consider different, homogenous groups of annotators to check whether the reason for disagreement is the heterogenicity of the annotators participating our study.

Another important challenge to be talked by further studies is to explore the use of additional tools that would allow for a more reliable categorisation of certain tasks. Perhaps it would be most appropriate to involve children of different ages in the problem-solving process. We can then use paper-based tests with selected competitors of different ages, which allows detailed monitoring of the solution process, or we can consider using the method of "thinking aloud" during the processes of task reading and solving. Both hold a potential to contribute to the further clarification of the current ambiguous definitions and categorizations of the CT skills.

Acknowledgements. We would like to acknowledge the financial support of the Slovenian Research Agency, via the grants *P5-0093*, *V5-1930* and *N2-0056*, as well as the University of Rijeka, via the grant *uniri-drustv-18-20*.

References

1. Bebras – International Challenge on Informatics and Computational Thinking. https://www.bebras.org/, Accessed 22 May 2020
2. Banerjee, M., Capozzoli, M., McSweeney, L., Sinha, D.: Beyond kappa: a review of interrater agreement measures. Can. J. Stat. **27**(1), 3–23 (1999)
3. Bollin, A., Demarle-Meusel, H., Kesselbacher, M., Mößlacher, C., Rohrer, M., Sylle, J.: The bebras contest in Austria–do personality, self-concept and general interests play an influential role? International Conference on Informatics in Schools: Situation. Evolution, and Perspectives, pp. 283–294. Springer, Cham (2018)
4. Barendsen, E., et al.: Concepts in K-9 computer science education. In: Proceedings of the 2015 ITiCSE on Working Group Reports, pp. 85–116 (2015)
5. Budinská, L., Mayerová, K., Veselovská, M.: Bebras task analysis in category little beavers in Slovakia. In: Dagiene, V., Hellas, A. (eds.) ISSEP 2017. LNCS, vol. 10696, pp. 91–101. Springer, Cham (2017). https://doi.org/10.1007/978-3-319-71483-7_8
6. Budinská, L., Mayerová, K., Šimandl, V.: Differences between 9–10 years old pupils' results from Slovak and Czech bebras contest. In: Pozdniakov, S.N., Dagienė, V. (eds.) ISSEP 2018. LNCS, vol. 11169, pp. 307–318. Springer, Cham (2018). https://doi.org/10.1007/978-3-030-02750-6_24
7. Dagienė, V., Futschek, G.: Bebras international contest on informatics and computer literacy: criteria for good tasks. In: Mittermeir, R.T., Sysło, M.M. (eds.) ISSEP 2008. LNCS, vol. 5090, pp. 19–30. Springer, Heidelberg (2008). https://doi.org/10.1007/978-3-540-69924-8_2
8. Dagienė, V., Sentance, S., Stupurienė, G.: Developing a two-dimensional categorization system for educational tasks in informatics. Informatica **28**(1), 23–44 (2017)
9. Denning, P.J., Tedre, M.: Computational Thinking. The MIT Press, Cambridge (2019)
10. Grover, S., Pea, R.: Computational thinking in K–12: a review of the state of the field. Educ. Res. **42**(1), 38–43 (2013)
11. Izu, C., Mirolo, C., Settle, A., Mannila, L., Stupuriene, G.: Exploring bebras tasks content and performance: a multinational study. Inf. Educ. **16**(1), 39–59 (2017)

12. Kabatova, M., Kalaš, I., Tomcsanyiova, M.: Programming in Slovak primary schools. Olympiads Inf. **10**, 125–159 (2016)
13. Kalas, I., Tomcsanyiova, M.: Students' attitude to programming in modern informatics. In: Proceedings of the 9th WCCE 2009, Education and Technology for a Better World (2009)
14. Landis, J.R., Koch, G.G.: An application of hierarchical kappa-type statistics in the assessment of majority agreement among multiple observers. Biometrics **33**, 363–374 (1977)
15. NSW Government: coding and computational thinking: what is the evidence? https://education.nsw.gov.au/our-priorities/innovate-for-the-future/education-for-a-changing-world/media/documents/future-frontiers-education-for-an-ai-world/Coding-and-Computational-Report_A.pdf. Accessed 5 Nov 2019
16. Opmanis, M., Dagiene, V., Truu, A.: Task types at "Beaver" contests. In: Information Technologies at School, pp. 509–519 (2006)
17. Papert, S.: Mindstorms: Children, Computers, and Powerful Ideas. Basic Books, New York (1980)
18. Tekmovanja Bober, ACM. Naloge in rešitve (2015/16; 16/17; 17/18; 18/19). https://tekmovanja.acm.si/?q=bober/naloge-re%C5%A1itve. Accessed 22 May 2020
19. Ternik, Ž.: Analiza rezultatov tekmovanja Bober skozi prizmo razumevanja konceptov računalništva ter računalniškega mišljenja = Analysis of the results of the Beaver contest based on the understanding of the computer science concepts and on computational thinking: MSc thesis, Ljubljana (2019)
20. Vaníček, J.: What makes situational informatics tasks difficult? In: Brodnik, A., Tort, F. (eds.) ISSEP 2016. LNCS, vol. 9973, pp. 90–101. Springer, Cham (2016). https://doi.org/10.1007/978-3-319-46747-4_8
21. Wing, J.: Computational thinking. Commun. ACM **49**(3), 33–36 (2006)

A Two-Dimensional Classification Model for the Bebras Tasks on Informatics Based Simultaneously on Subfields and Competencies

Valentina Dagiene[1(✉)], Juraj Hromkovic[2(✉)], and Regula Lacher[2(✉)]

[1] Institute of Data Science and Information Technologies, Vilnius University, Vilnius, Lithuania
valentina.dagiene@mif.vu.lt
[2] ETH Zürich, Zurich, Switzerland
{juraj.hromkovic,regula.lacher}@inf.ethz.ch

Abstract. The Bebras challenge on informatics originated 15 years ago, by now involves over 60 countries, and consists of short problem-solving tasks based on informatics (computing, computer science) and computational thinking. This paper deals with learning taxonomies and models that do not focus merely on partitioning computer science into its subareas, but rather on competencies that the learners can reach by working with information, data, algorithms, and automation processes. The contribution of this paper is a new concept for classifying tasks that also offers new ideas for generating tasks and which is used for creating spiral curricula for teaching informatics. One advantage of our approach is that the classes are not mutually exclusive, which reflects the fact that a task can support the development of different competencies in several areas. This allows to specify the benefits of working on a given task much more precisely and can thus help teachers to design and choose adequate tasks. Another advantage of this approach is the inclusion of important competencies that are not subject specific but are nevertheless important for the holistic development of school education. In addition, the proposed model can be used to develop informatics tasks (assignments), that are not only described by the topics to be covered, but also in competencies for the learners to reach.

Keywords: Bebras challenge · Classification · Competence · Competency model · Computational thinking · Informatics education · Learning taxonomy

1 Introduction

Recently, the importance of computer science education in primary and secondary schools has received more and more attention. Children's and students' interests and motivation in computing related fields are highly influenced by their educators.

While the term "Computer Science" (CS) (or "computing", mainly settled in England in recent years) are used in a very similar way internationally, the term "Informatics" (respectively the German "Informatik" or the French "Informatique") is understood

K. Kori and M. Laanpere (Eds.): ISSEP 2020, LNCS 12518, pp. 42–54, 2020.
https://doi.org/10.1007/978-3-030-63212-0_4

differently, depending on the country or the social or cultural background. In this paper we will use the mentioned terms synonymously.

During the last decade Computational Thinking (CT) has been actively promoted through K-12 curriculum as a part of an informatics subject or in an integrated way. CT encompasses a set of concepts from informatics that aid in formulating problems and solving in different fields [1]. However, CT has its roots in early years of human society. It "evolved from ancient origins over 4,500 years ago to its present, highly developed, professional state" as Denning and Tedre summarized in their deep-thought book [2, p. 19] and Hromkovic and Lacher pointed it out in [3]. CT is based on involving fundamental informatics components, such as data collection and analysis, data representation, logical reasoning, abstraction, algorithm design, decomposition, parallelization, automation, pattern recognition, generalization, simulation, and defining algorithms as part of a detailed solution [4, 5].

To introduce informatics to schools, both formal and non-formal education contribute to build the necessary foundations in knowledge and skills. Visual gaming environments and tangible interfaces provide tools to learn informatics in early years [6], computer science unplugged activities [7–9] provide possibilities to develop CT without computer, and Bebras international challenge [10] inspires students to discover informatics concepts and foster computational thinking, which involves systematical information processing needed to solve tasks (problems). Problem solving is one of the most important components for developing CT and the Bebras model [10].

In this paper we discuss learning taxonomies and competency models with the intention of developing a combined subject-based and competence-based classification system (a model) for Bebras tasks. The aim is not to present a complete list of informatics subfields and related keywords or to offer a final classification for Bebras tasks. What we offer is a classification strategy for tasks that can be helpful in designing Bebras competitions (designing tasks and tasks sequences, choosing the right formulations) and even in developing textbooks based on sequences of short challenging tasks.

We suggest a model for a new classification that can be updated and extended going forward. This classification model has two levels (dimensions), namely "subject" and "competency". The first dimension branches informatics into fields and subfields. The second dimension presents a list of competencies which the pupils can reach in this subfield, and additionally these competencies are presented with respect to their hardness according to the revised Bloom's taxonomy [11]. In this way one can simultaneously see which informatics topic and which competency with respect to CT a concrete task approaches and how it fits the Bloom's hierarchy.

2 Reviewing of Existing Classification Models of Learning

2.1 Research Methodology

Our research is a part of long going mixed methods research. After more than a decade of active involvement in creating and reviewing Bebras tasks, the various learning taxonomies as well as models are discussed. We have reviewed a number of taxonomies described in the educational literature and studies in the computer science education research literature that use of one or more taxonomies as an analytic tool. In addition, we have looked at the practice of developing assignments (exercises, tasks) in informatics both for formal and non-formal education, drawing on our and colleagues' experience.

We have kept in mind the methodology of Mayring [12], who had combined several techniques for systematic text analysis to a very systematic process by (1) either using deductive strategy when the category system is derived from suitable existing theories or (2) using inductive strategy when the category system is developed during the analysis from the text corpus. Our reasoning is based on combining both strategies.

In order to improve the Bebras task classification, we have reviewed a number of learning taxonomies described in the educational literature as well as studies in the informatics education research area. We reviewed hundreds of Bebras tasks developed by various countries during the last decade. We have used this evidence to propose a new informatics-specific model based on competency. Our attention is focused essentially on cognitive domain in informatics.

2.2 Existing Learning Taxonomies and Competency Models

A taxonomy is a classification system that is ordered in some way. Learning taxonomies and models describe and categorize the stages in cognitive, affective and other dimensions of a learner during the learning process. Learning taxonomies are widely used in a variety of educational contexts, i.e., to describe the learning stages at which a learner is operational in a certain topic. Of these taxonomies, the most widely cited is the Bloom's taxonomy [11] which describes the cognitive domain. The SOLO taxonomy uses a set of categories that describe a mixture of quantitative and qualitative differences at the performance of students [13]. Both Bloom's taxonomy and the SOLO taxonomy are increasingly used in the design and assessment of courses in informatics.

Shifting attention to the outcomes of the educational process has increased the interest in defining competencies in terms of what makes students successful in their future endeavors, irrelevant whether this success relates to personal development, employment, or participation in society. Since CT has become a part of computing school curricula in many countries, the paradigm of competence orientation has led to very detailed curricula which describe a large variety of detailed competencies.

Competencies describe what the individual is or should be able to do, behavior however is always shaped and constrained by the environment. We can only observe 'manifested competence', i.e., competence as it becomes manifest in a situation and in an environment. Competence integrates knowledge, skills, and dispositions and is context-situated. These integral components of competence manifest in observable and tangible form within a work context.

Existing competence frameworks provide insights into different types of competencies and different ways of their modelling. Competence models are the foundation of assessment and evaluation in terms of educational goals and thereby provide major information for revision and improvement of education [14].

Frezza et al. [15] have discussed a competence based approach that was well suited for constructing learning environments challenged by developing, describing and including competencies relevant to informatics education.

In order to be able to represent competencies more strictly, Schlüter and Brinda have defined a competence as an integrative function consisting of a set of knowledge elements, a set of skill elements, and a set of disposition elements [16]. These three sets have represented the knowledge, skills, and dispositions associated with performing the competence in a context.

PISA (the Program for International Student Assessment) together with OECD (The Organisation for Economic Co-operation and Development) has prioritized education for global citizenship and global competencies and proposed an assessment framework for which they introduced the notion of global competence as a multidimensional capacity [17]. Structurally, global competency in the PISA OECD framework is composed of knowledge, cognitive skills, and social skills and attitudes.

In Germany, a three-dimensional competence model was designed a decade ago for use in K-12 informatics education [18]. It is argued that learners develop competency by engaging with content in different processes. Content and skills are seen as interwoven, the content can be identified from analyzing a skill and vice-versa. The third dimension describes a quality of engaging with content and skill, how much the learner makes the content and skills his or her own, which relates to dispositions. Hereby, the informatics related topics and methods of the competencies cover a broad range of subject areas of informatics.

The persistently challenging problem of transferring learning to new situations coupled with the move from knowledge to learning has created favorable conditions for the popularity of the terms competence and competency. Kramer et al. have identified five dimensions that are common to many competence models [19]. Furthermore, they have excluded the context factor and came out with a four dimensional competency model that can be applied to informatics education: (1) Knowledge structure, (2) Content representation, (3) Cognitive processes, and (4) Metacognitive processes. This competency model has structural similarities with a model proposed by Havenga et al. [20] that aimed to measure the students' abilities in an introductory programming course.

3 Bebras Challenge

3.1 What Is a Bebras Task

Since the beginning of the Bebras challenge in 2004, development of new questions (tasks) based on informatics concepts is the crucial point [10]. The initial motivation to develop short challenging tasks was to introduce main computing concepts and principles in schools. Short tasks and small problem-solving activities should develop computational thinking skills and promote the creativity of students as well as of teachers.

Over the years, the Bebras community has developed thousands of tasks. Most of them are proposed as interactive and/or open-ended questions. However, even when answers have to be chosen from a list, there is no unique way of getting to the solution. The tasks can be used in the annual contests, but they can also be the starting point for in-depth educational activities [21, 22].

The tasks are related to concepts such as algorithms (sequential and concurrent); data structures (heaps, stacks and queues, trees, and graphs); modelling of states, control flow and data flow; human-computer interaction; and graphics. Students do not formally study these topics, instead, the topics are introduced implicitly by letting the students think about interesting problems. A "narrative cover story" is used to relate the tasks to an underlying topic.

We need to design suitable short tasks based on informatics concepts and aimed to develop CT. A Bebras task should be related to at least one informatics concept, attract children's attention with a story, picture, interactivity, or challenge and not require specific technical knowledge. The tasks should be short (fit on a computer screen), and the solving time should be set according to pupils' age. Bebras-like tasks are no longer than 15 lines and can be solved in 3–5 min. The short tasks support the idea of addressing a wider audience of, for example, varying background and knowledge. The attribute "short" does not necessarily mean that the short tasks are easy to solve. However, a short task should have an easy-to-understand problem statement. The short tasks should be complex enough to allow creativity in the solution process.

The Bebras community has approved a basic definition [23] whereby a good task proposal: (1) introduces or reinforces a topic in computer science, (2) is quick and easy to understand, but (3) is challenging to solve, and (4) is usable after the contest as a good example.

Besides this internal definition there have been some attempts to define or at least hint at what a good task proposal is. Vanícek [24] tried to provide a closer definition by refining the four criteria and relating them to some formal and practical aspects.

3.2 Bebras Tasks Categorization

Classifying Bebras tasks is important in two ways: (1) to organize the tasks collected each year, and (2) to guide countries in creating new tasks and thereby influencing informatics education over the world. Since the Bebras challenge began, there has been an interest in classifying and categorizing tasks. Early on in the project, the following seven categories were used [25]: (1) General logic; (2) ICT (Information and Communication Technology) in everyday life; (3) Practical and technical issues; (4) Information comprehension; (5) Algorithms and programming; (6) Mathematics underlying computer science; (7) History and trivia.

These categories were also used for developing new tasks as the main criteria to know which informatics topics and concepts need to be covered. Few years later the Bebras tasks' categories were revised and a modified system was proposed [23]:

1. Information comprehension (representation, coding, encryption)
2. Algorithmic thinking (including programming aspects)
3. Structures, patterns and arrangements (discrete structures: graphs, trees)
4. Puzzles (logical puzzles, games)
5. Using computer systems
6. ICT and Society (social, ethical, cultural, international, legal issues).

Since then there have been several attempts to refine these categories [26–28]. One category of task proposals, "Using computer systems", has been debated again and again. Many typical task proposals for this category require pre-knowledge that is not available to students of most participating countries, and therefore it has been not used for task proposals in the recent years. This criticism, together with the fact that almost all tasks are related to data and algorithms (the first two categories), shows that the current categories are not state of the art.

A further reason to renew the Bebras task categorization system is the demand for a combination of computational thinking skills with areas of "content competences" used to define educational standards for computer science education in school. Incorporating both described categorization systems a two-dimensional system was proposed [29].

4 The Proposed Two-Dimensional Classification Model of the Bebras Tasks Based on Subfields and Competency

4.1 Basic Concept of Classification

The choice of Bebras tasks and the strategy of building informatics curricula for schools are not based on splitting computer science into many subfields as in research and university studies. The central point is the development of the fundamentals that are the common core and unavoidable prior knowledge for all these subfields and simultaneously the fundament of computer scientists' way of thinking. Because of this, we follow the historical approach of three roots (information and data, automation and algorithms, technology) of informatics as presented in [3, 8, 9]. Another reason for taking this approach is to follow the concept of constructionism of S. Papert merged with critical thinking. We want to follow the history of developing computer science concepts and enable pupils to re-discover them by "learning by getting things to work".

Additionally, our classification has to be able to help us to design sequences of tasks that fit school curricula in such a way that we can follow the deepening in particular topics by learning taxonomies.

4.2 The Resulting Model of the Bebras Tasks

The following implementation of our classification strategy is not a final product. The main idea is to motivate and encourage colleagues to extend it appropriately by further subjects and related competencies that are available in a corresponding age group in school education.

All competencies listed below start with "Pupils can" and so we omit to write this at the beginning of the sentences here (Table 1).

One very important advantage of this classification model is that with a task or sequence of tasks (teaching material) one is encouraged to approach as many different competencies as doable, i.e., this classification is not exclusive, but the opposite of it.

Our approach takes care on competences and Bloom taxonomy, and we believe that this way of thinking is the best starting point to create good training and textbooks and tasks for pupils. This enables also to relate teaching informatics to other subjects as math and other discipline and taking care of cognitive load over all subjects and see everything in a broad context.

Table 1. Two dimensional classification model of the Bebras tasks based on Competency of informatics and Bloom's taxonomy

Subfields of informatics		R	U	Ap	An	E	C
Data	1.1 Information and data representation by symbols						
	Recognize patterns in sequences	+					
	Classify sequences with respect to some attributes	+	+	+	+		
	Use recognized patterns to prolong sequences or filling in missing items		+	+			
	Discover principles used to create a sequence and apply these principles		+	+			
	Understand concepts of different number representations and transform them into decimal system	+	+				
	Particularly transform number representations between binary and decimal numbers		+	+			
	Count and execute addition in different number representation system		+	+			
	Understand different systems for creating self-verifying and self-correcting codes and use them by coding data	+	+	+			
	Communicate with given sequences of symbols that represent messages (in advance agreed codes for different messages)	+	+				
	Choose alphabets (symbols, signals) and use them to create coding for a given collection of words or messages and apply them in communication	+	+	+			
	Compare two number representations with respect to different attributes (length, understandability, efficient computing)				+	+	
	Apply fundamental principles in order to design new systems for number representations and to work with the new systems						+
	Compare different self-verifying (self-correcting) codes with respect to the number of additional control bits and create new codes by optimizing their length					+	+
	1.2 Data representation and visualization by graphs and drawings						
	Understand the process of abstraction by reducing the complexity of drawings that represent the real world tasks	+	+	+			
	Use graphs for model networks of different kinds	+	+	+			
	Use graphs to represent relations between objects	+	+	+			
	Visualize data in different ways and compare the usefulness of the different approaches		+	+	+	+	
	Estimate the saved information and the lost information for different graphical representations				+		
	Use matrices to represent graphs in a symbolic way		+	+			
	1.3 Data protection and security						

(*continued*)

Table 1. *(continued)*

Subfields of informatics		R	U	Ap	An	E	C
	Use secret writings based on exchanging the position of particular symbols	+	+				
	Use secret writings and cryptosystems based on coding letters by other symbols of sequences of symbols	+	+				
	Analyze crypto-texts and cryptosystems with stochastic methods to break them		+	+	+		
	Create new original cryptosystems based on known principles, use them, and judge their strengths and weaknesses				+	+	+
	Understand and apply statistical methods for designing and for breaking cryptosystems				+	+	+
	Understand the requirements for the choice of passwords and judge whether a password is good or not	+	+				
	Create appropriate passwords			+			
	1.4 Organization of data collections and search						
	Use trees with subfolders to organize data collections		+	+			
	Use hashing (for classification into groups) to organize data collections		+	+			
	Understand and use sorting and binary search in sorted sequences		+	+			
	Analyze and compare the efficiency of different approaches of data organization with respect to searching				+	+	
	Create own hashing strategies for given data and compare them				+	+	+
	Compare different tree (subfolders) strategies for a given data collection				+	+	
	Analyze the computational complexity of different searching strategies				+	+	
	Analyze the amount of work needed to organize data				+	+	
	Reorganize data collections after updates			+	+	+	+
	1.5 Compression						
	Understand and apply simple algorithms for compressions of texts (symbol sequences)	+	+	+			
	Understand the digital representations of pictures by pixels	+	+				
	Apply simple algorithms for picture compressions		+	+			
	Combine different strategies for text compression to develop better ones			+	+	+	+
Algorithms	2.1 Description of computing problems						
	Recognize symbolic and visual tools (matrices, graphs, etc.) for describing problems	+					

(continued)

Table 1. (*continued*)

Subfields of informatics		R	U	Ap	An	E	C
	Understand the descriptions of an instance of a computing problem and interpreting them correctly		+				
	Decide for a problem description and whether a solution candidate is a feasible solution		+				
	Search for a feasible solution by experiment (trial and error)		+	+			
	Understand the language of logic in describing computing problems		+	+	+		
	Apply different criteria to assign costs to feasible solutions		+				
	2.2 Solving problems by Brute-force strategies						
	Classify objects with respect to their properties		+				
	Count the number of objects with given properties		+	+	+		
	Use tables or trees to list all feasible solutions of concrete problem instances		+	+			
	Compare different feasible solutions with respect to a cost measure		+				
	Apply the brute-force strategy to find optimal solutions of concrete problem instances		+	+			
	Compare different criteria for assigning values to feasible solutions			+	+		
	Create new criteria for evaluating feasible solutions that better capture the reality (our optimization goals)					+	+
	2.3 Automata and describing processes						
	Understand the model of automata as an acceptor or as a generator of symbol sequences	+	+				
	Recognize whether a symbol sequence is accepted/generated by a given automaton		+	+			
	Execute/simulate computations by a finite automaton			+			
	Recognize the equivalence of two finite automata				+	+	
	2.4 Data structures in data processing						
	Understand the concept of arrays and lists	+	+				
	Recognize stack or queue in a data structure in real processes	+					
	Apply stacks and queues to different solutions and for casting the results of running processes		+	+	+		
	Use trees for object classification		+	+			
	Use trees for data organization			+	+		
	2.5 Solving strategies for algorithmic problems						
	Understand concrete algorithms as strategies for solving successfully infinitely many instances of a problem		+	+	+	+	
	Verify and test algorithms		+	+	+	+	

(*continued*)

Table 1. (*continued*)

Subfields of informatics		R	U	Ap	An	E	C
	Prove the correctness of algorithms				+	+	
	Understand the concepts: divide and conquer, recursion, local search, and dynamic programming for algorithm design				+	+	+
	Recognize the design method of a presented algorithm	+	+				
	Apply algorithm design to solve concrete problem instances			+	+	+	+
	2.6 Sorting and searching						
	Find a minimum, maximum or medium in unsorted sequences	+	+	+			
	Understand and apply binary search to any sorted sequence of objects with a linear index		+	+			
	Analyze the computational complexity of binary search				+	+	
	Understand and apply different sorting algorithms		+	+			
	Analyze and compare the efficiency of different sorting strategies			+	+	+	
	2.7 Parallel processes						
	Recognize parallel processes in real situations	+					
	Understand the modelling of parallel processes		+	+			
	Solve instances of scheduling tasks		+	+			
	Simulate the execution of parallel processes following given description	+	+	+			
	Recognize and analyze conflicts that can occur in parallel processing		+	+	+		
	Plan and control parallel processes			+	+	+	+
	2.8 Artificial intelligence						
	Understand heuristics and apply them in order to solve instances of concrete problems	+	+	+			
	Analyze the work of heuristics on concrete problem instances and recognize why they fail		+	+	+		
	Compare the success of different heuristics for a concrete problem and choose an appropriate one			+	+	+	
	Simulate learning processes of simple models of machine learning	+	+	+			
	Use machine learning for classifying data			+			
	Evaluate the statistics success of concrete machine learning approaches for concrete classification tests			+	+	+	
Technology: programming, robotics, networks	3.1 Programming						
	Execute programs as sequences of instructions	+	+	+			
	Design programs for describing the movement in two dimensional space or drawing pictures		+	+	+	+	+
	Understand and apply the concept of repeat-loop		+	+			

(*continued*)

Table 1. (*continued*)

Subfields of informatics		R	U	Ap	An	E	C
	Understand and apply the concept of modular program design		+	+	+	+	+
	Understand and apply the concept of variables		+	+	+		
	Test programs and search for syntactic and logical errors		+	+	+	+	
	Understand and apply conditional instruction as if-then-else and while-loop		+	+	+		
	Formalize constraints and conditions in the language of logic and apply them by conditional instructions		+	+	+		
	Develop programs solving given problems			+	+	+	+
	Building robots from different components and program them			+	+	+	+
	3.2 Robotics						
	Navigate robots along a given path or trajectory	+	+	+			
	Execute or simulate robot's activities by following sequences of instructions	+	+				
	Understand processes as transformations between states	+	+	+			
	3.3 Networks						
	Recognize and understand the abstract representations of networks by graphs	+	+				
	Find path for information transmission or goods delivery	+	+	+			
	Broadcast information or goods in parallel in concrete networks		+	+			
	Measure the time needed to broadcast, accumulate or gossip information in networks			+	+		
	Design strategies for broadcasting information in concrete networks			+	+	+	+

R – Remember, **U** – Understand, **Ap** – Apply, **An** – Analyze, **E** – Execute, **C** – Create

5 Discussion and Further Work

In the process of developing spiral curricula for schools and corresponding textbooks, we applied this classification model in school projects with more than 550 schools and 15 000 pupils. This broad experience was the base for teaching and deepening different computer science topics in the right order. More detailed comments on this effort can be found in textbooks for teachers in the series "Einfach Informatik" [8].

But this experience is not enough to validate completely our classification model. We have a large amount of data that is awaiting evaluation, and we are starting research projects measuring the knowledge transfer with respect to different competencies. We also plan to classify a large sample of Bebras tasks to find out how well the tasks fit to our model. Last but not least, this in an invitation to the community to join us in the validation of our classification as well as to try to refine or revise it.

References

1. Wing, J.M.: Computational thinking. Commun. ACM **49**(3), 33–35 (2006)
2. Denning, P.J., Tedre, M.: Computational Thinking. The MIT Press, Cambridge (2019)
3. Hromkovic, J.: Homo informaticus – why computer science fundamentals are an unavoidable part of human culture and how to teach them. Olympiads Inform. **10**, 99–109 (2016)
4. Grover, S., Pea, R.: Computational thinking in K-12: a review of the state of the field. Educ. Res. **42**(1), 38–43 (2013)
5. Heintz, F., Mannila, L., Färnqvist, T.: A review of models for introducing computational thinking, computer science and computing in K-12 education. In: IEEE Frontiers in Education Conference (FIE) (2016)
6. Garneli, V., Giannakos, M., Chorianopoulos, K.: Computing education in K-12 schools: a review of the literature. In: IEEE Global Engineering Education Conference, pp. 543–551 (2015)
7. Bell, T., Alexander, J., Freeman, I., Grimley, M.: Computer science unplugged: school students doing real computing without computers. New Zealand J. Appl. Comput. Inf. Technol. **13**(1), 20–29 (2009)
8. Hromkovic, J., Lacher, R., et al.: Einfach Informatik. Series of 19 textbooks for teaching informatics from kindergarten to high school. Klett and Balmer (2018–2021) (in German)
9. Hromkovič, J., Lacher, R.: The computer science way of thinking in human history and consequences for the design of computer science curricula. In: Dagiene, V., Hellas, A. (eds.) ISSEP 2017. LNCS, vol. 10696, pp. 3–11. Springer, Cham (2017). https://doi.org/10.1007/978-3-319-71483-7_1
10. Dagiene, V., Stupuriene, G.: Bebras – a sustainable community building model for the concept based learning of informatics and computational thinking. Inform. Educ. **15**(1), 25–44 (2016)
11. Anderson, L.W., et al.: A Taxonomy for Learning and Teaching and Assessing: A Revision of Bloom's Taxonomy of Educational Objectives. Addison Wesley Longman, Inc., Boston (2001)
12. Mayring P.: Qualitative content analysis. Forum: Qual. Soc. Res. **1**(2). Retrieved from http://www.qualitative-research.net/index.php/fqs/article/view/1089. Accessed Sept 2020
13. Biggs, J.B., Collis, K.F.: Evaluating the Quality of Learning: The SOLO Taxonomy (Structure of the Observed Learning Outcome). Academic Press, New York (1982)
14. Klieme, E., Hartig, J., Rauch, D.: The concept of competence in educational contexts. In: Hartig, J., Klieme, E., Leutner, D. (eds.) Assessment of Competencies in Educational Contexts, pp. 3–22. Hogrefe, Göttingen (2008)
15. Frezza, S., et al.: Modelling competencies for computing education beyond 2020. In: Proceedings of the Companion of the 23rd Annual ACM Conference on Innovation and Technology in Computer Science Education, pp. 148–174. ACM (2018)
16. Schlüter, K., Brinda, T.: From exercise characteristics to competence dimensions exemplified by theoretical computer science in secondary education. In: Proceedings of the Joint Open and Working IFIP Conference on ICT and Learning for the Net Generation, Malaysia (2008)
17. PISA Organization for Economic Co-operation and Development: Preparing Our Youth for an Inclusive and Sustainable World: The OECDPISA Global Competency Framework (2018). Retrieved from http://www.oecd.org/pisa/pisa-2018-global-competence.htm
18. Gesellschaft für Informatik (GI): Bildungsstandards Informatik fürdie Sekundarstufe II (2016). Retrieved from https://dl.gi.de/bitstream/handle/20.500.12116/2350/57-GI-Empfehlung-Bildungsstandards-Informatik-SekII.pdf . Accessed Sept 2020
19. Kramer, M., Hubwieser, P., Brinda, T.: A competency structure model of object-oriented programming. In: International Conference on Learning and Teaching in Computing and Engineering (LaTICE). IEEE-CS, Mumbai, India, pp. 1–8 (2016)

20. Havenga, M., Mentz, E., De Villiers, R.: Knowledge, skills and strategies for successful object-oriented programming: a proposed learning repertoire. South Afr. Comput. J. SACLA, Spec. Ed. **42**, 1–8 (2008)
21. Dagienė, V., Sentance, S.: It's computational thinking! Bebras tasks in the curriculum. In: Brodnik, A., Tort, F. (eds.) ISSEP 2016. LNCS, vol. 9973, pp. 28–39. Springer, Cham (2016). https://doi.org/10.1007/978-3-319-46747-4_3
22. Dagiene, V., Futschek, G., Stupuriene, G.: Teachers' constructionist and deconstructionist learning by creating Bebras tasks. In: Sipitakiat, A., Tutiyaphuengprasert, N. (eds.) Constructionism in Action, pp. 257–264. Suksapattana Foundation, Bangkok (2016)
23. Dagienė, V., Futschek, G.: Bebras international contest on informatics and computer literacy: criteria for good tasks. In: Mittermeir, R.T., Sysło, M.M. (eds.) ISSEP 2008. LNCS, vol. 5090, pp. 19–30. Springer, Heidelberg (2008). https://doi.org/10.1007/978-3-540-69924-8_2
24. Vaníček, J.: Bebras informatics contest: criteria for good tasks revised. In: Gülbahar, Y., Karataş, E. (eds.) ISSEP 2014. LNCS, vol. 8730, pp. 17–28. Springer, Cham (2014). https://doi.org/10.1007/978-3-319-09958-3_3
25. Opmanis, M., Dagiene, V., Truu, A.: Task types at "Beaver" contests. Inf. Technol. Sch. 509–519 (2006). DOI:ISIP:BFP69-509
26. Lonati, V., Malchiodi, D., Monga, M., Morpurgo, A.: Bebras as a teaching resource: classifying the tasks corpus using computational thinking skills. In: Proceedings of the 2017 ACM Conference on Innovation and Technology in Computer Science Education, pp. 366–366, ACM (2017)
27. Pohl, W., Westmeyer, J.: Content categories for informatics tasks. LNCS, vol. 9378, p. 61 (2015)
28. Tomcsányiová, M., Tomcsányi, P.: Little beaver – a new Bebras contest category for children aged 8–9. In: Kalaš, I., Mittermeir, R.T. (eds.) ISSEP 2011. LNCS, vol. 7013, pp. 201–212. Springer, Heidelberg (2011). https://doi.org/10.1007/978-3-642-24722-4_18
29. Dagiene, V., Sentance, S., Stupurienė, G.: Developing a two-dimensional categorization system for educational tasks in informatics. Informatica **28**(1), 23–44 (2017)

Participants' Perception of Tasks in an Informatics Contest

Jiří Vaníček(✉) and Václav Šimandl

University of South Bohemia, České Budějovice, Czech Republic
{vanicek,simandl}@pf.jcu.cz

Abstract. Bebras is a contest organized for schools to promote computational thinking and new tasks are developed for it every year. The contest is held online in over 50 countries around the world and its results provide a great deal of information regarding difficulty levels of particular tasks and factors influencing participants' success in the contest. Our paper brings an analysis of such hard data in relation to statements of those participants who expressed their opinion on the difficulty of particular tasks and whose statements could be matched with their actual academic performance in the contest. Questionnaires were voluntarily completed by contestants participating in the Senior category (for the oldest participants aged over 16) from the Czech Republic.

Statistical analysis of contest results and perceived task difficulty provided new findings. There is no relationship between the proportion of participants with wrong answers to tasks and participants' subjective perception of task difficulty. Subjective difficulty is more aptly expressed in terms of the proportion of participants who did not answer the task. The contest was perceived as being easier by those participants who achieved higher scores in it. Male participants demonstrate a higher level of self-esteem in terms of IT skills than female participants. However, female participants' self-perceptions of their IT skills are slightly more accurate than males'. Results presented in the article could help the authors of the contest to improve compilation of contest tasks and have them included in the Informatics curriculum.

Keywords: Bebras · Informatics contest · Task difficulty · Participant perception · Self-esteem

1 Introduction

The situational informatics tasks used in the Bebras contest [1, 2] can be viewed from various angles. One view sees them as practical problems, developing various elements of computational thinking such as algorithmization, abstraction, decomposition and evaluation. From another angle, they can be seen as tasks involving various parts of computer science like programming, optimization, data representation, structures, processes, hardware, coding, cryptography, robotics and social aspects [3–6].

Bebras tasks are examined in a large number of studies. Some of them deal with creating good informatics tasks [7–9] or criteria influencing task difficulty [10–13]. Other

K. Kori and M. Laanpere (Eds.): ISSEP 2020, LNCS 12518, pp. 55–65, 2020.
https://doi.org/10.1007/978-3-030-63212-0_5

papers deal with the use of Bebras tasks - in assessing levels of computational thinking [14], bringing change into the classroom [6, 15] or preparing teachers as curriculum makers [16, 17]. School course books include Bebras tasks [18] or similar situational tasks that are adapted to a particular method of teaching [19].

A considerable proportion of research focuses on the difficulty of particular tasks or their types [13, 20–22]. As stated by Lonati et al. [13], predicting task difficulty is far from being an exact science and understanding difficulties and mistakes afterwards is not that easy either. Bellettini et al. [22] point out that in one third of the cases the tasks were either easier or more difficult than expected. According to van der Vegt and Schrijvers [20], category data structures and representations seem to be easier than algorithmization and programming tasks, while combining these categories increases the difficulty even further. Moreover, open ended tasks turned out to be the hardest as opposed to interactive or multiple choice tasks [20].

Other studies explore the issue of age suitability [22] and gender balance of contest tasks [23–26]. Hubwieser et al. [24] and Izu et al. [26] inquire into motivating younger girls to solve informatics tasks. Stupurienė et al. [25] point out that girls from the 3rd to 8th grades are as interested in solving informatics problems as boys. However, the proportion of 11th and 12th grade girls in the contest drops. Izu et al. [26] state that a declining performance trend of girls vs. boys can be recognized from primary to high school level, with boys outperforming girls in all countries in the Senior category. Other studies focus on international and long-term comparisons of tasks [25, 27, 28].

Given the online nature of the contest, it is not difficult to acquire data that measures achievement. As long as personal data protection rules are complied [29], an online contest can provide a large amount of data on how participants coped with various tasks. Statistical analysis of such data can indeed enable us to ascertain which type of task is difficult.

However, such data cannot ascertain how participants perceive contest tasks, their difficulty, and the motivational effect or "discouraging effect" of task settings. Very few studies actually inquire into this issue. One exception is Lonati et al. [13], who used interviews to uncover difficulties that participants encountered while completing tasks. Our paper is focused on participants' feedback, providing their retrospective self-perceptions of contest tasks and a comparison of that feedback with their actual results. The aim of our study is to shed light on participants' perceptions of contest tasks. The following research questions (RQ) were formulated on the basis of the research aim:

- Is there a relationship between perceived difficulty of a task and the proportion of participants who did not answer (RQ1a), gave the correct answer (RQ1b) or gave the wrong answer (RQ1c)?
- Is there a relationship between perceived difficulty of the test as a whole and performance in it (RQ2)?
- Is there a relationship between respondents' self-perceptions of IT ability and their performance in the test (RQ3) or their perception of tasks difficulty (RQ4)?
- Are self-perceptions of IT ability higher (RQ5) and more accurate (RQ6) for male or for female participants?

2 Methodology and Design

2.1 Bebras Contest and Questionnaire Survey

In the Bebras contest, participants take an online test, comprising of situational informatics tasks. In a situational task, solvers emerge into a described situation in which they must grasp, get to understand the used concepts and terms, find an informatics principle the task is based on, solve the problem using cognitive and thinking skills and select the right answer from the options [12]. The Senior category for students aged 16 to 19 consists of 15 tasks. These are completed by selecting the correct answer from a number of options or by typing a number or some text. In interactive tasks, objects are to be checked or moved with a mouse. Participants have 40 min to complete the test. For correct answers, participants are awarded a varying number of points according to predefined task difficulty levels. For incorrect answers, a proportional number of points are deducted. Points are not deducted for unanswered tasks (this rule has an impact on deciding whether to answer a task if a participant is not sure about the correct answer). As soon as the test is over, participants can see their points total but cannot see which tasks they got right and where they made mistakes. Such feedback could have an impact on their perception of the difficulty of the test as a whole.

In order to determine how participants perceive the difficulty of contest tasks, we compiled an anonymous online questionnaire. This comprised of questions concerning issues such as pupils' self-perceptions of their IT ability and their opinion on the difficulty of particular tasks in the contest. Where participants agreed, their questionnaire responses were correlated with their test score.

In the research, we used the term IT ability instead of informatics/computer science ability because a school subject known by research participants is called IT. This subject is based on digital technology handling and rarely contains topics from informatics, such as algorithmization. Since most Czech pupils might not properly understand the term informatics, asking a question about their informatics ability could bring unclear results.

The *self-perceptions of IT ability* and *perceived difficulty* of contest task variables express participants' subjective opinion in the six-point Likert scales, whose extreme ends were "I know nothing" and "I am very good at it", or "Easy" and "Hard". Participants also had the possibility of indicating that they are "unable to say".

2.2 Research Sample

All Senior category participants in the 2018 contest were notified with a request to complete a questionnaire. In that year 5898 participants took part in that category designated for pupils aged over 16 and our questionnaire was completed by 595 of them. 565 of the questionnaires were sent shortly after completing the test at a time when participants had already been informed of the scores they had achieved in the test but had not yet been given the correct answers to particular tasks and did not know whether their answers were right or wrong. The remaining 30 questionnaires were sent at a time when this information had been made available to them. 294 participants gave their consent to having their questionnaire answers correlated with their contest test scores (for details see Table 1).

Table 1. Numbers of participants and received questionnaires according to gender. Some respondents did not state their gender in the questionnaire.

	Men	Women	Total
Total number of participants	4093	1805	5898
Number of questionnaires received	385	131	595
Number of participants agreeing to have their responses correlated with their test scores	220	74	294

2.3 Data Analysis

To answer the above mentioned research questions, we developed research hypotheses, as presented in the Appendix to the paper available at https://www.ibobr.cz/papers/ISSEP2020.pdf. Data analysis was carried out using the following statistical methods: Pearson's correlation coefficient, Spearman's rank correlation coefficient and Mann–Whitney U test.

Pearson's correlation coefficient was used for linear expression of the relationship between two variables as per Cohen [30]. According to Chráska [31], a test value of 0 indicates a statistical independence between the two variables, while a value of +1 (or −1) indicates a perfect correlation between the two variables.

As per King and Eckersley [32], we could not use Pearson's correlation coefficient for data that are not discrete or continuous and are not normally distributed. For such cases we used Spearman's rank correlation coefficient, which is used to calculate a measure of correlation and works on the ranked values of the data.

As per Chráska [31], we used the nonparametric Mann–Whitney U test to verify whether two samples can come from the same basic set. This test is used to analyze two-sample unpaired data [33] and is based on pooling all original sample values and then ranking them. The following null hypothesis is used: The two populations have identical distributions. The following alternative hypothesis is stated: The two populations have different medians, but otherwise are identical.

Some items acquired from the questionnaire survey were unsuitable for analysis in certain respects as they did not include all the required information. Consequently, they were eliminated, as detailed in the Appendix.

The statistical software R was used for data analysis.

3 Results

3.1 Relationship Between Perceived Difficulty of a Task and Type of Answer Participants Gave

We used the variable *average perceived difficulty* of a particular task to answer research questions RQ1a to RQ1c. We also used the proportion of a certain type of answer (did not answer, gave the correct answer, gave the wrong answer) within the total number of participants. For the observed variables, the Anderson-Darling test and the Shapiro-Wilk test for normality failed to reject the null hypothesis of normal sample distribution. Consequently, we treated that data as data from a normal distribution. Pearson's correlation coefficient was used for testing.

To answer RQ1a, we verified the hypothesis whether the *average perceived difficulty* and *proportion of no answers* variables are independent. Pearson's correlation coefficient is equal to R = 0.91. There is a relationship between the variables at a significance level of 0.05. It can therefore be said that the proportion of no answers does express participants' perceptions of their difficulty (Fig. 1).

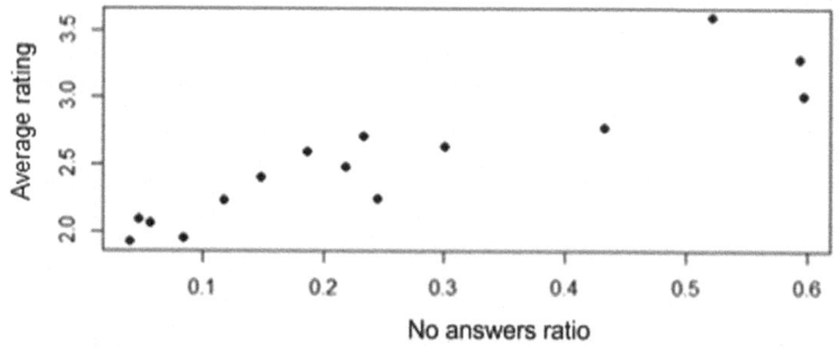

Fig. 1. Relationship between *average perceived difficulty* of a task and *proportion of respondents* who did not answer

To answer RQ1b, we tested whether the *average perceived difficulty* and *proportion of correct answers* variables are independent. Pearson's coefficient is equal to R = −0.89 and there is negative relationship between the variables at a significance level of 0.05. It can therefore be said that the proportion of correct answers also expresses participants' perceptions of the difficulty of contest tasks – tasks which are perceived by participants as more difficult have fewer correct answers (Fig. 2).

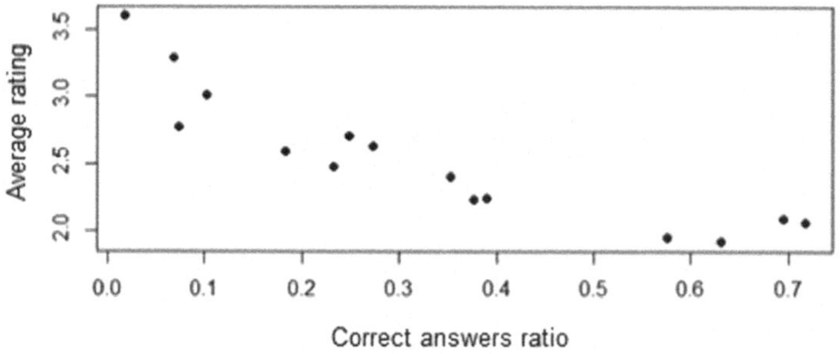

Fig. 2. Relationship between *average perceived difficulty* of a task and *proportion of correct answers*

To answer RQ1c, we tested whether the *average perceived difficulty* and *proportion of incorrect answers* variables are independent. Pearson's coefficient is equal to R = 0.27. We cannot reject the null hypothesis at a significance level of 0.05 so we cannot claim to have evidence of any relationship between these two variables. This can lead us to infer that the proportion of wrong answers does not express participants' perceptions of the difficulty of contest tasks (Fig. 3).

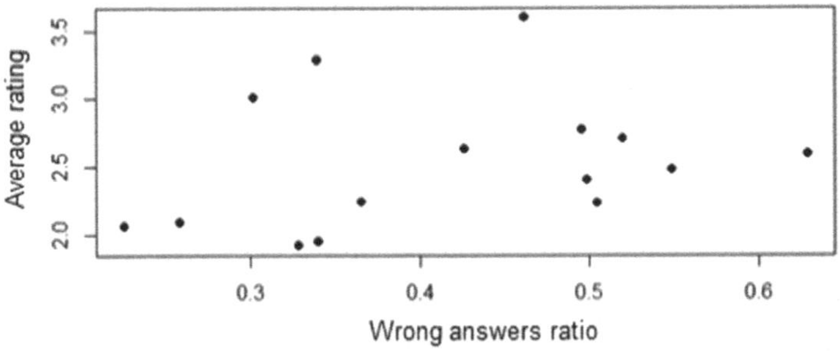

Fig. 3. Relationship between *average perceived difficulty* of a task and *proportion of wrong answers*

3.2 Relationship Between Perceived Difficulty of the Test as a Whole and Performance in It

In research question RQ2, we use the *points scored* and *perceived difficulty of the test* variables, for which all implemented tests (Shapiro-Wilk, Anderson-Darling, Kruskal-Wallis) rejected normality. We used Spearman's coefficient to calculate correlation, which is equal to $\rho_S = -0.37$. Its result at a significance level of 0.05 clearly rejects the null hypothesis of no relationship between the variables. There is indirect rank correlation between number of points scored in the test and perception of its difficulty. This can be interpreted to mean that the test was perceived as being more difficult by participants with lower scores in the test (Fig. 4).

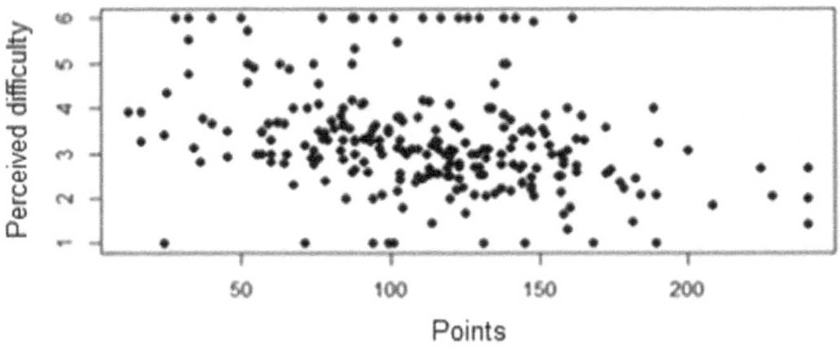

Fig. 4. Comparison of *points scored* in the test and *perceived difficulty of the test*

3.3 Self-perceptions of IT Ability and Performance

The following two research questions concern respondents' self-perceptions of IT ability, their test score and perception of test difficulty:

- RQ3: Is there a relationship between respondents' self-perceptions of IT ability and their performance in the test?
- RQ4: Is there a relationship between respondents' self-perceptions of IT ability and their perception of tasks difficulty?

To answer these questions, we used the *self-perception* variable, which is an ordinal variable that cannot have normal distribution, even asymptotically. For that reason, we used Spearman's coefficient of rank correlation.

To answer RQ3, we used *points scored* as the second variable, Spearman's coefficient being equal to $\rho_s = 0.26$. The null hypothesis of no rank correlation between the variables was rejected at a significance level of 0.05. A certain weak correlation between self-perceptions of IT ability and number of points scored is identified.

To answer RQ4, we used the variable *perceived difficulty of the test*. Spearman's coefficient being equal to $\rho_s = -0.27$, identifying almost the same weak negative correlation as in the previous research question RQ3. The test again rejected the null hypothesis of no correlation, indicating a certain weak negative correlation between these variables.

To a certain extent, this confirms expectations that participants who perceive themselves as having above-average IT ability actually achieve higher scores in the test and perceive the test as being rather easy. However, this is not a particularly strong corroboration.

3.4 Gender Differences in Self-perceptions of IT Ability

Participants provided data regarding their gender both in the contest and the questionnaire, the collected data enabling us to answer research questions concerning male and female participants' self-perceptions:

- RQ5: Do male or female participants have higher self-perceptions of IT ability?
- RQ6: Are self-perceptions of IT ability more accurate for male or for female participants?

To answer RQ5, we used the *gender* and *self-perception* variables. The *self-perception* variable being of an ordinal type, we cannot compare the expected value. We can only compare the median of *self-perception*, the male median equaling $M_M = 3.86$ and the female median equaling $M_F = 3.11$. The result of the nonparametric Mann–Whitney U test rejected the null hypothesis of both genders having the same self-perceptions of IT ability at a significance level of 0.05.

To answer RQ6, we used a comparison of the *self-perception* and *points scored* variables. To be able to test which gender perceives their IT ability more accurately, we transformed the *points scored* continuous variable into an ordinal variable called *categorized points* by dividing the interval of 0–240 points into 6 equal intervals of 40 points. The median of the absolute value of the difference between *self-perception* and *categorized points* was calculated at: $\rho_{sM} = 1.25$ for men, $\rho_{sF} = 1.04$ for women. The Mann–Whitney U test does not reject the null hypothesis of both genders self-perceiving their IT ability with equal accuracy at a significance level of 0.05 but does reject it at a significance level of 0.1.

These results can be interpreted to mean that male participants have higher self-perceptions of IT ability than female participants. Contrarily, female participants' self-perceptions of their IT ability are slightly more accurate than male participants', the difference being negligible (Fig. 5).

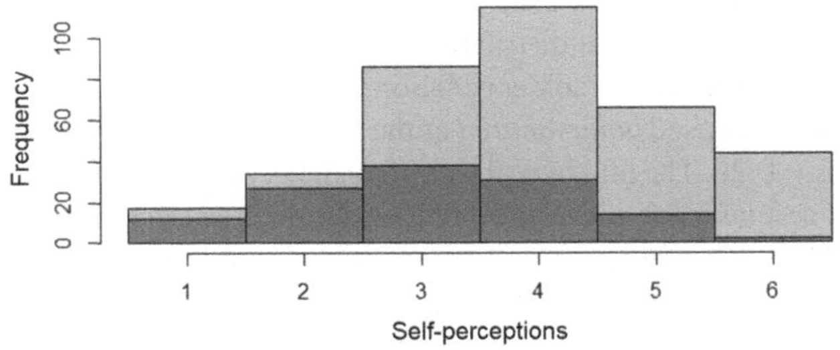

Fig. 5. Stacked chart showing distribution of female (dark grey) and male (light grey) participants' self-perceptions of IT ability.

4 Discussion and Conclusion

By comparing participants' statements with their actual score, it was discovered that perceived difficulty of a particular task is not expressed by the proportion of participants who answered incorrectly. Perceived difficulty of a task is expressed by the proportion of those participants who did not answer and also of those who gave the correct answer. This result corresponds to findings of Vaníček [12] that the no answer indicator describes task difficulty very well. The perceived difficulty of contest tasks can be considered an important parameter, as per Keller and Landhäußer [34] a perceived fit of skills and task demands is a prerequisite for emergence of flow, which means the state in which according to Engeser and Schiepe-Tiska [35] an individual is completely immersed in an activity without self-consciousness but with a deep sense of control.

Our research also shows that participants who achieved higher scores in the test do actually perceive it as being easier. Moreover, participants who have higher self-perceptions of IT ability perceive the test as being easier and achieve higher scores in it. These conclusions correspond to findings of Li et al. [36], Mangos and Steele-Johnson [37] that self-perceptions of ability are negatively related to perceptions of task difficulty; self-perceptions of ability have a positive correlation with performance; and perceptions of task difficulty are negatively associated with performance.

In addition, our research identifies findings relating to gender differences. Male participants of this age were found to have higher self-perceptions of their IT ability than female participants but female participants' self-perceptions of their IT ability are slightly more accurate than male participants'. The finding that men have higher self-perceptions of IT ability than women corresponds to earlier research of Cussó-Calabuig et al. [38] and Birol et al. [39] relating to self-perception in IT. As Vekiri claims, perceived teacher expectations are more strongly associated with girls' than with boys' self-efficacy beliefs in IT [40], thus there seems to be a need to encourage and support girls to cope with informatics problems. This is a particularly important task as self-confidence and perceived self-efficacy seem to play a big role for students' choice of further studies, as Dagienė et al. quote Ashcraft et al. [41].

The limit of our study is that some participants could have based their self-perceptions of IT ability on the score they had achieved in the test that they had just taken. In a certain way, time delay between the test and the questionnaire could have influenced perceived difficulty of contest tasks. While some responded to the questionnaire shortly after completing the test, other responses were delayed or sent after being provided with the correct answers, knowing whether their answers to particular tasks were right or wrong. As only 5% of respondents completed the questionnaire after finding out which questions they had got wrong, this aspect has a negligible influence on the results.

Further studies should focus on identifying factors that make participants perceive contest tasks as being more difficult, features that have a positive impact on task popularity and the relationship between task popularity and perceived task difficulty. Such factors could be connection of the story of the task with the world of a child, including gender aspects, or connection of the theme of the task with a part of informatics or elements of computational thinking. Other factors could be the attractiveness of interactive tasks (in terms of visual aspect or user-friendliness) and potential laboriousness, for example the assumption that a number of variations will have to be tested to determine an answer or the need to fully understand the task instructions before anything else.

If we can understand the factors that cause participants to perceive task difficulty or popularity in different ways, we will be able to improve the way we classify task difficulty. We will also be able to design or modify tasks to increase participant motivation and to include the more useful ones in the school curriculum.

References

1. Bebras website. http://bebras.org. Accessed 21 May 2020
2. Dagienė, V.: Information technology contests – introduction to computer science in an attractive way. Inf. Educ. **5**(1), 37–46 (2006)
3. Wing, J.M.: Research notebook: computational thinking: what and why? In: The Link. Carneige Mellon, Pittsburgh (2010)
4. Selby, C., Woollard, J.: Computational thinking: the developing definition. In: Special Interest Group on Computer Science Education (SIGCSE) 2014. ACM, Atlanta (2014)
5. ISTE, CSTA: Operational Definition of Computational Thinking for K-12 Education (2011). https://id.iste.org/docs/ct-documents/computational-thinking-operational-definition-flyer.pdf
6. Dagienė, V., Sentance, S.: It's computational thinking! Bebras tasks in the curriculum. In: Brodnik, A., Tort, F. (eds.) ISSEP 2016. LNCS, vol. 9973, pp. 28–39. Springer, Cham (2016). https://doi.org/10.1007/978-3-319-46747-4_3
7. van der Vegt, W.: Predicting the difficulty level of a Bebras task. Olympiads Inform. **7**, 132–139 (2013)
8. van der Vegt, W.: How hard will this task be? Developments in analyzing and predicting question difficulty in the Bebras challenge. Olympiads Inform. **12**, 119–132 (2018). https://doi.org/10.15388/ioi.2018.10

9. Pohl, W., Hein, H.-W.: Aspects of quality in the presentation of informatics challenge tasks. In: Jekovec, M. (ed.) The Proceedings of International Conference on Informatics in Schools: Situation, Evolution and Perspectives, ISSEP 2015, pp. 21–32. University of Ljubljana, Ljubljana (2015)
10. Dagienė, V., Futschek, G.: Bebras international contest on informatics and computer literacy: criteria for good tasks. In: Mittermeir, R.T., Sysło, M.M. (eds.) ISSEP 2008. LNCS, vol. 5090, pp. 19–30. Springer, Heidelberg (2008). https://doi.org/10.1007/978-3-540-69924-8_2
11. Vaníček, J.: Bebras informatics contest: criteria for good tasks revised. In: Gülbahar, Y., Karataş, E. (eds.) ISSEP 2014. LNCS, vol. 8730, pp. 17–28. Springer, Cham (2014). https://doi.org/10.1007/978-3-319-09958-3_3
12. Vaníček, J.: What makes situational informatics tasks difficult? In: Brodnik, A., Tort, F. (eds.) ISSEP 2016. LNCS, vol. 9973, pp. 90–101. Springer, Cham (2016). https://doi.org/10.1007/978-3-319-46747-4_8
13. Lonati, V., Malchiodi, D., Monga, M., Morpurgo, A.: How presentation affects the difficulty of computational thinking tasks: an IRT analysis. In: Proceedings of the 17th Koli Calling International Conference on Computing Education Research, pp. 60–69. ACM, New York (2017). https://doi.org/10.1145/3141880.3141900
14. Chiazzese, G., Arrigo, M., Chifari, A., Lonati, V., Tosto, C.: Educational robotics in primary school: measuring the development of computational thinking skills with the Bebras tasks. Informatics **6**(4), 43 (2019). https://doi.org/10.3390/informatics6040043
15. Černochová, M., Vaníček, J.: Informatics education: current state and perspectives of development within the system of field didactics in the Czech Republic. Int. J. Inform. Commun. Technol. Educ. **4**(3), 14–31 (2015). https://doi.org/10.1515/ijicte-2015-0011
16. Dagienė, V., Futschek, G., Stupurienė, G.: Teachers' constructionist and deconstructionist learning by creating Bebras tasks. In: Sipitakiat, A., Tutiyaphuengprasert, N. (eds.) Constructionism in Action 2016, pp. 257–264. Suksapattana Foundation, Bangkok (2016)
17. Manabe, H., Tani, S., Kanemune, S., Manabe, Y.: Creating the original Bebras tasks by high school students. Olympiads Inform. **12**, 99–110 (2018). https://doi.org/10.15388/ioi.2018.08
18. Berki, J., Drábková, J.: Základy informatiky pro 2. stupeň ZŠ. Textbook. Technical University of Liberec, Liberec (2020)
19. Hromkovič, J., Lacher, R.: Einfach informatik. Lösungen finden. Textbook. Klett und Balmer, Baar (2019)
20. van der Vegt, W., Schrijvers, E.: Analyzing task difficulty in a Bebras contest using cuttle. Olympiads Inform. **13**, 145–156 (2019). https://doi.org/10.15388/ioi.2019.09
21. Yagunova, E., Podznyakov, S., Ryzhova, N., Razumovskaia, E., Korovkin, N.: Tasks classification and age differences in task perception. Case study of international on-line competition "Beaver". In: Jekovec, M. (ed.) The Proceedings of International Conference on Informatics in Schools: Situation, Evolution and Perspectives, ISSEP 2015, pp. 33–43. University of Ljubljana, Ljubljana (2015)
22. Bellettini, C., Lonati, V., Malchiodi, D., Monga, M., Morpurgo, A., Torelli, M.: How challenging are Bebras tasks?: an IRT analysis based on the performance of Italian students. In: Proceedings of the 2015 ACM Conference on Innovation and Technology in Computer Science Education, pp. 27–32. ACM, New York (2015). https://doi.org/10.1145/2729094.2742603
23. Tort, F., Drot-Delange, B., Mano, M.: Filles et informatique: qu'en est-il du concours Castor?. In: Henry, J., Aude, N., Vandeput, E. (eds.) L'informatique et le numérique en classe. Qui, quoi, comment?, pp. 69–84. Presses Universitaires Namur, Namur (2017)
24. Hubwieser, P., Hubwieser, E., Graswald, D.: How to attract the girls: gender-specific performance and motivation in the Bebras challenge. In: Brodnik, A., Tort, F. (eds.) ISSEP 2016. LNCS, vol. 9973, pp. 40–52. Springer, Cham (2016). https://doi.org/10.1007/978-3-319-46747-4_4

25. Stupurienė, G., Vinikienė, L., Dagienė, V.: Students' success in the Bebras challenge in Lithuania: focus on a long-term participation. In: Brodnik, A., Tort, F. (eds.) ISSEP 2016. LNCS, vol. 9973, pp. 78–89. Springer, Cham (2016). https://doi.org/10.1007/978-3-319-46747-4_7
26. Izu, C., Mirolo, C., Settle, A., Mannila, L., Stupurienė, G.: Exploring Bebras tasks content and performance: a multinational study. Inform. Educ. **16**(1), 39–59 (2017). https://doi.org/10.15388/infedu.2017.03
27. Budinská, L., Mayerová, K., Šimandl, V.: Differences between 9–10 years old pupils' results from Slovak and Czech Bebras contest. In: Pozdniakov, S.N., Dagienė, V. (eds.) ISSEP 2018. LNCS, vol. 11169, pp. 307–318. Springer, Cham (2018). https://doi.org/10.1007/978-3-030-02750-6_24
28. Tomcsányi, P., Vaníček, J.: International comparison of problems from an informatic contest. In: Mechlová, E., Valchař, A. (eds.) Proceedings of the Information and Communication Technology in Education 2009, pp. 219–223. University of Ostrava, Ostrava (2009)
29. Šimandl, V.: Ochrana osobních údajů podle GDPR v soutěži Bobřík informatiky. In: DidInfo 2019, pp. 146–151. Univerzita Mateja Bela, Banská Bystrica (2019)
30. Cohen, J.: Statistical Power Analysis for the Behavioral Sciences, 2nd edn. Lawrence Erlbaum Associates, New Jersey (1988)
31. Chráska, M.: Metody pedagogického výzkumu, 2nd edn. Grada, Praha (2016)
32. King, A.P., Eckersley, R.J.: Descriptive statistics II: bivariate and multivariate statistics. In: Statistics for Biomedical Engineers and Scientists, pp. 23–56. Academic Press (2019). https://doi.org/10.1016/b978-0-08-102939-8.00011-6
33. King, A.P., Eckersley, R.J.: Inferential statistics III: nonparametric hypothesis testing. In: Statistics for Biomedical Engineers and Scientists, pp. 119–145. Academic Press (2019). https://doi.org/10.1016/b978-0-08-102939-8.00015-3
34. Keller, J., Landhäußer, A.: The flow model revisited. In: Engeser, S. (ed.) Advances in Flow Research. Springer, New York (2012). https://doi.org/10.1007/978-1-4614-2359-1_3
35. Engeser, S., Schiepe-Tiska, A.: Historical Lines and an overview of current research on flow. In: Engeser, S. (ed.) Advances in Flow Research. Springer, New York (2012). https://doi.org/10.1007/978-1-4614-2359-1_1
36. Li, W., Lee, A., Solmon, M.: The role of perceptions of task difficulty in relation to self-perceptions of ability, intrinsic value, attainment value, and performance. Eur. Phys. Educ. Rev. **13**(3), 301–318 (2007). https://doi.org/10.1177/1356336X07081797
37. Mangos, P.M., Steele-Johnson, D.: The role of subjective task complexity in goal orientation, self-efficacy, and performance relations. Hum. Perform. **14**(2), 169–185 (2001). https://doi.org/10.1207/S15327043HUP1402_03
38. Cussó-Calabuig, R., Farran, X.C., Bosch-Capblanch, X.: Are boys and girls still digitally differentiated? The case of Catalonian teenagers. J. Inf. Technol. Educ. Res. **16**(1), 411–435 (2017). https://doi.org/10.28945/3879
39. Birol, C., Bekirogullari, Z., Etci, C., Dagli, G.: Gender and computer anxiety, motivation, self-confidence, and computer use. Eurasian J. Educ. Res. **34**, 185–198 (2009)
40. Vekiri, I.: Boys' and girls' ICT beliefs: do teachers matter? Comput. Educ. **55**(1), 16–23 (2010). https://doi.org/10.1016/j.compedu.2009.11.013
41. Dagiene, V., Mannila, L., Poranen, T., Rolandsson, L., Stupuriene, G.: Reasoning on children's cognitive skills in an informatics contest: findings and discoveries from Finland, Lithuania, and Sweden. In: Gülbahar, Y., Karataş, E. (eds.) ISSEP 2014. LNCS, vol. 8730, pp. 66–77. Springer, Cham (2014). https://doi.org/10.1007/978-3-319-09958-3_7

Engagement and Gender Issues in School Informatics

Upper- and Lower-Secondary Students' Motivation to Study Computer Science

Külli Kori[1(✉)] and Piret Luik[2]

[1] Tallinn University, Tallinn, Estonia
kulli.kori@tlu.ee
[2] University of Tartu, Tartu, Estonia

Abstract. There is a growing need for upper- and lower-secondary education institutions to provide computer science (CS) knowledge and skills to learners. As learners' motivation plays an important role in their learning and female students have shown to be less motivated to study CS, the current study focuses on developing a scale for measuring lower- and upper-secondary students' motivation to study CS and investigating the motivation of female and male students.

Data was collected from 740 Estonian students from 9th and 12th grade (55.1% female) by online questionnaire, which was based on value-expectancy theory. Nine factors of student's motivation to study CS were differentiated by Confirmatory Factor Analysis: value of future work, importance, altruistic motivation, positive learning experiences from school, self-efficacy, positive learning experiences, social pressure, perceived abilities, interest. Multivariate analyses of variance with the Bonferroni adjustment for multiple comparisons revealed that the factor 'value of future work' was the highest and factor 'interest' was ranked the lowest among motivational factors. Multivariate test between-subjects' effects with Bonferroni adjustment indicated that in all of these factors, boys showed higher motivation to study CS than girls.

The results are valuable for teachers who teach CS in school. When planning CS lessons, the teachers should consider the type of motivation that drives the students and put more effort on motivating the girls as the boys are generally more motivated to study CS. E.g., the teacher can raise students' interest towards CS by bringing in real life CS problems and linking the tasks with possible future work, encouraging girls to participate in CS competition and giving them more recognition to increase girls' self-efficacy and interest, which were more highly rated by boys than girls.

Keywords: Motivation · Computer science · Gender differences

1 Introduction

Increasingly, all countries need people with computer science (CS) skills for various occupations [1], and there is a growing need for educational institutions, including upper- and lower-secondary education institutions, to provide CS knowledge and skills to learners. However, students' motivation plays an important role in their learning, performing

K. Kori and M. Laanpere (Eds.): ISSEP 2020, LNCS 12518, pp. 69–78, 2020.
https://doi.org/10.1007/978-3-030-63212-0_6

(e.g., [2, 3]) and effectiveness [4]. Motivation is described as being either intrinsic or extrinsic [5] and can be explained with various aspects based on different motivation theories [6]. This paper bases on the expectancy-value model of motivation [7, 8], which involves task value and ability beliefs i.e. expectancies for success.

Historically, the field of CS was considered to be a male-dominated profession [9] and low numbers of females in CS courses from high school to graduate school diminishes [10]. The same problem is in Estonia. For example, there are 22.7% of women studying CS on bachelor and 24.6% on master level in the University of Tartu in the academic year 2019/2020 (http://www.ut.ee/oppijate-arv/). One reason for such a result might be lack of role models and encouragement, gender stereotyping, and lack of self-esteem among females [10], but also different misconceptions of CS such as CS is only programming, CS is difficult, careers in CS consist of little human interaction [11]. Yukselturk and Bulut [9] point out that men's and women's experiences in learning vary besides other aspects also by motivation including goal orientation, task value, self-efficacy. Using the expectancy-value model of motivation, the present paper seeks to understand more about the motivation to study CS on lower- and upper-secondary education levels and compare the motivation of female and male students.

2 Previous Studies

Many studies have focused on investigating higher education students' motivation to study CS, but less studies can be found about lower- and upper-secondary students. As student retention is an issue in higher education CS studies, a group of studies have focused on students' motivation to find solutions for dropout [12–14]. In addition, a group of studies have looked into teaching methods used in higher education to motivate students. For example, different gaming methods have been found to have a positive impact on students' motivation to learn programming concepts [15] and students' learning on CS courses [16], and organizing teaching around small groups have found to have benefit on students' achievement motivation, desire to pursue their studies, self-confidence etc. [17]. Also, a group of studies have focused on the reasons why students choose to study CS in higher education. For the first year higher education CS students in Estonia it has been found that interest in the topic with perceived abilities in CS and usefulness in the future were the main motivators for choosing CS studies [18]. This interest in CS forms mostly when students are in upper secondary school and have hands-on experience of doing something related to computers [19]. These activities include solving computer-related issues, building a computer, trying programming or making a computer game or web-page. These activities happened both at home and at school. Therefore, CS lessons in school have a potential of causing students' interest in CS and even have an effect on students to choose CS as a career.

On lower- or upper-secondary level several activities are done to motivate students to study CS. Teachers propose interesting real world CS-related problems, implement computer games and other graphical applications to the lessons [20], students interest is increased through using educational robots [21] and games that support the development of computational thinking skills (e.g., AutoThinking [22]), schools and students are invited to participate in informatics competitions (e.g., Bebras [23]) to increase the motivation to study CS and to develop students' CS skills; and even escape games have been developed for introducing CS through problem solving in attractive and motivating environment [24].

As female students are a minority in higher education CS studies, many studies have looked into this problem. For example, Spieler et al. [25] conducted literature review and concluded that when female teenagers between 12–15 years decide their future careers, many factors steer them away from a CS, e.g., stereotypes, preconceptions about coding, absence of female role models, cultural and social factors, non-supportive CS classroom, inequality in CS education. Also, males have reported higher motivation and perceived-usefulness than females among 10th grade high school students [26]. However, integrating art and animation in teaching computer programming have increased high school girls' interest in programming and in pursuing a degree in CS after graduation, while among boys this change has not been significant [27]. An interesting result has been found by Papastergiou [11] who declared that there were no gender differences in motivation for or against studying CS, but girls' motivation towards studying CS was more extrinsic than intrinsic, while for boys those two motivational aspects were almost the same. Also, there were gender differences in perceptions of CS: girls perceived CS as more hardware- and programming-oriented, but boys perceived it as more human- and application-oriented [11]. In addition, interesting results have been presented by Pedaste et al. [14] who found on higher education level that the female students who have chosen to enroll in CS curricula show higher motivation than the male students in the same studies. This suggests that the small amount of females who choose CS as a career are very motivated.

However, when looking at young children, the gender differences do not appear clearly. A study carried out in Estonia showed that in kindergarten and primary education both boys and girls are equally interested in the digital world, but the change happens when students are 10 to 13 years old [28]. At this age, boys become more interested in CS and girls may lose their interest. Moreover, upper- and lower secondary students who have special interest in CS often study it independently outside the school because school lessons are not sophisticated enough for these students. Some studies have also focused on increasing the opportunities for females in the CS field. For example, Kindsiko, Türk and Kantšukov [29] found that the obstacles in the way of increasing the role of females in CS include cultural-gender attitudes, CS studies in general education level, individual and extra-individual barriers related to CS. In regard to general education schools, a problem presents itself where in some schools, the boys are encouraged to take programming lessons and the girls are recommended to take drawing, photography, etc. classes. Students also may have false understanding that CS is only programming and they lack the picture of the broad opportunities available in the CS field.

As many studies have looked into students' motivation to study CS, several instruments have been used. To measure lower- and upper-secondary students' ICT motivation, a scale has been developed and validated for 13–17 years old students in Germany [30]. However, the authors did not find the scale to be useful for measuring motivation to study CS in Estonian schools. Still, increasing the number of students who want to pursue CS profession after graduation from high school is important. Therefore, this study aims to (1) develop the scale measuring motivation to study CS among lower- and upper-secondary students and to validate it in Estonian context; (2) describe the motivation of students at the end of lower- and upper-secondary education and to compare motivation of female and male students. Tho research questions will be answered: (1) What are the motivational orientations toward CS of 9th and 12th grade students in specially recognised Estonian schools? (2) What gender differences can be found in motivation to study CS among 9th and 12th grade students in specially recognised Estonian schools?

3 Methodology

3.1 Sample

The sample consisted of 740 students from 9th (age 15–16) and 12th (age 18–19) grade. The students were studying in 25 schools in Estonia which have shown positive experiences of teaching CS (e.g., have received golden recognition from Information Technology Foundation for Education or have a field of study in CS for upper-secondary students). 156 of the participants were studying in 9th grade and 584 were studying in 12th grade. 55.1% of the participants were female. We chose to look at the 9th and 12th grade students together and not separate them because they both soon have to face a choice whether to continue studying, and if so, what to study.

3.2 Instrument

The data was collected with an online questionnaire based on expectancy-value theory [7, 8]. The developed questionnaire was based on the FIEM scale [31] measuring motivation for enrolment in programming MOOC and was developed in cooperation by university experts in educational theory and CS. Expectations were divided into different constructs: Positive experiences (e.g., My experiences related to studying IT (e.g. programming, robotics, etc.) have been positive), self-efficacy (e.g., I am sure that if I would study IT, I would be successful in my studies) and Perceived ability (e.g., I have good programming skills.). Expectancy-value components - intrinsic, subjective attainment and utility values - were represented following constructs: Interest (e.g., IT is interesting to me.), Importance (e.g., Studying IT and working in IT gives me a chance to develop myself), Social utility value (e.g., IT skills give me a chance to make people's lives easier) and Personal utility value (e.g., IT skills will get me a good salary in the future.). As in FIEM scale, we added items describing social influence (e.g., My parents direct me to pursue activities related to IT). All motivational items were on a 5-point Likert scale ranging from 1 (totally disagree) to 5 (totally agree). The prefacing statement to all motivational items was 'Assess the extent to which you agree with the following statements?'.

According to this model 32 items were created and questions about demographic data (gender, grade, etc.) were added. The questionnaire was piloted with 9th and 12th grade of students (all together 19 students). In the pilot study respondents wrote comments about how they understood each item. Items, which were misunderstood, were corrected.

3.3 Procedure

Initially, the schools who had shown positive experience in teaching CS (e.g., who had received golden recognition from Information Technology Foundation for Education or had a field of study in CS for upper secondary students) were contacted. If the school agreed to participate in the study, then online questionnaires were sent to the schools and they organized how and when the students filled in the questionnaires. Some schools did it during a lesson and some asked the students to answer the questionnaire at home. It is possible that the less motivated students did not answer the questionnaire if they were asked to do it at home, and this can be considered as one limitation of the procedure.

3.4 Data Analysis

Exploratory and confirmatory factor analyses were performed with Mplus 7.31 program to analyze the items of motivation and validate the scale. IBM SPSS Statistics 25 was used for descriptive statistics and comparing the motivation of male and female students. Multivariate analyses of variance with the Bonferroni adjustment was used for multiple comparisons.

4 Results

4.1 Validation of the Scale Measuring Students' Motivation to Study CS

To confirm whether the items divide into factors in this manner, a confirmatory factor analysis was carried out. The results of the confirmatory factor analysis showed that the items do not divide into 11 factors in this manner, as the model fit indices were not good enough (especially in the case of TLI and CFI). To find a fitting model that would characterize the responses of students, an exploratory factor analysis was carried out. Based on this, a 9-factor model was chosen as having the best fit (TLI = 0.956, CFI = 0.977, RMSEA = 0.041, SRMR = 0.017).

The 9 factors were:

1. Factor 'Positive learning experience' (Cronbach's alpha 0.717) contained three items and the standardized factor loadings ranged from 0.57 to 0.74 (estimated residual variance from 0.389 to 0.566),
2. Factor 'Self-efficacy' (Cronbach's alpha 0.890) contained three items with the standardized factor loadings from 0.78 to 0.92 (estimated residual variance from 0.158 to 0.303),
3. Factor 'Value of future work' (Cronbach's alpha 0.896) contained two items with the standardized factor loadings 0.90 and 0.91 (estimated residual variance from 0.174 to 0.194),
4. Factor 'Interest' (Cronbach's alpha 0.915) contained four items and the standardized factor loadings ranged from 0.75 to 0.94 (estimated residual variance from 0.089 to 0.324),
5. Factor 'Importance' (Cronbach's alpha 0.836) contained four items and the standardized factor loadings ranged from 0.59 to 0.87 (estimated residual variance from 0.232 to 0.550),

6. Factor 'Perceived abilities' (Cronbach's alpha 0.860) contained five items with standardized factor loadings from 0.51 to 0.85 (estimated residual variance from 0.239 to 0.391),
7. Factor 'Altruistic motivation' (Cronbach's alpha 0.877) contained three items and standardized factor loadings ranged from 0.72 to 0.91 (estimated residual variance from 0.170 to 0.403),
8. Factor 'Social influence' (Cronbach's alpha 0.720) contained six items with standardized factor loadings from 0.43 to 0.66 (estimated residual variance from 0.232 to 0.508),
9. Factor 'Positive learning experiences from school' (Cronbach's alpha 0.801) contained four items and standardized factor loadings ranged from 0.53 to 0.86 (estimated residual variance from 0.242 to 0.564)

All standardized factor loadings and item reliabilities were moderate or high.

4.2 Students' Motivation to Study CS

An average rating of each factor on a 5-point scale is represented in Table 1. All the factors were statistically significantly different from each other ($F(1,717) = 14{,}470.226$, $p < 0.01$; multiply comparison with Bonferroni adjustment all $p < 0.05$). The results showed that students' motivation was highest in relation to the factor 'value of future work' (average rating 3.82). This factor comprised the items related to good job position and good pay in the CS field and clearly shows the importance of extrinsic variables. This was followed by factor 'importance', which put together items related to the usefulness of CS skills and to the opportunities of self-realization and self-development (average rating 3.55). This factor comprised items related to mostly intrinsic variables. These factors were followed by factors 'altruistic motivation' (average rating 3.39) and 'positive learning experiences from school' (average rating 3.34). The lowest rated factors were 'interest' (average rating 2.72) and 'perceived abilities' (average rating 2.86). However, all factors were evaluated higher than the neutral point of the scale (2.5).

The male students rated all the factors statistically significantly higher than female students. Comparing ratings of male and female students using multivariate analyses of variance with the Bonferroni adjustment for multiple comparisons revealed that there were statistically significant differences between the males and females in all motivational factors (see Table 1). The greatest differences between males and females emerged in factors 'self-efficacy' and 'interest', where the values of F statistics were over 90. F-value comparing factors 'social influence' and 'perceived abilities' was also greater than 60 indicating a bigger difference. Smaller gender differences were in factors 'value of future work' and 'positive learning experiences from school', where F value was less than 10.

Table 1. Students' average rating of factors related to motivation.

Factor	Overall average rating (SD)	Female students' average rating (SD)	Male students' average rating (SD)	F statistic (p-value)
Value of future work	3.82 (1.00)	3.74 (1.02)	3.93 (0.95)	6.958 (<0.001)
Importance	3.55 (0.92)	3.42 (0.92)	3.72 (0.89)	19.220 (<0.001)
Altruistic motivation	3.39 (1.01)	3.28 (0.99)	3.53 (1.01)	11.210 (<0.001)
Positive learning experiences from school	3.34 (0.94)	3.25 (0.91)	3.44 (0.97)	7.456 (<0.001)
Self-efficacy	3.01 (1.05)	2.69 (1.00)	3.41 (0.96)	97.613 (<0.001)
Positive learning experiences	2.98 (1.03)	2.76 (0.97)	3.24 (1.04)	39.566 (<0.001)
Social influence	2.88 (0.72)	2.67 (0.65)	3.13 (0.73)	77.332 (<0.001)
Perceived abilities	2.86 (0.75)	2.67 (0.68)	3.09 (0.76)	60.085 (<0.001)
Interest	2.72 (0.75)	2.49 (0.66)	3.00 (0.75)	94.140 (<0.001)

5 Discussion and Conclusion

The study aimed to develop a scale for measuring motivation to study CS among lower- and upper-secondary students and to validate it in Estonian context. The aim was also to describe the motivation of students at the end of lower- and upper-secondary education and to compare the motivation of female and male students.

Scale for measuring motivation to study CS was created and tested with 9th and 12th grade students. The 9-factor model was found to be the best for the scale. Four of these factors represented expectancies: 1) self-efficacy, 2) perceived abilities; and positive experiences which splitted into two factors: 3) positive learning experiences and 4) positive learning experiences from school. Four factors represented expectancy-value components: 5) interest, 6) importance, 7) value of future work as personal utility value and 8) altruistic motivation as social utility value. The ninth factor described was 9) social influence. The factors accorded to the theoretical model based on the value-expectancy theory [7, 8] and the model showed sufficient indices in CFA. Therefore, we can conclude that the instrument is validated in Estonian schools which have received special recognition for CS teaching and the instrument can be used in future studies as well.

Based on the results we can answer the first research question "What are the motivational orientations toward CS of 9th and 12th grade students in specially recognised Estonian schools?". In general, Estonian students' motivation to study CS was rather high. This supports the facts that there is a high competition every year for CS related curricula in Estonian higher education institutions [32] and a lot of people in Estonia choose to enroll in CS related MOOCs where the completion rates are unusually high [33]. The lower- and upper-secondary students who participated in the study evaluated the highest 'value of future work', and 'importance' among the motivational factors. The lowest rated motivational factor was 'interest'. This differs from the results that have previously been found while investigating higher education students. For the first year CS students in Estonia 'interest in a topic with perceived abilities in CS' and 'usefulness in the future' were the main motivators for choosing CS studies [18].

As CS is considered male-dominated profession [9], gender differences in motivation to study CS were seeked and the answer to the second research question "What gender differences can be found in motivation to study CS among 9th and 12th grade students in specially recognised Estonian schools?" was found. Male students showed higher motivation than females in all the factors. The greatest differences emerged in the factors 'self-efficacy' and 'interest', also high differences emerged in 'social influence' and 'perceived abilities'. The students who participated in the study were over 15 years old and as it was concluded previously [28] boys between age 10 to 13 become more interested in CS and girls at the same age may lose their interest.

Differences between male and female students were the smallest in factors 'value of future work' and 'positive learning experiences from school'. This suggests that both male and female students see similarly the value of CS skills at future work and have got positive CS related learning experiences from school. This result does not support findings by Papastergiou [11] who found that there are no gender differences in motivation for or against studying CS. Also, we can't conclude that female students' motivation towards studying CS was more extrinsic than intrinsic and in the case of male students' these aspects were almost the same as was found previously [11].

The results of the current study are valuable for teachers who teach CS in lower- or upper-secondary level as the teacher should consider the type of motivation that drives students. When planning the CS lessons, the teacher should put more effort on motivating girls to study CS as boys are generally more motivated than girls. For example, the teacher can raise students' interest towards CS by bringing in real life CS problems and linking the tasks with possible future work, encouraging girls to participate in CS competition and giving them more recognition to increase girls' self-efficacy and interest, which were more highly rated by boys than girls.

Acknowledgements. This research was partnered with TransferWise to research the technology skills gap in Estonian schools and how to fix it.

References

1. OECD: Education at a Glance 2018: OECD Indicators. OECD Publishing, Paris (2018)

2. Anderman, E., Wolters, C.: Goal, values, and affect. In: Alexander, P., Winne, P. (eds.) Handbook of Educational Psychology, 2nd edn., pp. 369–389. Erlbaum Publishers, Mahwah (2006)
3. Munoz-Merino, P.J., Fernandez, M., Munoz-Organero, M., Delgado, C.: Motivation and emotions in competition systems for education: an empirical study. IEEE Trans. Educ. **57**(3), 82–187 (2014)
4. Cerasoli, C.P., Ford, M.T.: Intrinsic motivation, performance, and the mediating role of mastery goal orientation: a test of self-determination theory. J. Psychol. **148**(3), 267–286 (2014)
5. Ryan, R.M., Deci, E.L.: Self-determination theory and the facilitation of intrinsic motivation, social development, and well-being. Am. Psychol. **55**(1), 68–78 (2000)
6. Schunk, D.H., Pintrich, P.R., Meece, J.L.: Motivation in Education: Theory, Research, and Applications, 4th edn. Boston Pearson (2014)
7. Eccles, J.S., Wigfield, A.: Motivational beliefs, values, and goals. Annu. Rev. Psychol. **53**, 109–132 (2002)
8. Wigfield, A., Eccles, J.S.: Expectancy-value theory of achievement motivation. Contemp. Educ. Psychol. **25**, 68–81 (2000)
9. Yukselturk, E., Bulut, S.: Gender differences in self-regulated online learning environment. Educ. Technol. Soc. **12**(3), 12–22 (2009)
10. Cantwell Wilson, B.: A study of factors promoting success in computer science including gender differences. Comput. Sci. Educ. **12**(1–2), 141–164 (2002)
11. Papastergiou, M.: Are computer science and information technology still masculine fields? High school students' perceptions and career choices. Comput. Educ. **51**(2), 594–608 (2008)
12. Peteranetz, M.S., Flanigan, A.E., Shell, D.F., Soh, L.K.: Future-oriented motivation and retention in computer science. In: Proceedings of the 49th ACM Technical Symposium on Computer Science Education, pp. 350–355 (2018)
13. Kori, K., Pedaste, M., Altin, H., Tõnisson, E., Palts, T.: Factors that influence students' motivation to start and to continue studying information technology in Estonia. IEEE Trans. Educ. **59**(4), 225–262 (2016)
14. Pedaste, M., et al.: How do cognitive ability and study motivation predict the academic performance of IT students? In: Gómez Chova, L., López Martínez, A., Candel Torres, I. (eds.) ICERI2015, 8th International Conference of Education, Research and Innovation, pp. 7167 – 7176. IATED Academy (2015)
15. Barnes, T., Powell, E., Chaffin, A., Lipford, H.: Game2Learn: improving the motivation of CS1 students. In: Proceedings of the 3rd International Conference on Game Development in Computer Science Education, pp. 1–5 (2008)
16. Borrego, C., Fernández, C., Blanes, I., Robles, S.: Room escape at class: escape games activities to facilitate the motivation and learning in computer science. JOTSE **7**(2), 162–171 (2017)
17. López-Fernández, D., Tovar, E., Raya, L., Marzal, F., Garcia, J.J.: Motivation of computer science students at universities organized around small groups. In: 2019 IEEE Global Engineering Education Conference (EDUCON), pp. 1120–1127. IEEE (2019)
18. Säde, M., Suviste, R., Luik, P., Tõnisson, E., Lepp, M.: Factors that influence students' motivation and perception of studying computer science. In: SIGCSE 2019 Proceedings of the 50th ACM Technical Symposium on Computer Science Education, pp. 873–878 (2019)
19. Kori, K., Altin, H., Pedaste, M., Palts, T., Tõnisson, E.: What influences students to study information and communication technology? In: L. Gómez Chova, A. López Martínez, I. Candel Torres (eds.) INTED2014 Proceedings, pp. 1477 – 1486. IATED Academy (2014)
20. Scapin, E., Mirolo, C.: An exploration of teachers' perspective about the learning of iteration-control constructs. In: Pozdniakov, S.N., Dagienė, V. (eds.) ISSEP 2019. LNCS, vol. 11913, pp. 15–27. Springer, Cham (2019). https://doi.org/10.1007/978-3-030-33759-9_2

21. Altin, H., Pedaste, M.: Learning approaches to applying robotics in science education. J. Balt. Sci. Educ. **12**(3), 365–377 (2013)
22. Hooshyar, D., Lim, H., Pedaste, M., Yang, K., Fathi, M., Yang, Y.: AutoThinking: an adaptive computational thinking game. In: Rønningsbakk, L., Wu, T.-T., Sandnes, F.E., Huang, Y.-M. (eds.) ICITL 2019. LNCS, vol. 11937, pp. 381–391. Springer, Cham (2019). https://doi.org/10.1007/978-3-030-35343-8_41
23. Dagienė, V., Futschek, G.: Bebras international contest on informatics and computer literacy: criteria for good tasks. In: Mittermeir, R.T., Sysło, M.M. (eds.) ISSEP 2008. LNCS, vol. 5090, pp. 19–30. Springer, Heidelberg (2008). https://doi.org/10.1007/978-3-540-69924-8_2
24. Hacke, A.: Computer science problem solving in the escape game "Room-X". In: Pozdniakov, S.N., Dagienė, V. (eds.) ISSEP 2019. LNCS, vol. 11913, pp. 281–292. Springer, Cham (2019). https://doi.org/10.1007/978-3-030-33759-9_22
25. Spieler, B., Oates-Indruchova, L., Slany, W.: Female teenagers in computer science education: understanding stereotypes, negative impacts, and positive motivation. J. Woman Minor. Sci. Eng. (2019)
26. Chen, M.: The effects of prior computer experience and gender on high school students' learning of computer science concepts from instructional simulations. In: 10th IEEE International Conference on Advanced Learning Technologies, Sousse, pp. 610–612 (2010)
27. Jawad, H.M., Tout, S., Abualkibash, M., Xie, Y.: Integrating art and animation in teaching computer programming for high school students experimental study. In: 2018 IEEE International Conference on Electro/Information Technology (EIT), pp. 0311–0317 (2018)
28. Tuleviku tegija teekond startup ökosüsteemi. Uuringu raport. Rakendusliku Antropoloogia Keskus (2018). https://media.voog.com/0000/0037/5345/files/Raport%2015.11.18.pdf. Accessed 02 May 2020
29. Kindsiko, E., Türk, K. Kantšukov, M.: Naiste roll ja selle suurendamise võimalused Eesti IKT sektoris: müüdid ja tegelikkus 1-27 (2015). https://majandus.ut.ee/sites/default/files/www_ut/naiste_roll_ikt._tu_mj-skype_uuring_2015.pdf. Accessed 02 May 2020
30. Senkbeil, M.: Development and validation of the ICT motivation scale for young adolescents. Results of the international school assessment study ICILS 2013 in Germany. Learn. Individ. Differ. **67**, 167–176 (2018)
31. Luik, P., et al.: What motivates enrolment in programming MOOCs? Br. J. Educ. Technol. **50**(1), 153–165 (2019)
32. Kori, K., et al.: Why do students choose to study Information and Communications Technology? Procedia Soc. Behav. Sci. **191**, 2867–2872 (2015)
33. Lepp, M., et al.: MOOC in programming: a success story. In: Proceedings of the International Conference on e-Learning, pp. 138–147 (2017)

Tips and Tricks for Changing the Way Young People Conceive Computer Science

Cécile Lombart, Anne Smal, and Julie Henry(✉)

Namur Digital Institute, Computer Science Department,
University of Namur, Namur, Belgium
{school-it,julie.henry}@unamur.be

Abstract. Many youths have an incomplete perception of what computer science is, which leads to a lack of interest in studies on information and communication technologies. However, there is a large gap to be filled in terms of jobs in this field. It is therefore important to make young people aware of what computer science is about and of the jobs associated with it, specifically at this age as they do not yet have a precise vision of their future career. To meet this challenge, workshops have been organized to expose 12 to 15-year-olds to the basic concepts of computer science and its subfields, such as programming, robotics, computer networking, artificial intelligence, and cybersecurity. Over three years, data were collected to measure the influence of hands-on workshops conducted in the classroom on young people's conceptions. The workshops offered an introduction to a field of computer science poorly understood by most young people. Analysis of the data collected from more than 200 pupils across six different schools shows the important role played by both the themes addressed and the teacher's discourse. In particular, comparisons with workshops conducted by experts highlight the problem of the lack of teacher training.

Keywords: Computer science education · K12 · Didactic · Workshops

1 Introduction

In the French-speaking part of Belgium (Wallonia), computer science, including computational thinking, is almost missing from compulsory education, namely for 5 to 18-year-old students [16,22]. Because no specific computing course is organized, few solutions are available to introduce children to computer science within their school curriculum. Moreover, teachers are not trained [15] to teach digital skills [17]. However, Belgian education has been undergoing a major and complete reform[1] that stipulates that "from primary school, an introduction to digital logic can be achieved by programming simple machines" and also evokes a "minimum mastery of tool logic - *program or be programmed.*" A forthcoming polytechnic education curriculum between 3 and 15 years is also envisioned,

[1] "Le Pacte pour un Enseignement d'Excellence".

K. Kori and M. Laanpere (Eds.): ISSEP 2020, LNCS 12518, pp. 79–93, 2020.
https://doi.org/10.1007/978-3-030-63212-0_7

including digital literacy. Despite the desire to develop digital skills from an early age, the content of such education has yet to be defined [18], and currently only algorithms and programming are mentioned with regard to computer science.

Companies cite a lack of workers trained in digital skills and experts in various fields related to information and communication technologies. Although enrolments in computer-related studies are increasing, they are still insufficient and the "gender gap" is still not being bridged. But how can Walloon teenagers enrol in a discipline they do not understand? One solution could be short workshops that can be directly integrated into an existing technology-related course, and which could be integrated into the future digital literacy course. That is what the school-IT project[2] is all about.

This project was started in September 2017, partly funded by a plan for digital equipment in schools[3]. It promotes digital literacy for K12 students with three objectives: teach computer science as a fundamental discipline, modify the conceptions of computer science among teenagers to encourage their integration into recruitment channels, and aim at a civic education to enable them to be autonomous and reflective in their digital practices.

The workshops developed in this context[4] give priority to variety in the fields covered (communication, network, human-machine interaction, artificial intelligence, etc.), in the processes highlighted (analysis, coding, testing, etc.), and in the equipment used (unplugged activities, micro:bit[5], Makeblock[6], thymio[7], Bee-Bot, etc.). The goal of such workshops is to increase teenagers' interest in computer science in the hope that they realize the richness and diversity that characterize this discipline. But changing the teenagers' conceptions is not simple and undesired conceptions can appear. In consequence, attention must be paid to the design of such workshops.

This paper proposes to inform future workshops designs by answering the following research question: *How can workshops aimed at discovering computer science change the children's conceptions of computer science and computer scientists?*. In order to provide insights into this question, we have been conducting workshops under real conditions with children aged 12 to 15 for two years.

2 Related Work

It is not easy for learners to discard their existing conceptions and adopt new ones [8], especially if these conceptions are fuelled by the media. Existing conceptions are sometimes incorrect, and thus called misconceptions.

According to Ben-Ari [1], the constructivism theory "claims that knowledge is actively constructed by the learner (...). Since the construction builds recursively on knowledge that the learner already has, each learner will construct an

[2] https://school-it.info.unamur.be/.
[3] "École Numérique".
[4] Available on the school-IT website.
[5] http://microbit.org/.
[6] https://www.makeblock.com/.
[7] https://www.thymio.org/.

idiosyncratic version of knowledge. To the extent that such knowledge is not identical with 'standard' scientific knowledge, the learner is said to have misconceptions."

According to Maier [24], the way to resolve or prevent misconceptions is to directly confront the learner with an experience that causes an imbalance. Challenging learners' existing ideas encourages them to detect problems in their understanding and to motivate them to build appropriate understandings [29]. Generally, a cognitive conflict teaching strategy involves three steps: investigating learners' prior knowledge and existing conceptions; challenging learners with contradictory information; evaluating the conceptual change between learners' prior ideas and current ones [23]. Thus, because learners have to be confronted with their misconceptions, these are a prime source of material for teachers to build teaching resources.

In this section, related work is organized under three main topics: conceptions of computers, computer science and computer scientists.

2.1 Children's Conceptions of Computers

Children grow up surrounded by computers and interact with them. As a consequence, children start forming conceptions of how computers work and what their basic capabilities are. Rücker [26] presented five distinct conceptions identified from a literature review.

First, "the computer is often anthropomorphized and seen as some kind of living entity that is better understood in terms of psychology rather than technology". Children attribute to the computer "some form of mind or brain as well as various mental states like motivations, intentions or even emotions". Second, the computer is an omniscient database: it knows everything (unlimited storage of data) and knows everything by heart (by providing access to information). Consequently, the computer does not really compute anything at all. Third, the computer is mechanical because of how it is built. The computer is seen as an intricate clockwork, where data and processes are physical entities. Fourth, the computer is a network of different components connected together because it is a very complex electronic device. "what exactly is wired to what initially remains a complete mystery". Last but not least, the computer is programmable: their "behaviour and capabilities are determined by humans and can be changed by humans". According to Rücker [26], not all of these conceptions appear to be equally persistent over time: intrinsic capabilities are more tenacious while the conceptions related to hardware are logically more influenced by technological developments. Moreover, a child may hold several conceptions simultaneously, which may or may not be selected in a given context or situation". For Rücker [26], "education needs to take this into account and make children aware of such advantages and limitations".

Investigating children's current conceptions of computers is essential, as is communicating the results of such research to teachers in charge of introductory computer courses.

2.2 Children's Conceptions About Computer Science

In the past decade, there have been a number of studies on 12–18-year-old students' misconceptions about the nature of computer science, and related career prospects. These studies suggest that students are unaware of what computer science is. Their misconceptions impact both their interest in computer science and their affinity for this specific academic field.

In 1998, Greening [9] asked a fundamental question: "Is it the case that many students who enroll for a first computer science course do so with some very limiting misconceptions of what the discipline entails?". He considered that "students might also not be enrolling in computer science courses due to misconceptions". This belief that students choose not to major in computer science because they have an incorrect or inadequate conception of the field (or none at all) is supported by several studies [2,5,6,27]. For Brinda [5], pupils develop inadequate beliefs in computer science because they often only have experiences in information and communication technology.

The solution is to be found in the introduction to computer science which is proposed from the earliest age. Greening [9] proposed "a basis for evolving coursework in such a way that it increases the likelihood that students become excited about their learning". Yardi and Bruckmann [32] suggested that "there is an opportunity to increase interest in computing among teenagers by bridging the gap between their conceptions of programming and the actual opportunities that are offered in computing disciplines". He proposed a curriculum "to prepare and motivate teenagers for careers in today's expanding, Internet-based, global economy". Taub [31] suggested additions to unplugged activities to increase the shift in students' conceptions of computer science. More recently, Grover [10] presented the results of "a curricular intervention that aims to show computer science to [12–14 year-old] students in a new light–in real world contexts and as a creative and problem-solving discipline; as something bigger and broader than the computer-centric view that many students are known to harbor". Two years later, she reported on middle and high school students' engagement with an understanding of the question "what is a computer?" [11]. She urged "educators to shift the initial focus of introductory courses to the deeper ideas of computing, computation and computability".

According to the constructivist perspective on learning [1], the suggestions made by these experts all point in the same direction: teaching resources must be written with an awareness of students' existing conceptions of computer science.

But that seems easier said than done. According to Hewner [21], teaching teenagers about computer science with introductory courses designed to be engaging, relevant to student interests, and focused on the practice of programming do not have a significant effect on the students' attitude about computing. For him, it is not a viable way to significantly increase interest in computer science as a major [21]. Taub is slightly more optimistic [31]. His results show that "computer science unplugged activities did start a process of changing the students' views, but that this process was partial". Among the difficulties in overcoming, Taub cites "students' difficulties in identifying relationships between computer science unplugged activities and central ideas in computer science". This optimistic vision is shared by Henry [17]. She developed workshops to expose children aged 12–14 to core concepts in programming by letting them manipulate widespread tangible embedded systems and measured its influence on children's conceptions of computer science. Among the lessons to be drawn from this study, the meaning of the workshops and their objectives must be well thought out, governed by the vision of computer science to be transmitted to children.

2.3 Children's Conceptions of Computer Scientists

For many years, the draw-a-"something" technique is used to determine attitudes and beliefs about whatever the "something" is. According to Martin [25], children most often depict computer scientists as "white males in various degrees of geekiness" (described as including features such as glasses, pocket protectors, acne, messy hair, eyes glued to a computer monitor, overweight, eating junk food, wearing t-shirt with obscure computer code, etc.). These results are similar to those described by Hansen. She used a Draw-A-Scientist-Test [13] with children (ages 9–10) before and after a computer science curriculum [14]. After the curriculum, more female students drew female computer scientists than before, and the featured actions were more specific to computer science (not to technology in general: typing, printing, etc.).

So, understanding children's conceptions helps to identify when stereotypes begin and taking into account these conceptions is essential to counter these stereotypes.

3 Methodology

In order to measure the impact of short workshops on children's conceptions of computer science and computer scientists, a study was conducted in a real-world setting, extended over two years (between September 2017 and June 2019).

3.1 Sample and Workshops

The workshops were given in five schools. For each school, one teacher volunteered. These teachers were responsible for a course entitled "education through technology" (ETT) in which it is common practice to introduce students to office software. Eleven classes took part in the study, i.e. 232 students between 12 and 15 aged.

In 2017–2018, the workshops were given by one of the authors (Anne Smal), a computer scientist by training. In 2018–2019, the workshops were given by the teachers in charge of the classes. They did not have computer science training. In total, 134 students (Sample 1) were given by the expert in computer science, and 98 students (Sample 2) followed the workshops with their regular ETT teachers. However, it should be noted that the teachers observed, during the first year, the workshops given by the expert.

The students had between four and eight periods of classes dedicated to workshops. Not all students had the same workshops, depending on the time available in each school and the teacher affinity. However, two workshops were mandatory: a 2-period one introducing digitization, and a 1-period one explaining the working of a computer through the discovery of the inputs and outputs of a tangible device (laptop, micro:bit, thymio, tablet, or smartphone). Then, it was suggested to choose among the workshops introducing the programming concepts and implemented them with a tangible device (micro:bit or makeblock).

3.2 Data Collection and Analysis

During the study, a survey was set up to collect data, inspired by pretest-posttest design [28]. This survey was administered to the children before and after all the workshops given. A period of up to four months elapsed between the two tests.

The survey consists of open-ended questions: *What is computer science? What is a computer? What can it do? What can it not do?* Then, the children were asked to list the positive and negative points of computer jobs.

Survey responses were manually coded to identify key concepts and to count the most frequently cited words. A comparison was then made between the results obtained in the first year (workshops given by the expert) and the results of the second year (workshops given by the teachers).

4 Results

The results of the study are structured in four sections, taking into account the questions from the tests administered to the children: the view of the computer science, the view of the computer, the view of its capabilities, and the view of computer jobs. The full results are presented in tables in the appendix and only the most striking observations are included in the text.

4.1 Students' View of Computer Science

For the sentence to be completed "For you, computer science is ..." (Table 1), before the workshops, 50.0% of the Sample 1 pupils mentioned the word "computer" at least once. After the workshops, that number drops to 41.8%. Considering Sample 2 pupils, the number of times the word "computer" is mentioned is almost constant changing from 39.4% to 38.8%. In French, "computer" translates to "informatique", so the word computer does not appear in the question.

Whereas pupils talk about hardware (mouse, keyboard) before the workshops, this is mostly no longer the case afterwards. However, after the expert's intervention, more of the pupils in Sample 1 talk about input/output (+7.5%).

Sample 2 pupils talk more about robots after the workshops (+11.8% vs. +3.8% for Sample 1 pupils). In both samples, the pupils mention the word "code" more after the workshops (+16.2% for Sample 2 and +5.9% for Sample 1 pupils).

The association between computer science and the Internet is more present in 2017–2018, but it decreases with the impact of the workshops (−5.3%). The following year, a small increase is observed in Sample 2 after the teachers' intervention (+2.2%).

For software, the trends are reversed. Whereas in 2017–2018 they were mentioned by nearly 9% of pupils before the workshops, this was the case for only 1% of the pupils in Sample 2. However, after the workshops, only 1.5% of the pupils in Sample 1 talk about software, compared to 9.5% of the pupils in Sample 2. The same pattern is observed for video games.

Finally, artificial intelligence is evoked by more Sample 2 pupils after the workshops (+5.4%).

4.2 Pupils' View of Computer

To the question on what a computer is (Table 2), before the workshops, the Sample 1 pupils mostly talk about a machine, with a screen, a keyboard and a mouse, having a memory and capable of acting alone. They also talk about a very common use, the search for information. After the workshops, these pupils talk more about input/output, always referring to memory, but associate it to the processor.

When a teacher gives the workshops, the observations differ. Sample 2 pupils describe the computer from a hardware point of view (screen, mouse, keyboard) before and after the workshops. Few pupils mentioned the component aspect (processor, memory) before the workshops, this number decreases after the workshops. Furthermore, the number of pupils describing the uses of the computer (communication, research) increases slightly. Finally, nearly 12.8% of the Sample 2 pupils (+9.8%) mention artificial intelligence after workshops.

4.3 Pupils' View of Computer Capacity

Pupils had to answer two questions: "What can a computer do?" and "What can't a computer do?" (Table 3 and 4).

Results highlight that pupils think first of all about the computer being able to do research, to go online, and to store data. After the workshops, use for research is still cited by more than one third of the pupils.

The evoking of video games decreases strongly after the workshops for both samples.

There is an increase in the number of pupils thinking that a computer can do everything (+7.3% for Sample 1 and +2.4% for Sample 2) before and after the workshops. These results are confirmed by the results of what the computer can't do question, with some pupils answering "nothing" (+4.5% for Sample 1 and +7.5% for Sample 2).

When the workshops are given by the expert, 6.0% of the pupils think after the workshops that the computer cannot do anything without the human.

Finally, after the workshops, Sample 2 pupils talk more about "coding" (+15.6%).

4.4 Pupils' View of Computer Jobs

Pupils were asked what they found positive and negative about working in computer science (Table 5 and 6).

Concerning the positive aspects of computer jobs, there is an increase in the number of children who find them useful for society. This increase is the same for the workshops presented by the expert and by the teachers. Sample 1 pupils think that computer science helps people.

The pupils in Sample 1 move away from the idea that a computer job requires the use of a computer, while this idea is reinforced among the pupils in Sample 2.

The fun side decreases for all pupils, while creativity only increases for the pupils in Sample 1.

For the negative aspects of computer jobs, Sample 1 pupils' responses decrease in almost all points except for the attractiveness. When the workshops are presented by the teachers, negative health aspects and the static side of jobs are mentioned by more pupils after the workshops.

5 Discussion

A first observation to be made is the confusion that is always present among children between computers, the computer jobs, and the computer in its most classic form (with a screen, keyboard, and mouse). Although distinct, the questions asked suffered from this confusion. However, lessons can be learned from the responses.

In general, the computer scientist was more careful to keep the child away from the computer (in its classic form) to make him/her understand its internal functioning, including the functioning of its components (memory, processor). This is not surprising since this study is part of a project aimed at changing children's conceptions of computer science. The computer scientist aims at a better view of computing. Given the mandatory workshops, the teachers also had to delve into these ideas (computing, computation and computability). The measured difference between the two samples could be explained by the teacher's lack of training, by a lack of confidence in the teaching to be imparted, or by the fact that the teacher probably insisted less on these ideas, which the expert considered crucial.

Teachers seem to draw inspiration from the media to develop their knowledge of the computer field. This certainly explains the evocation, by their pupils, of robots and artificial intelligence, notions not present in the workshops given, but which are regularly in the media headlines. The evocation of software and video games, more cited by the pupils of Sample 2 also shows that the teachers rely on their knowledge and frequent uses.

The increase in discussions around programming is logically due to the content of the workshops. However, it is much more pronounced among Sample 2. Once again, this can be explained by the expert's attention to showing the variety that exists in computer jobs.

The capacities of the computer are limited to current use or extrapolated (capable of anything). Here again, the expert tried to give back to the human what is due to him/her, i.e. the intentions of the computer. Teachers seem to have been less insisting on this point.

The reactions concerning the jobs once again highlight the precaution taken by the expert to enhance the value of her job. The intervention of the teachers seems to have a relatively weak, even rather negative impact.

In concluding this study, it appears that it is difficult to change children's conceptions if certain conditions are not met. But what are those conditions?

- *Being clear about the message to be conveyed: don't teach computer science to only teach computer science.* Whereas the expert is aware of what she has to bring, things are different for the teachers who are struggling in a field they do not master.
- *Becoming as much as possible a role model or promote inspiring role models.* The expert becomes a role model for the pupils who then have in front of them someone who should work daily in front of a computer (according to their conceptions) but who says she does much more than that. If it is not possible for teachers to be role models themselves, they can make their pupils discover inspiring ones through personal stories. Accessible role model should be preferred to rare cases of success [30].
- *Taking sufficient time.* It is clear that it is difficult to change deeply rooted conceptions, especially if the time devoted is short. Unfortunately, it seems that the solution will not be a one-shot introduction to computer science.
- *Being careful what is said.* Teachers have to be informed of existing stereotypes in order to deconstruct them and not feed them. This would also allow them to take a critical look at the media and the metaphors commonly used [4].
- *Discovering different sub-fields of computer science.* It is important to show different sub-fields of computer science (AI, cybersecurity, human-machine interface, etc.) to avoid reinforcing stereotypes and changing the way young people view it.
- *Training to master.* If it is necessary to play on the themes addressed (AI, cybersecurity, human-machine interface, etc.), this forces teachers to master more than the skills increasingly demanded in teaching, which are algorithmic and programming. Mastering the material means mastering the basic concepts and mastering the associated vocabulary, being confident, and being able to detach oneself from the material itself, but also from the media in order to take a step back. This step back is essential if pupils are to be encouraged to take a critical stance with regard to computer science.
- *Detaching from the computer in its most classic form (screen, mouse, and keyboard).* As pupils mainly talk about computers when referring to computer

science, the ideal is to get as far away from them as possible to develop their view and to show them other aspects and devices (micro:bit, makeblock, thymio, etc.). An unplugged activity can be just as effective in changing mentalities.

6 Conclusion

In an increasingly digital world, there is a lack of human resources in the computer job market. The misconceptions that teenagers have of what computer science is and what it implies in terms of jobs is a possible cause. Therefore, we are interested in the following research question: *How can workshops aimed at discovering computer science change the children's conceptions of computer science and computer scientists?*.

Short workshops have been developed to introduce teenagers to computer science. During two years, these workshops were organized in 5 schools with over 200 pupils aged 12–15 years. The first year, the workshops were given by a computer scientist, and the second year, by the regular teachers of the pupils. To collect data, a survey was conducted before and after each sequence of workshops, following a pretest-post-test design. The purpose of the survey was to identify changes in teenagers' conceptions of computer, computer science, and computer scientist.

Several elements were highlighted by this study. The most important is that there is a big difference in impact between workshops given by a computer scientist and the same workshop given by a teacher. The computer scientist with an in-depth knowledge of stereotypes knows how to orient the workshops because he/she has the time to make some research about those stereotypes. It is also logically easier for him/her to convey key concepts. Special attention should be paid to deconstructing the erroneous stereotypes that teenagers have about computers. The idea is to start from the representations that teenagers have and to propose workshops asking them to revise their knowledge by confronting them with the reality of people working in this field. This action is not possible without a training, unfortunately often absent or incomplete among teachers.

Another insight we can draw from this study is that the choice of workshops proposed is also very important. It is important to enrich the vision of teenagers by avoiding to propose only workshops that present sub-fields already known to computer science (programming, among others). It is important to target sub-fields that people think less of when they think about computer science (often because of stereotypes and the vision diffused by the media), such as human-machine interaction, cybersecurity, modelling, etc.

Finally, particular attention must also be paid to the choice of the equipment used. It is at the price of respecting these conditions that we can hope to improve teenagers' view of computers, computer science, and computer scientist.

A Results Tables

Table 1. What is computer sciences?

	Sample 1		Sample 2	
	Pretest(%)	Post-Test(%)	Pretest(%)	Post-Test(%)
Computer	50.0	41.8	39.4	38.9
Screen/Mouse/Keyboard	6.7	0.0	8.1	2.1
Smartphone	14.2	4.5	6.1	3.2
Television	2.2	0.7	1.0	3.2
Electronic machine	10.4	8.2	13.1	10.5
Robot	0.7	4.5	7.1	18.9
Internet	7.5	2.2	2.0	4.2
Communication	1.5	0.0	3.0	0.0
Networks	2.2	1.5	1.0	1.1
Video games	5.2	0.7	0.0	4.2
Code/program	7.5	13.4	10.1	26.3
Technology	21.6	9.7	13.1	8.4
AI	2.2	1.5	3.0	0.0
Data	10.4	0.0	5.1	3.2
Software	8.2	1.5	1.0	9.5
Job	11.2	6.0	0.0	0.0
Input/Output	0.0	7.5	0.0	0.0

Table 2. What is a computer?

	Sample 1		Sample 2	
	Pretest(%)	Post-Test(%)	Pretest(%)	Post-Test(%)
Machine	27.9	18.0	21.0	27.7
"Box"	12.0	10.5	2.0	13.8
Screen/Mouse/Keyboard	25.3	6.0	16.0	19.1
Input/Output	0.0	36.1	3.0	1.1
Processor	2.7	13.5	3.0	1.1
Memory	20.0	24.1	3.0	2.1
Code/program	4.0	2.3	3.0	6.4
Internet	9.3	1.5	6.0	6.4
Communication	6.7	0.0	0.0	1.1
Research	27.9	5.3	3.0	8.5
Software	6.7	6.0	4.0	6.4
AI	5.3	6.0	3.0	12.8
Following orders	6.7	3.0	7.0	8.5
Doing things on its own	23.9	3.0	4.0	8.5

Table 3. What can a computer do?

	Sample 1		Sample 2	
	Pretest(%)	Post-Test(%)	Pretest(%)	Post-Test(%)
To do research	31.6	30.8	36.0	35.5
To go online	13.5	5.3	12.0	12.9
To program	2.3	3.0	7.0	22.6
To store date	13.5	4.5	12.0	9.7
To do word processing	3.8	3.0	8.0	5.4
To communicate	5.3	5.3	7.0	4.3
To play	8.3	1.5	11.0	1.1
Everything	12.8	20.3	3.0	5.4
Nothing without human action	0.8	6.0	0.0	1.1

Table 4. What can't a computer do?

	Sample 1		Sample 2	
	Pretest(%)	Post-Test(%)	Pretest(%)	Post-Test(%)
To move	14.3	12.0	22.0	29
To talk	14.3	12.8	19.0	18.3
To mundane tasks (eat, drink,...)	10.0	15.0	31.0	33.3
To think like a human	7.5	5.3	3.0	1.1
Nothing	4.5	9.0	0.0	7.5

Table 5. Positive points of computer jobs

	Sample 1		Sample 2	
	Pretest(%)	Post-Test(%)	Pretest(%)	Post-Test(%)
Static	0.8	3.0	5.0	3.0
Helping people	3.8	6.0	1.0	1.0
Useful	15.8	24.1	22.0	35.0
Computer use	10.5	6.8	4.0	6.0
Continual learning	11.3	8.3	13.0	11.0
Fun	6.0	3.0	9.0	4.0
A job with a future	8.2	8.9	4.0	6.0
Creativity	4.5	5.3	2.0	1.0

Table 6. Negative points of computer jobs

	Sample 1		Sample 2	
	Pretest(%)	Post-Test(%)	Pretest(%)	Post-Test(%)
Bad for your eyesight	31.9	16.5	10.0	25.0
Bad for your health (addiction, migraine, etc.)	14.6	7.5	6.0	6.0
Static	37.2	21.1	16.0	21.0
Loneliness	10.6	7.5	2.0	2.0
Not attractive	5.3	6.8	15.0	5.0
Difficult	16.0	6.8	11.0	8.0
Scary	1.3	0.0	3.0	4.0

References

1. Ben-Ari, M.: Constructivism in computer science education. J. Comput. Math. Sci. Teach. **20**(1), 45–73 (2001)
2. Biggers, M., Brauer, A., Yilmaz, T.: Student perceptions of computer science: a retention study comparing graduating seniors with cs leavers. ACM SIGCSE Bull. **40**(1), 402–406 (2008)
3. Olivier, B., Smal, A., Frenay, B., Henry, J.: Intelligence Artificielle: Éduquer pour modifier la représentation qu'en ont les jeunes. In: Une école numérique pour émanciper? Colloque scientifique, Actes de la conférence, pp. 34–37 (March 2018)
4. Boraita, F., Henry, J., Collard, A.-S.: Developing a critical robot literacy for young people from conceptual metaphors analysis. In: Proceedings of the 2020 IEEE Frontiers in Education Conference (FIE) (2020)
5. Brinda, T., Puhlmann, H., Schulte, C.: Bridging ICT and CS: educational standards for computer science in lower secondary education. ACM SIGSE Bull. **41**(3), 288–292 (2009)
6. Carter, L.: Why students with an apparent aptitude for computer science don't choose to major in computer science. ACM SIGCSE Bull. **38**(1), 27–31 (2006)
7. Collard, A.S., Henry, J., Hernalesteen, A., Jacques, J.: Déconstruire les représentations médiatiques sur l'intelligence artificielle en jouant à "Qui est-ce?". In: Actes du Colloque International TICEMED (2020)
8. Davis, J.: Conceptual change. In: Emerging Perspectives on Learning, Teaching, and Technology, vol. 19 (2001)
9. Greening, T.: Computer science: through the eyes of potential students. In: Proceedings of the 3rd Australasian Conference on Computer Science Education, pp. 145–154 (1998)
10. Grover, S., Pea, R., Cooper, S.: Remedying misperceptions of computer science among middle school students. In: Proceedings of the 45th ACM Technical Symposium on Computer Science Education, pp. 343–348 (2014)
11. Grover, S., Rutstein, D., Snow, E.: "What is a computer" what do secondary school students think? In: Proceedings of the 47th ACM Technical Symposium on Computer Science Education, pp. 564–569 (2016)

12. Gutierrez, F.J., Simmonds, J., Casanova, C., Sotomayor, C., Hitschfeld, N.: Coding or hacking? Exploring inaccurate views on computing and computer scientists among K-6 learners in Chile. In: Proceedings of the 49th ACM Technical Symposium on Computer Science Education, pp. 993–998 (2018)
13. Hansen, A.K., Dwyer, H., Harlow, D.B., Franklin, D.: What Is a Computer Scientist? Developing the Draw-A-Computer-Scientist-Test for Elementary School Students. AERA Online Paper Repository (2016)
14. Hansen, A.K., et al.: Assessing children's understanding of the work of computer scientists: the draw-a-computer-scientist test. In: Proceedings of the 2017 ACM (SIGCSE) Technical Symposium on Computer Science Education, pp. 279–284 (2017)
15. Henry, J., Joris, N.: Maîtrise et usage des TIC: la situation des enseignants en Belgique francophone (2013). https://edutice.archives-ouvertes.fr/edutice-00875643/. Accessed 6 July 2020
16. Henry, J., Joris, N.: Informatics at secondary schools in the French-speaking region of Belgium: myth or reality. In: International Conference on Informatics In Schools Situation, Evolution and Perspective, vol. 2016, p. 13 (2016)
17. Henry, J., Dumas, B.: Perceptions of computer science among children after a hands-on activity: a pilot study. In: 2018 IEEE Global Engineering Education Conference (EDUCON), pp. 1811–1817 (2018)
18. Henry, J., Hernalesteen, A., Dumas, B., Collard, A.S.: Que signifie éduquer au numérique? Pour une approche interdisciplinaire. In: Didapro 7 - DidaSTIC. De 0 à 1 ou l'heure de l'informatique à l'école (2018)
19. Henry, J., Smal, A.: Et si demain je devais enseigner l'informatique? Le cas des enseignants de Belgique francophone. In Didapro: De 0 à 1 ou l'heure de l'informatique à l'école, p. 129 (2018)
20. Henry, J., Hernalesteen, A., Collard, A.S.: Designing digital literacy activities: an interdisciplinary and collaborative approach. In: 2020 IEEE Frontiers in Education Conference (FIE) (2020)
21. Hewner, M., Guzdial, M.: Attitudes about computing in postsecondary graduates. In: Proceedings of the 4th International Workshop on Computing Education Research, pp. 71–78 (2008)
22. Joris, N., Henry, J.: L'enseignement de l'informatique en Belgique francophone: état des lieux. 1024: Bulletin de la Société Informatique de France **2**, 107–116 (2014)
23. Limón, M.: On the cognitive conflict as an instructional strategy for conceptual change: a critical appraisal. Learn. Instr. **11**(4–5), 357–380 (2001)
24. Maier, S.: Misconception research and Piagetian models of intelligence. In: Proceedings of the 2004 Oklahoma Higher Education Teaching and Learning Conference (2004)
25. Martin, C.D.: Draw a computer scientist. ACM SIGCSE Bull. **36**(4), 11–12 (2004)
26. Rücker, M.T., Pinkwart, N.: Review and discussion of children's conceptions of computers. J. Sci. Educ. Technol. **25**(2), 274–283 (2016)
27. Ruslanov, A.D., Yolevich, A.P.: College student views of computer science: opinion survey. J. Comput. Sci. Coll. **25**(4), 142–148 (2010)
28. Shuttleworth, M.: Pretest-Posttest Designs (2009). https://explorable.com/pretest-posttest-designs. Accessed 7 July 2020
29. Scott, P.H., Asoko, H.M., Driver, R.H.: Teaching for conceptual change: a review of strategies. In: Research in Physics Learning: Theoretical Issues and Empirical Studies, pp. 310–329 (1992)

30. Spieler, B., Oates-Indruchova, L., Slany, W.: Female Teenagers in Computer Science Education: Understanding Stereotypes, Negative Impacts, and Positive Motivation (2019). arXiv preprint arXiv:1903.01190
31. Taub, R., Ben-Ari, M., Armoni, M.: The effect of CS unplugged on middle-school students' views of CS. ACM SIGCSE Bull. **41**(3), 99–103 (2009)
32. Yardi, S., Bruckman, A.: What is computing? Bridging the gap between teenagers' perceptions and graduate students' experiences. In: Proceedings of the 3rd International Workshop on Computing Education Research, pp. 39–50 (2007)

Engagement Taxonomy for Introductory Programming Tools: Failing to Tackle the Problems of Comprehension

Tomas Šiaulys(✉)

Institute of Data Science and Digital Technologies, Vilnius University, Vilnius, Lithuania
tomas.siaulys@mif.vu.lt

Abstract. A large number of introductory programming environments for K-12 education have become widely used across the world. One of the main ideas behind these environments is introducing basic programming concepts more effectively by incorporating different visualization strategies. There have been attempts to classify introductory programming tools, however, certain critical aspects have not yet been discussed within the existing classifications, especially those related to user engagement in the programming environment. In this paper we introduce an engagement taxonomy for introductory programming tools (ETIP) built on a concept of engagement taxonomy for software visualization and previous classifications of programming learning tools. The new taxonomy is then used to inclusively review introductory programming environments for secondary education used today with a focus on user engagement in a learning environment. Our review illustrates how majority of introductory programming tools do not fully explore the ways visualizations could help with tackling the problems of beginner programming comprehension. There is still a lack of knowledge about the importance of the level of engagement in visual introductory programming tools and the suggested taxonomy could be used for future research of computer science education.

Keywords: Introductory programming · Software visualization · Engagement taxonomy

1 Introduction

Since the introduction of Logo programming language and turtle graphics in 1967, as well as the new vision for computer science education (Papert 1980), there has been a huge interest of educators, scientists and engineers in designing introductory programming tools for school-age children. At present there are hundreds of introductory programming environments employing different strategies for easing the access to the world of programming, which would otherwise be out of reach for the children. Robots, tangible programing, virtual worlds, e-textiles, music composition, visualizations, 3D models are just a few ways to help students understand the basic programming concepts, motivate and engage children of all ages. This study focuses on the role of visualization

K. Kori and M. Laanpere (Eds.): ISSEP 2020, LNCS 12518, pp. 94–106, 2020.
https://doi.org/10.1007/978-3-030-63212-0_8

in improving student comprehension of the basic concepts and practices of programming in introductory programming environments for K-12 education.

It is important to note that visual programming environments that are widely used across the secondary education, employ both visualization types - programming code visualizations as well as visualizations of program execution. While the role of code visualization has been extensively studied (Xu et al. 2019, Weintrop and Wilensky 2019), the impact of execution-time visualizations on students' comprehension is less clear.

Previous works of Sorva et al. (2013) and Hidalgo-Céspedes (2016) made extensive reviews of generic program visualization systems for introductory programming with a focus on higher education and professional programming languages. This work covers the visualization systems for K-12 education including visual programming environments. The following research questions were addressed:

RQ1: What levels of engagement in visual programming learning environments could be defined based on their design?
RQ2: What levels of engagement do the introductory programming tools for K-12 support?

To answer the first research question we briefly discuss engagement taxonomies for software visualization and previous classifications of programming learning environments (Sect. 2). Then a new, revised engagement taxonomy for program visualization is presented (Sect. 3). To answer the second research question we inclusively review 70 introductory programming environments for K-12 education (Sects. 4 and 5). The results are discussed in Sect. 6.

2 Related Work

Recently there has been an increasing amount of research about introductory programming tools for higher education (Luxton-Reilly et al. 2018). While some of this work is relevant to K-12 education as well, there are factors that require special consideration when approaching secondary education. Firstly, environments for higher education mostly focus on professional programming or make a transition from educational languages to professional programming languages at some point during introductory programming course with a final goal of mastering professional programming languages. Secondly, it is important to take into consideration student mental development, since concepts of computer science are of an abstract nature, and abstract thinking might not be developed to the same extent when considering most of K-12 age groups (Mladenović et al. 2018, Rijke et al. 2018) In this section we briefly touch upon the subject of misconceptions that novice programmers have about programming and discuss the previous classifications of introductory programming environments and software visualization tools forming a clearer picture of what might be the key factors in creating visualizations for learner engagement in learning.

2.1 Misconceptions of Novice Programmers

According to literature review by Qian and Lehman (2017) novice programmers tend to have misconceptions about most of the basic programming concepts including variables, conditionals, parameters, loops and even the idea of states and sequential execution. Tracing programs step by step is probably the most important strategy to overcome these misconceptions, however, Lister et al. (2004) and Simon (2011) show that it's the ability that most of the novices struggle with. Grover and Basu (2017) show that even students, who completed introductory visual programming courses, keep misconceptions about the basic programming concepts. Authors argue, that even though visual programming environments like *Scratch*, do help learners with the syntactic aspects of programming, conceptual and strategic aspects of programming require additional effort. Role of pedagogy in overcoming these misconceptions also leaves many unknowns as instructors tend to show weak understanding about students' mistakes (Brown and Altadmri 2014). One of the most popular approaches in trying to tackle the problems of student comprehension is visualization. Visualizations can make abstract programming concepts and hidden automatic runtime processes visible and controllable.

2.2 Taxonomies of Programming Learning Tools

Taxonomy of programming environments and languages for novice programmers by Kelleher and Pausch (2005) is the most cited attempt to classify introductory programming tools. While proposed taxonomy could be criticized for vague descriptions and overlapping categories, it provides an overall view of the key aspects in making programming accessible for novices (K-12 as well as higher education). Taxonomy suggested the category of code visualization with an emphasis of avoiding syntax errors, as well as the category for visualizing program execution, including examples of strategies that programming environments use for visualization. Authors argue that different visualization techniques are similar to "the supports found in many debuggers". Article provides brief descriptions of 86 systems, some dating back to 1960's.

Built upon the work of Kelleher and Pausch, Taxonomy of programming learning tools (Saito et al. 2017) attempts to describe each learning tool across 11 categories. However, due to the lack of clarity in category definitions, it is not fully clear what certain categories of the taxonomy represent. While taxonomy doesn't explicitly focus on visualization of execution, *support to understand programs* category provides some information about visualization strategies of the learning tools. Proposed taxonomy is then used to classify 43 introductory programming environments designed for kids.

João et al. (2019) used similar approach analyzing 26 most popular block-based and visual programming apps across 27 categories with a focus on pedagogical usefulness. As with the previous classifications, some categories are vaguely defined, particularly those concerning the execution environment.

Different approach was taken by Duncan et al. (2014) in loose classification of 47 tools for introductory programming according to the difficulty level, concepts being introduced, as well as student age, without focusing on visualization. Authors introduce heuristics to classify introductory programming tools into 5 approximately defined categories leaving the classification rather subjective.

2.3 Engagement Taxonomies

Meta-analysis of visualization systems by Hundhausen et al. (2002) concludes that visualization proved to be effective in only 13 out of 28 studies and that different learner engagement forms were connected to the effectiveness of visualizations. Following this work Naps et al. (2002) introduced original engagement taxonomy (OET) for program visualization, which defined six different forms of learner engagement in the context of using visualization tools: *no viewing*, *viewing*, *responding*, *changing*, *constructing* and *presenting*. It has been hypothesized that increasing level of engagement would result in better learning outcomes and that the mix of different forms of engagement would be more beneficial than a single engagement form. A survey partially supporting OET was carried out by Urquiza-Fuentes and Velázquez-Iturbide (2009) regarding program visualization and algorithm animation systems.

Building upon the original engagement taxonomy Myller et al. (2009) and Sorva et al. (2013) attempted to improve the categorization of engagement levels. Hypothesizing that collaborative activities of the students and engagement levels are correlated, Myller et al. introduced an extended engagement taxonomy (EET) defining 10 engagement levels: *no viewing*, *viewing*, *controlled viewing*, *entering input*, *responding*, *changing*, *modifying*, *constructing*, *presenting* and *reviewing*. Sorva et al. (2013) criticized OET and EET for mixing different engagement forms and introduced a revised 2-dimentional engagement taxonomy (2DET) differentiating between direct engagement dimension: *no viewing*, *viewing*, *controlled viewing*, *responding*, *applying*, *presenting*, *creating*; and content ownership dimension: *given content*, *own cases*, *modified content*, *own content*. Then 22 systems were classified into categories according to 2DET.

3 Engagement Taxonomy for Introductory Programming Tools (ETIP)

Previously defined taxonomies of engagement in software visualization, even though have theoretical basis, are still problematic in using them practically for classification and research of program visualization systems. Attempts to classify programming environments tend to distribute all the systems across two or three groups and for the further analysis other factors have to be chosen. Sorva et al. (2013) found that 18 out of 22 generic program visualization systems fall under controlled viewing engagement level and own content in ownership dimension of 2DET. Hence understanding what is meant by controlled viewing may be the key in explaining user engagement in using visualization tools. This is especially relevant when discussing introductory programming tools for K-12 since these tools tend to employ visualizations different from the ones used in higher education that were analyzed using previous taxonomies.

Another argument for introducing a new taxonomy for introductory programming is that most of the visualizations cannot be categorized as specially designed for presenting (Sorva 2013) and even if they were, this would give us more information about the use of visualization in social interactions rather than about individual interaction with the visualization. This remark is consistent with the survey of Urquiza-Fuentes and Velázquez-Iturbide (2009) classifying all the systems that support *changing* level of OET, as well supporting *presenting* level of engagement.

We propose a new engagement taxonomy for introductory programming tools (ETIP) focusing on student engagement in studying the visual execution of programs (Table 1). The lower levels of engagement (*no viewing* and *viewing)* in our proposed taxonomy are the same as in 2DET. *Following* is added and *controlled viewing* is split into three levels of engagement in respect to tracing the execution of a program in visual environment. Highlighting the code during execution was suggested by Naps et al. (2002) in the context of algorithm visualization. Nevertheless, this might not be enough to engage learners into tracing the visualization, especially when the certain steps being executed are too complex or the bugs are present. Tracing the execution of visualization can be partially helped by *changing the speed*. Finally, engagement levels of *executing step-by-step* and *rewinding* are adapted from the requirements for the algorithm visualization systems (Karavirta and Shaffer 2016). For the reasons described above, *presenting* level was not included. *Creating*, *responding* and *applying* levels were omitted as well for being not consistent with the concept of visual student-written program execution. Given that all of the introductory programming environments involving program visualization are expected to promote content ownership of the students, content ownership dimension is as well omitted in the presented taxonomy.

Table 1. The categories of the engagement taxonomy for introductory programming tools

Level of engagement		Description
No viewing		There is no visualization, only material in textual format
Viewing		The learner views a visualization with no control over execution of visualization, can only zoom/navigate the environment of program execution
Following		The learner views the visualization with the executed code being highlighted
Controlled viewing	Changing the speed	The learner can change the speed of visualization being executed
	Executing step by step	The learner can view the visualization being executed step-by-step
	Rewinding	The learner can rewind the visualization at any time during the visualization

4 Method to Select Tools

To answer the second research question, as many as possible of all the available programming environments for secondary education were categorized according to the highest level of user engagement of ETIP they allow. All the tools from the previous classifications of programming environments for K-12 education (Duncan et al. 2014, Saito et al. 2017, Joao et al. 2019) were included in the list for the study as well as additional environments from the web search. The general overview of 70 selected environments can be found in the Appendix 1. The list could not be seen as complete, since the number of introductory learning environments for K-12 education is difficult to track. However, most of the most popular visual introductory programming environments are included.

Of course, it is not possible to distinguish clearly between introductory programming for K-12 and higher education. Even though there are differences in final goals they are trying to achieve, these systems do overlap to a large extent. Even the block-based programming environments (usually designed for primary and middle schools' students in mind) are being used in universities. Tools based on textual execution environments were omitted as there could be rarely a clear focus on K-12 regarding the design. Finally, environments developed for learning with robots or electronics were not included in this study.

Another problem with selection was the language, since the environments for younger students happen to be implemented in native languages of the learners. Since it would be really difficult to evaluate such systems, only the ones that were available in English were included.

There was also a problem in determining whether particular programming environments are still in use. While the latest web-based applications dominate the searches, some older visualization systems are still compatible with modern OS systems and might be still used for education. There is no basis to consider these systems obsolete. To tackle this problem, we included only the systems that could be found in a web search and were showing some activity during the last 5 years (updates, community posts, etc.).

After analyzing each tool, a classification of all the 70 tools was made according to the proposed taxonomy. The results could be found in the Appendix 2.

5 Results

The results from the Appendix 1 table suggest that majority of the tools cover most of the basic programming concepts with exception of the tools focusing on primary education. Also, majority of the tools use the same block model for code construction as well as the same game/puzzle activity type (*Blockly games*, *Code Studio*, etc.). Another common group of introductory programming environments are the classical turtle visualization environments (*Scratch*, *Snap!*, etc.) focusing on the motion of the sprites and drawing. The most common programming languages used for learning were Python and JavaScript. Systems based on gamification elements are just as common as tools allowing for free creation of games, animations, etc.

Appendix 2 shows that only 2 programming tools allow rewinding and only 20% of the introductory programming environments allow executing step by step level of engagement, while majority (47%) allows only viewing of program execution visualization. What is somewhat surprising is that tools created for primary education to a great extent employ low engagement levels, while the systems that fall into high engagement level categories are targeted towards older students.

6 Discussion

The results of the study bring some new insights into K-12 programming education. First of all, it seems that in relation to such a large number of educational programming environments, most of the tools stick to the same old models. Of course, new technologies gave visualizations the quality and the possibilities never seen before, but as noted before, even though more enjoyable and emotionally engaging, visualizations are not always effective in improving the learning results. Secondly, having in mind the misconceptions of novice programmers about most of the basic programming concepts, it seems puzzling why so many tool designs do not address the issue of learners' comprehension. In particular, the ability to track the program execution, a skill at the core of understanding the basic programming concepts, seems to be unrepresented in most of the programming environments for schools. These systems could borrow strategies for program visualization from the systems targeted more at higher education. It could be argued that tracing the program execution in a visual environment involves the same strategies as tracing an algorithm visualization, while the systems for algorithm visualization often employ much richer tools for user engagement. Vieira et al. (2019) argues that one of the problems might be a lack of reliable design and usability evaluation models for educational tools.

This work proposed a new engagement taxonomy of introductory programming visualization systems, however, it is worth mentioning that taxonomy only points out the highest engagement level supported by the visualization tool and does not necessarily reflect the level of engagement of every learner. Even at a viewing level of engagement supported by the tool, the learners can engage in the process of learning at a higher than viewing level. On the other hand, even the engagement at the level of execution step by step does not ensure that the learner will necessarily use the visualization to track the program execution and construct a better understanding. Research suggests that misuse of visualization tools might occur often as novices may not be inclined to trace their programs (Thomas et al. 2004).

There are still a lot of unknowns in studying engagement in K-12 introductory programming education. It is not clear to what extent engagement in tracing the program execution visually can help improve comprehension of the basic programming concepts. Also it is not clear how pedagogy, motivation and collaboration can work in combination with design of the visualization tools. To answer these questions more empirical research is needed.

7 Conclusion

This work introduced Engagement taxonomy for introductory programming tools (ETIP) - a model to measure learners' engagement in tracing the program execution in visual environments. The new tool was used to classify 70 visual programming environments for secondary education. Results show that majority of introductory programming environments for K-12 education are not developed in line with theoretical models of the basic programming concepts' comprehension. There is still a lack of knowledge about the importance of engagement levels in designing introductory programming tools as well as different types of engagement involved. Suggested taxonomy could be used for future research in studying these issues.

Appendix 1

General information of introductory programming environments for K-12 sorted by the age of target audience.

Name	Code representation	Activity type	Visualization type	release date	age group	conditionals	loops	variables	functions	objects
Code Studio (courses)	blocks	game-puzzle	moving sprite, drawing	2013	4 and up	x	x	x	x	
BotLogic.us	picture-blocks	game-puzzle	moving sprite	2013	4–11					
Kodable	picture-blocks, JavaScript	game-puzzle	moving sprite	2014	4–11	x	x	x	x	x
Lightbot Jr	picture-blocks	game-puzzle	moving sprite	2014	4–8	x	x			
Cargo-bot	picture-blocks	game-puzzle	moving sprite	2012	5 and up	x	x			
Tynker	Blocks, Python, JavaScript, HTML	game-puzzle, creating	moving sprite, drawing, animation, music	2012	5 and up	x	x	x	x	x
Code avengers	Java, JavaScript, Python	game-puzzle, creating	moving sprite/drawing	2012	5 and up	x	x	x	x	x
Lego Bits and bricks	picture-blocks	game-puzzle	moving sprite	2017	5–11	x				
Move the Turtle	picture-blocks	game-puzzle	moving sprite	2012	5–11		x	x	x	
My robot friend	picture-blocks	game-puzzle	moving sprite	2013	5–12					
Cato's Hike	picture-blocks	game-puzzle	moving sprite	2012	5–12	x	x			
Junior Coder	picture-blocks	game-puzzle	moving sprite	2015	5–12	x	x		x	
ScratchJr	picture-blocks	creating	moving sprite, game design	2014	5–7	x	x			
Daisy the dinosaur	blocks	game-puzzle	moving sprite	2012	5–7	x	x			
the Foos (CodeSpark)	picture-blocks	game-puzzle	moving sprite, game design	2014	5–9	x	x			
Codable Crafts	picture-blocks	game-puzzle	moving sprite	2015	5–9	x	x			
Swift Playgrounds	swift	game-puzzle	moving sprite	2016	6 and up	x	x	x	x	x
Run Marco (All can code, hour of code)	blocks	game-puzzle	moving sprite	2014	6–12	x	x			
Codemancer	picture-blocks	game-puzzle	moving sprite	2013	6–12		x		x	
Rapid router (Blockly, Code for life)	blocks/Python	game-puzzle	moving sprite	2014	6–13	x	x	x	x	

Gamefroot	blocks	creating	game design	2017	7 and up	x	x	x	x	x
Bee-bot app / bee-bot emulator	no code	game-puzzle	moving sprite	2012	7–11					
Alice	blocks	creating	game design	1998	7–13	x	x	x	x	x
RobotMagic (Blockly)	blocks, JavaScript	game-puzzle, creating	moving sprite, simulation, game design	2017	7–16	x	x	x	x	x
Code Monkey	CoffeeScript, Python	game-puzzle	moving sprite	2014	8 and up	x	x	x	x	x
Blockly games (Blockly)	blocks	game-puzzle	moving sprite, drawing, animation, music	2012	8 and up	x	x	x	x	
mBlock (Blockly)	blocks, Python	creating	moving sprite, drawing, game design	2011	8 and up	x	x	x	x	
Pencil Code (Droplet editor)	blocks, coffee-Script, JavaScript	creating	moving sprite, drawing, animation, game design, music	2013	8 and up	x	x	x	x	x
Microsoft MakeCode Arcade	blocks	creating	game development	2020	8 and up	x	x	x	x	x
Open Roberta Lab (robot simulation)	blocks	creating	simulation	2016	8 and up	x	x	x	x	
CodeBug (electronics simulation)	blocks	creating	simulation	2015	8 and up	x	x	x		
LearnToMod (Minecraft)	blocks, JavaScript	creating	game design	2015	8 and up	x	x	x	x	x
Penjee	Python	game-puzzle	moving sprite	2014	8 and up	x	x	x	x	x
RoboMind	RoboMind	game-puzzle	moving sprite	2005	8 and up	x	x	x	x	
Turtle Academy	jslogo	creating	moving sprite, drawing, animation	2011	8 and up	x	x	x	x	
Robo Logic	picture-blocks	game-puzzle	moving sprite	2013	8 and up				x	
StarLogo TNG/Nova	blocks	creating	moving sprite, drawing, animation, game design, simulation	2008	8 and up	x	x	x	x	x
NetsBlox	blocks	creating	moving sprite, drawing, game design, simulation	2016	8 and up	x	x	x	x	x
Logo Interpreter	UCBLogo	creating	moving sprite, drawing, game design	2013	8 and up	x	x	x	x	x
SpriteBox Coding	picture-blocks, Swift	game-puzzle	moving sprite	2018	8–13		x		x	
Code Kingdoms (Minecraft, Roblox)	blocks, Java, Lua	creating	game design	2013	8–14	x	x	x	x	x
Hopscotch	blocks	creating	animation, game design	2012	8–14	x	x	x	x	x
Scratch	blocks	creating	moving sprite, drawing, game design	2007	8–16	x	x	x	x	
Snap!	blocks	creating	moving sprite, drawing, game design	2011	8–16	x	x	x	x	x
SmalRuby	blocks/Ruby	creating	moving sprite,	2014	8–16	x	x	x	x	

			drawing, game design							
Pyonkee	blocks	creating	moving sprite, drawing, game design	2014	8–16	x	x	x	x	
Kodu	picture-blocks	creating	game design	2009	9 and up	x	x	x		x
Lightbot	picture-blocks	game-puzzle	moving sprite	2008	9 and up	x	x		x	
Code Combat	python, JavaScript, CoffeeeScript	game-puzzle, creating	moving sprite	2013	9 and up	x	x	x	x	x
Crunchzilla/Code Monster	JavaScript	creating	animation, game design	2015	9 and up	x	x	x	x	x
NetLogo	NetLogo	creating	moving sprite, drawing, animation, game design, simulation	1999	9 and up	x	x	x	x	x
Khan Academy	JavaScript	creating	animation, game design	2014	9 and up	x	x	x	x	x
RoboZZle	picture-blocks	game-puzzle	moving sprite	2010	9 and up	x	x		x	
MIT App Inventor (Blockly)	blocks	creating	app	2010	10 and up	x	x	x	x	x
Kodular (MIT AppInventor)	blocks	creating	app	2018	10 and up	x	x	x	x	x
Thunkable	blocks	creating	app	2018	10 and up	x	x	x	x	x
Looking Glass	blocks	creating	game design	2012	10 and up	x	x	x	x	x
tickle app learn to code	blocks	creating	moving sprite	2014	10 and up	x	x	x	x	
AgentCubes	blocks	creating	game design	2006	10 and up	x	x	x	x	x
Codesters	Python	creating	moving sprite, drawing, game design	2014	11 and up	x	x	x	x	x
CodeSpells	blocks, JavaScript	creating	game design	2015	12 and up	x	x	x	x	x
Gameblox (Blocky)	blocks	creating	game design	2014	13 and up	x	x	x	x	x
App Lab (Code Studio)	blocks, JavaScript	creating	app	2016	13 and up	x	x	x	x	x
Grasshopper (Google)	JavaScript	game-puzzle, creating	animation	2018	13 and up	x	x	x	x	x
Game Lab (Code Studio)	blocks, JavaScript	creating	app	2016	13 and up	x	x	x	x	x
Karel the Dog (CodeHS)	Karel, Java	game-puzzle	moving sprite, drawing	2012	13–15	x	x	x	x	
Coding with Chrome (Blockly)	Blocks, Python, JavaScript, CoffeeScript	creating	drawing, animation, game design	2015	14 and up	x	x	x	x	x
Greenfoot	Java, Stride	creating	game design	2006	14 and up	x	x	x	x	x
Codea	Lua	creating	game design	2011	14 and up	x	x	x	x	x
CodeHS	Python, Java, JavaScript, C++, C	creating	drawing, animation	2012	16 and up	x	x	x	x	x

Appendix 2

Classification of introductory programming tools for K-12 education.

Name	Viewing	Following	Changing the speed	Executing step-by-step	Rewinding	Age group
Code Combat					x	9 and up
Karel the Dog (CodeHS)					x	13–15
RobotMagic (Blockly)				x		7–16
NetsBlox				x		8 and up
Snap!				x		8–16
Cargo-bot				x		5 and up
Rapid router (Blockly, Code for life)				x		6–13
CodeBug (electronics simulation)				x		8 and up
Penjee				x		8 and up
RoboMind				x		8 and up
RoboZZle				x		9 and up
AgentCubes				x		10 and up
App Lab (Code Studio)				x		13 and up
Game Lab (Code Studio)				x		13 and up
Greenfoot				x		14 and up
Code Studio (courses)			x	x		4 and up
Blockly games (Blockly)			x			8 and up
Lightbot Jr			x			4–8
Code Monkey			x			8 and up
Lightbot			x			9 and up
Swift Playgrounds		–	x			6 and up
Move the Turtle	x		x			5–11
StarLogo TNG/Nova	x		x			8 and up
NetLogo	x		x			9 and up
BotLogic.us		x				4–11
Kodable		x				4–11
Lego Bits and bricks		x				5–11
Junior Coder		x				5–12
ScratchJr		x				5–7
Daisy the dinosaur		x				5–7
the Foos (CodeSpark)		x				5–9
Codable Crafts		x				5–9
Run Marco (All can code, hour of code)		x				6–12
Codemancer		x				6–12
Robo Logic		x				8 and up
SpriteBox Coding		x				8–13
Tynker	x	x				5 and up
Logo Interpreter	x					8 and up
Code avengers	x					5 and up

My robot friend	x					5–12
Cato's Hike	x					5–12
Gamefroot	x					7 and up
Bee-bot app / bee-bot emulator	x					7–11
Alice	x					7–13
mBlock (Blockly)	x					8 and up
Pencil Code (Droplet editor)	x					8 and up
Microsoft MakeCode Arcade	x					8 and up
Open Roberta Lab (robot simulation)	x					8 and up
LearnToMod (Minecraft)	x					8 and up
Turtle Academy	x					8 and up
Code Kingdoms (Minecraft, Roblox)	x					8–14
Hopscotch	x					8–14
Scratch	x					8–16
SmalRuby	x					8–16
Pyonkee	x					8–16
Kodu	x					9 and up
Crunchzilla/Code Monster	x					9 and up
Khan Academy	x					9 and up
MIT App Inventor (Blockly)	x					10 and up
Kodular (MIT AppInventor)	x					10 and up
Thunkable	x					10 and up
Looking Glass	x					10 and up
tickle app learn to code	x					10 and up
Codesters	x					11 and up
CodeSpells	x					12 and up
Gameblox (Blocky)	x					13 and up
Grasshopper (Google)	x					13 and up
Coding with Chrome (Blockly)	x					14 and up
Codea	x					14 and up
CodeHS	x					16 and up

References

Brown, N.C., Altadmri, A.: Investigating novice programming mistakes: educator beliefs vs. student data. In: Proceedings of the Tenth Annual Conference on International Computing Education Research, pp. 43–50, July 2014

Duncan, C., Bell, T., Tanimoto, S.: Should your 8-year-old learn coding? In: Proceedings of the 9th Workshop in Primary and Secondary Computing Education, pp. 60–69, November 2014

Grover, S., Basu, S.: Measuring student learning in introductory block-based programming: examining misconceptions of loops, variables, and boolean logic. In: Proceedings of the 2017 ACM SIGCSE Technical Symposium on Computer Science Education, pp. 267–272, March 2017

Hidalgo-Céspedes, J., Marín-Raventós, G., Lara-Villagrán, V.: Learning principles in program visualizations: a systematic literature review. In: 2016 IEEE Frontiers in Education Conference (FIE), pp. 1–9. IEEE, October 2016

Hundhausen, C.D., Douglas, S.A., Stasko, J.T.: A meta-study of algorithm visualization effectiveness. J. Vis. Lang. Comput. **13**(3), 259–290 (2002)

João, P., Nuno, D., Fábio, S.F., Ana, P.: A cross-analysis of block-based and visual programming apps with computer science student-teachers. Educ. Sci. **9**(3), 181 (2019)

Karavirta, V., Shaffer, C.A.: JSAV: the JavaScript algorithm visualization library. In: Proceedings of the 18th ACM Conference on Innovation and Technology in Computer Science Education, pp. 159–164. July 2013

Kelleher, C., Pausch, R.: Lowering the barriers to programming: a taxonomy of programming environments and languages for novice programmers. ACM Comput. Surv. (CSUR) **37**(2), 83–137 (2005)

Lister, R., et al.: A multi-national study of reading and tracing skills in novice programmers. ACM SIGCSE Bull. **36**(4), 119–150 (2004)

Luxton-Reilly, A., et al.: Introductory programming: a systematic literature review. In: Proceedings Companion of the 23rd Annual ACM Conference on Innovation and Technology in Computer Science Education, pp. 55–106, July 2018

Mladenović, M., Boljat, I., Žanko, Ž.: Comparing loops misconceptions in block-based and text-based programming languages at the K-12 level. Educ. Inf. Technol. **23**(4), 1483–1500 (2017). https://doi.org/10.1007/s10639-017-9673-3

Myller, N., Bednarik, R., Sutinen, E., Ben-Ari, M.: Extending the engagement taxonomy: software visualization and collaborative learning. ACM Trans. Comput. Educ. (TOCE) **9**(1), 1–27 (2009)

Naps, T.L., et al.: Exploring the role of visualization and engagement in computer science education. In: Working Group Reports from ITiCSE on Innovation and Technology in computer Science Education, pp. 131–152 (2002)

Papert, S.: Mindstorms: Computers, children, and Powerful Ideas, p. 255. Basic Books, New York (1980)

Qian, Y., Lehman, J.: Students' misconceptions and other difficulties in introductory programming: a literature review. ACM Trans. Comput. Educ. (TOCE) **18**(1), 1–24 (2017)

Rijke, W.J., Bollen, L., Eysink, T.H., Tolboom, J.L.: Computational thinking in primary school: an examination of abstraction and decom-position in different age groups. Inf. Educ. **17**(1), 77 (2018)

Saito, D., Sasaki, A., Washizaki, H., Fukazawa, Y., Muto, Y.: Program learning for beginners: survey and taxonomy of programming learning tools. In: 2017 IEEE 9th International Conference on Engineering Education (ICEED), pp. 137–142. IEEE, November 2017

Simon. Assignment and sequence: why some students can't recognise a simple swap. In: Proceedings of the 11th Koli Calling International Conference on Computing Education Research (Koli Calling 2011). Association for Computing Machinery, New York, NY, USA, pp. 10–15 (2011). https://doi.org/10.1145/2094131.2094134

Sorva, J., Karavirta, V., Malmi, L.: A review of generic program visualization systems for introductory programming education. ACM Trans. Comput. Educ. (TOCE) **13**(4), 1–64 (2013)

Thomas, L., Ratcliffe, M., Thomasson, B.: Scaffolding with object diagrams in first year programming classes: some unexpected results. ACM SIGCSE Bull. **36**(1), 250–254 (2004)

Urquiza-Fuentes, J., Velázquez-Iturbide, J.Á.: A survey of successful evaluations of program visualization and algorithm animation systems. ACM Trans. Comput. Educ. (TOCE) **9**(2), 1–21 (2009)

Vieira, E.A.O., Da Silveira, A.C., Martins, R.X.: Heuristic evaluation on usability of educational games: a systematic review. Inf. Educ. **18**(2), 427–442 (2019)

Weintrop, D., Wilensky, U.: Transitioning from introductory block-based and text-based environments to professional programming languages in high school computer science classrooms. Comput. Educ. **142**, 103646 (2019)

Xu, Z., Ritzhaupt, A.D., Tian, F., Umapathy, K.: Block-based versus text-based programming environments on novice student learning outcomes: a meta-analysis study. Comput. Sci. Educ. **29**(2–3), 177–204 (2019)

Ready for Computing Science? A Closer Look at Personality, Interests and Self-concept of Girls and Boys at Secondary Level

Andreas Bollin(✉), Max Kesselbacher, and Corinna Mößlacher

Universität Klagenfurt, 9020 Klagenfurt, Austria
{Andreas.Bollin,Max.Kesselbacher,Corinna.Moesslacher}@aau.at
https://www.aau.at/informatikdidaktik

Abstract. Among school children, the interest in dealing with computing science varies between different age groups and countries, but it can be observed that it tends to decline among young women, and it is mostly men who gain a foothold in this domain. Various programs and activities are meant to increase the interest of all our children, but measurement instruments to collect baseline data and interpret effects of (classroom) interventions are rare.

In this work, we present a framework that allows us for collecting measures (personality traits, interests, and self-concept) from different age groups, and we use it to take a closer look at girls and boys at lower secondary school level. We report on measurable similarities as well as differences and, in the context of our own teaching interventions, we come up with first recommendations and suggestions in order to encourage secondary school teachers and curriculum developers to also address the needs and interests of girls and boys.

Keywords: Gender issues · Secondary education · Personality · General interests · Self-concept · Computing science

1 Introduction

One of the greatest challenges facing society today is to instill in children and young people an interest in computing science as a skill of the 21st century. Even though starting ages and also the content differs between individual countries [18], computing science (thereinafter we are also using the term informatics instead) has found its way into the different curricula. Clearly, computing science does not appeal to everyone equally, and so many additional support programs were launched [7,13,15,20,25].

In Austria, among many others, there are now environments like Pocket-Code [21] in place, free MOOCs teaching computing science and digital literacy [11], but also implementations of CoderDojo or CodeClub [2], and in the field

K. Kori and M. Laanpere (Eds.): ISSEP 2020, LNCS 12518, pp. 107–118, 2020.
https://doi.org/10.1007/978-3-030-63212-0_9

of computational thinking and computing science the Bebras (Beaver) competition [9] attracts more and more young pupils. In Klagenfurt, we are running the "Informatikwerkstatt" (German for "Informatics-Lab" [22]) and, working together with teachers from primary and secondary education, it has attracted more than 13.500 visitors at the Institute for Informatics-Didactics since 2015.

But, a look in the direction of industry or tertiary education makes one rethink. There, you clearly see that, comparable to the situation at the end of the 1990s [12], on the one hand not enough young people have become enthusiastic about a computer science career, and on the other hand, the proportion of young women is still significantly lower compared to young men – a situation that became known as the gender-gap.

The objective of this paper is now to report on a baseline of traits that can inform and steer future research in computing science education at the lower secondary level. Related work (see Sect. 2) shows that interests and personality do influence the attitude towards computing science, and so we are interested in learning more about the pupils attending our Informatics-Lab and how to cope with gender issues. The analysis for more than 650 pupils attending our workshops was supported by a data collection framework (called KAUA, see Sect. 3), and the first findings are presented in this work.

The rest of this paper is structured as follows. Section 2 briefly summarizes literature related to personality, interests and self-concept. Section 3 introduces our data collection framework, Sect. 4 reports on the collected data for pupils aged 10 to 14 years, Sect. 5 reflects on the data found and derives initial recommendations. Finally, Sect. 6 concludes with the most important findings and future work.

2 Related Work

As mentioned above, it is well known that women are under-represented in many fields of STEM, but the percentage of women differs in the fields, e.g. women are not under-represented in biological sciences as they are in computer science. A cross-study paper of Cheryan et al. [8] found different potential factors that may result in these differences. They mention, inter alia, stereotypes of STEM fields, lack of role models, insufficient early experience in the field, as well as math ability, math performance and self-efficiency. Their paper also shows that most studies only evaluate one STEM field but lack a cross-study comparison which could give more insight on the influencing factors.

Stout et al. [24] show that female university students can be influenced by role models (like female professors). It increases their self-concept, attitudes and future career ideas.

A study on freshman undergraduate students chose personality, motivation, self-regulation, self-concept, self-estimates of ability as factors to survey on. It showed that men and women show different profiles on these criteria: A decisive factor for women leaving STEM majors are lower scores in Math and Science self-concept. So it can be a factor to predict STEM persistence [1].

Gender differences have been well reported [4,10,19], with respect to the RIASEC (Realistic - Investigative - Artistic - Social - Enterprising - Conventional) interests: Women show higher mean scores in the dimensions Artistic and Social. Men show higher mean scores in the Realistic dimension (independently from their background).

A study [10] on school students (n = 247, age cohort 12–19 years) shows also that students with high scores in self-concepts (verbal and mathematics) as well as students with higher interest in the subject Math show higher interests in all dimensions of the RIASEC model.

A study [4] in middle school students (n = 627, age 13) shows that boys have more interest in STEM occupation and activities (this is also confirmed by the participants in our Informatics-Lab) – with the highest difference to girls in technology and engineering. All correlations between RIASEC interests and STEM interest were observed as being positive but highest in Investigative, showing similarities between boys and girls. It can also be seen that the students differ in their interests in science technology, engineering, and mathematics. They do not see these fields uniformly.

A study [23] on high school students (n = 3023), tracked 10 years after graduating school, observed RIASEC interests and personality traits. It shows that the interests can predict many life outcome factors of work, health, and relationship. It does not show a significant difference by gender on influence of these measures in the life outcomes concerning work and health. It shows that specific interests at school can predict later working life and success, which makes them particularly interesting for further research and justifies the research in terms of a possible influence on students' interests.

The characteristics that benefit life outcomes are similar for female and male students. But, the characteristics differ between the gender cohorts. This makes a more detailed observation of these characteristics (and the evaluation of possible interventions to influence these factor) important for progress in educational processes.

3 Data Collection Framework

In 2016, we intensified our efforts to improve our teaching in Klagenfurt but also at our partner University in Košice. We also looked for ways to measure the sustainability of our classroom interventions. As our school systems differ, but as we also wanted to learn more about the characteristics of our pupils and (future) students, we implemented a framework called KAUA, which is an online survey system that supports anonymous, longitudinal studies.

From the very beginning, KAUA was designed with the General Data Protection Regulation of the European Union[1] in mind, guaranteeing that personal data is not stored while still being able to allow for tracing changes in participants' characteristics. To enable this, a KAUA survey works as follows:

[1] http://data.europa.eu/eli/reg/2016/679/2016-05-04.

1. In a first step participants supply personal information (name, birthday) and answer a security question (where the answer is likely stable over lifetime) from a list compiled by us. This personal information is then used as input to compute a SHA-512 hash that identifies the participant. With this setup, participants are anonymous, but will generate the same hash in longitudinal study designs.
2. In the second step, participants are authorized with their hash and complete the survey. The survey results are only linked to the anonymous hash.

KAUA was already used in a small-scale study to investigate the personality, self-concept, and general interests of pupils participating in informatics competitions (Bebras, Coding Contests) in Austria [3]. Since then, the survey has been expanded, additionally eliciting specific interest in computing science and study interests, and it has been adapted to be also usable by children. In its current version, it takes about 20 min to register and fill out a KAUA survey.

Table 1 provides an overview of the dimensions, the individual traits and corresponding scales collected by KAUA. The items for *I1) General Interests* follow the six dimensions of interests (RIASEC) established by Holland [14] and formulated by Bergmann and Eder [6]. The items for *I2) Personality* cover two dimensions (Dominant/Easygoing, Formal/Informal) of the Five-Factor and Stress Theory [17,27]. The items for *I3) Self-Concept* are formulations used in the PISA surveys [16] that elicit the verbal and mathematical self-concept with three items each. The item for *I4) CS Interest* is formulated by us and elicits interest in computing science specifically. The items for *I5) Study Interests* are formulated by us and are presented as check boxes of fields of study the participants might be interested in (now or in the future).

4 Traits of Lower Secondary Pupils

4.1 Methodology

In this publication, we describe differences in traits of lower secondary school pupils, aged 10 to 14, with regard to their personality, self-concept and interests. Our goal is to report on a baseline of traits, which can inform and steer future research - for example the design of classroom interventions to mitigate gender gaps. In a two-year span, we used the data collection framework KAUA to collect 676 survey responses (303 girls and 373 boys) from pupils attending computer science workshops at our Informatics-Lab. The pupils were from regional schools without any focus on computer science - their class teachers voluntarily decided to attend our workshops with their classes. The survey was conducted before each workshop. To better gauge differences in traits, we divide the cohorts by gender (female and male) and by age (5 groups from 10 to 14 years). For the mentioned traits, we investigate intra-gender progression (how the traits change with the pupils' age) and inter-gender differences (conditional to the pupils' age). The sizes of the different cohorts and age groups $\{10y/o, 11y/o, 12y/o, 13y/o, 14y/o\}$ are distributed as follows: $n_{Female} = \{15, 75, 106, 69, 38\}$, $n_{Male} = \{11, 53, 110, 130, 69\}$.

Table 1. Dimensions and items collected by the KAUA framework.

Dimension	Items	Scale
I1) General Interests [6,14]	Realistic, Investigative, Artistic, Social, Enterprising, Conventional	9-level Likert [−4; 4]
I2) Personality [17,27]	Dominant/Easygoing, Formal/Informal	13-level Likert [−6; 6]
I3) Self-Concept [16]	3x Verbal Self-Concept, 3x Mathematical Self-Concept	4-level [1; 4]
I4) CS Interest	Computing Science Interest	6-level [1; 6]
I5) Special Interests	History, Art, Music, Literature, Language, Economy, Law, Social fields, Health, Natural sciences, Informatics, Math, Engineering, None	Yes/no [0; 1]

4.2 General Interests

In the study of Bollin et al. [3] it turned out that pupils interested in computing science seem to be more interested in the investigative and artistic area, and, with the exception of the social dimension, they are more interested in all the other fields of interest. Figure 1 depicts the responses of interests of our cohorts and dimensions and shows relevant differences. Interests change and slightly decrease over time, but two features stand out. First, according to the realistic (a, b) and artistic (e, f) interests there is a notable difference between boys and girls. Secondly, while the interest in the social domain decreases for boys (h), it stays, with some exceptions, stable at a quite high level for girls (g).

4.3 Personality

Personality plays an important role when working together in teams [17], and pupils interested in Computing Science tend to be (significant) more easy-going compared to control-groups and not so formal as expected [3]. Figures 2(a) and (c) depict the differences between the two cohorts and show that girls are "moving" from dominant to easy-going, whereas boys are "moving" the other way round. Concerning formal/informal, both cohorts tend to be slightly more formal than informal. But, it is interesting to see that the age of 12 years seems to be a point where the personality tilts over for both, boys and girls.

4.4 Self-concept

The mathematical and verbal self-concept plays an important role when deciding for (or staying in) a STEM field. Figure 3 shows the answers to the questions "How well do you rate yourself in German?" and "How well do you rate yourself in mathematics?". There are no statistically significant differences between girls and boys; girls start at a slightly worse level (in our grading system 1 is the best grade) but are then overtaking the boys. In all the cases, the mathematical self-concept is better than the verbal self-concept, but both, verbal and mathematical self-concept are getting worse by nearly one grade over the time.

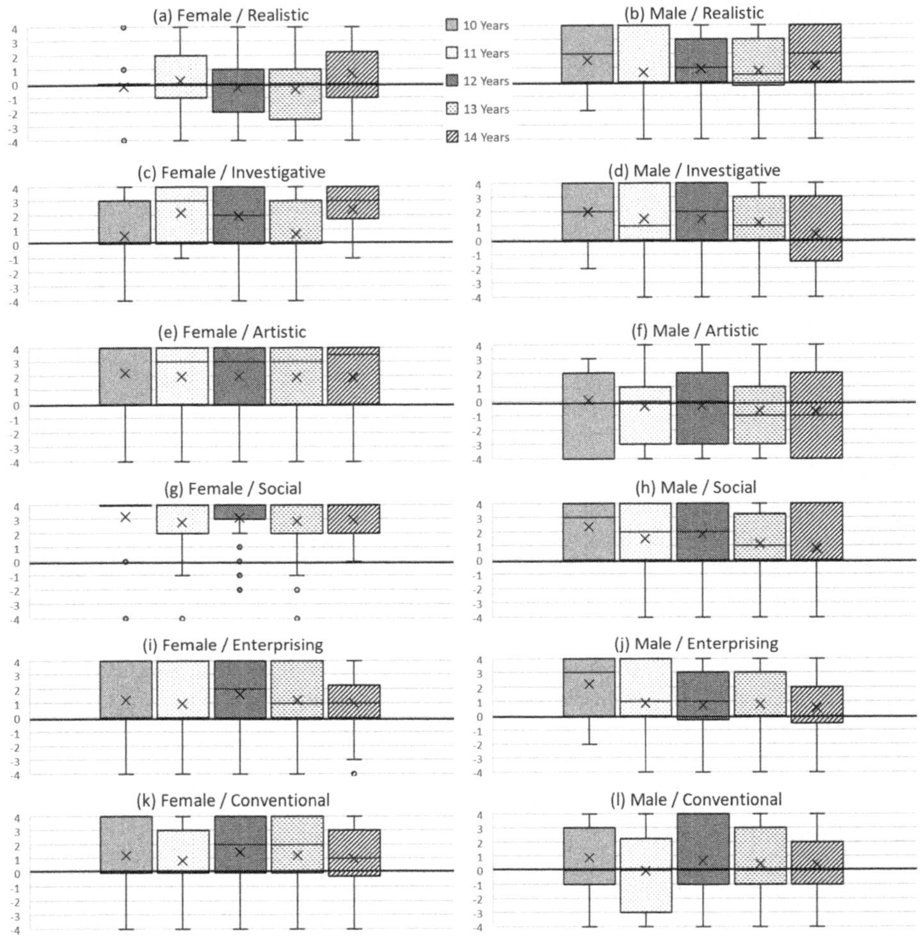

Fig. 1. Interests for female and male pupils. Values range [−4 .. not at all interested up to 4 .. very interested].

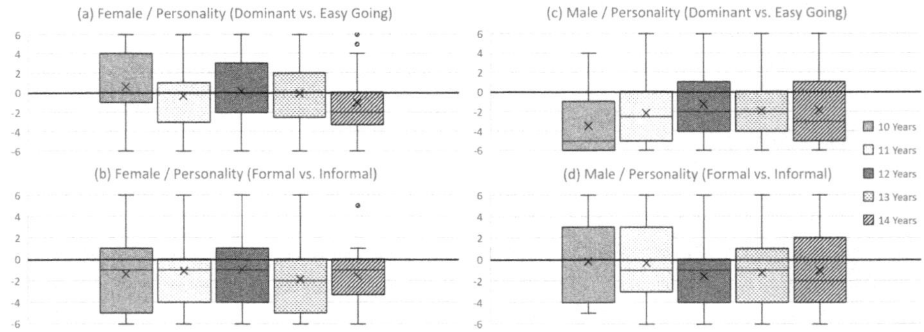

Fig. 2. Personality traits for male/female pupils. Scales in (a) and (c) are Dominant [−6] up to Easy-Going [6], (b) and (d) are Formal [−6] up to Informal [6].

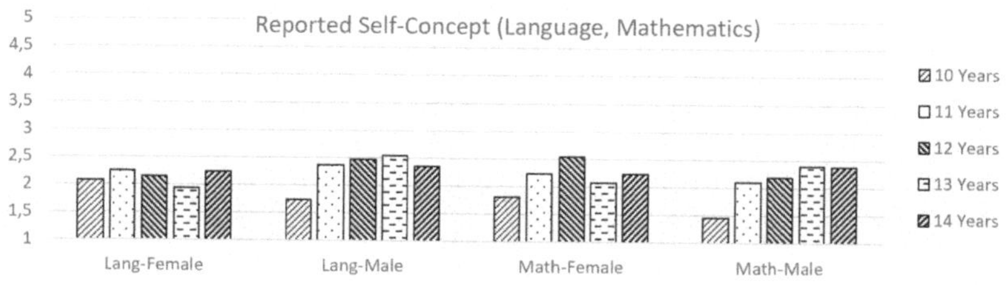

Fig. 3. Mean of reported grades (1 .. very good up to 5 .. insufficient) in language skills and mathematics for female and male pupils. Numbers and standard deviation are $(n_{Female}, \sigma_{lang}, \sigma_{math}) = \{$(10y/o, 1.03, 0.94), (11y/o, 0.93, 0.93), (12y/o, 0.81, 0.89), (13y/o, 0.83, 1.00), (14y/o, 0.71, 0.81)$\}$, and $(n_{Male}, \sigma_{lang}, \sigma_{math}) = \{$(10y/o, 0.64, 0.68), (11y/o, 0.92, 1.09), (12y/o, 0.93, 1.05), (13y/o, 0.90, 1.03), (14y/o, 0.87, 1.05)$\}$)

4.5 Interest in Computing Science and Special Interests

Figure 4 summarizes the differences in the interest in computing science between the two cohort of girls and boys. Whereas the interest of boys is quite stable across the different age groups, it declines a bit for girls. With the exception of age 10, the interest of boys is always higher than that of girls.

In addition to the RIASEC dimensions and the question about the interest in computing science, we also asked for additional fields of interests. Figure 5 shows the percentages of boys and girls who voted for one or more items. On the first sight, girls seem to be interested a bit more in art, music, literature, language, social sciences, health and nature, and boys are more interested in informatics, mathematics and the engineering domain. However, it is noticeable that for girls, with the exception of art and language, the interest is growing by time, whereas with the exception of history, economy and informatics the interest decreases for boys in general. It also shows that, when not asking for computing science (Informatics) directly, interest of girls is still there, but just at a lower percentage as for boys.

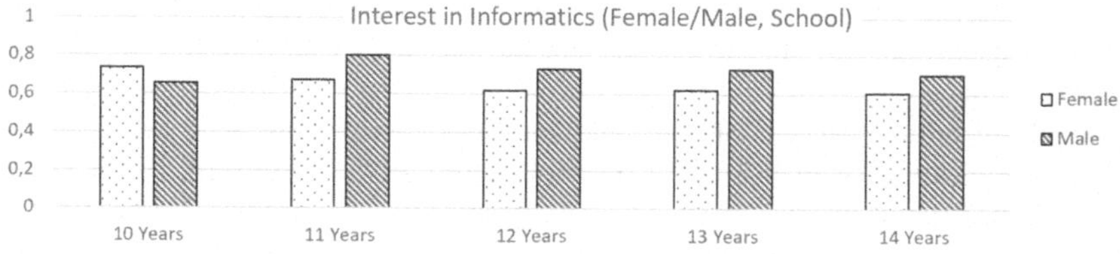

Fig. 4. Reported interest in computing science. Scale between [0 .. not interested to 1 .. very interested]. Numbers and standard deviation are: $(n_{Female}, \sigma) = \{$(10y/o, 0.26), (11y/o, 0.23), (12y/o, 0.28), (13y/o, 0.26), (14/yo, 0.27)$\}$ and $(n_{Male}, \sigma) = \{$(10y/o, 0.36), (11y/o, 0.22), (11y/o, 0.26), (13y/o, 0.25), (14y/o, 0.30)$\}$

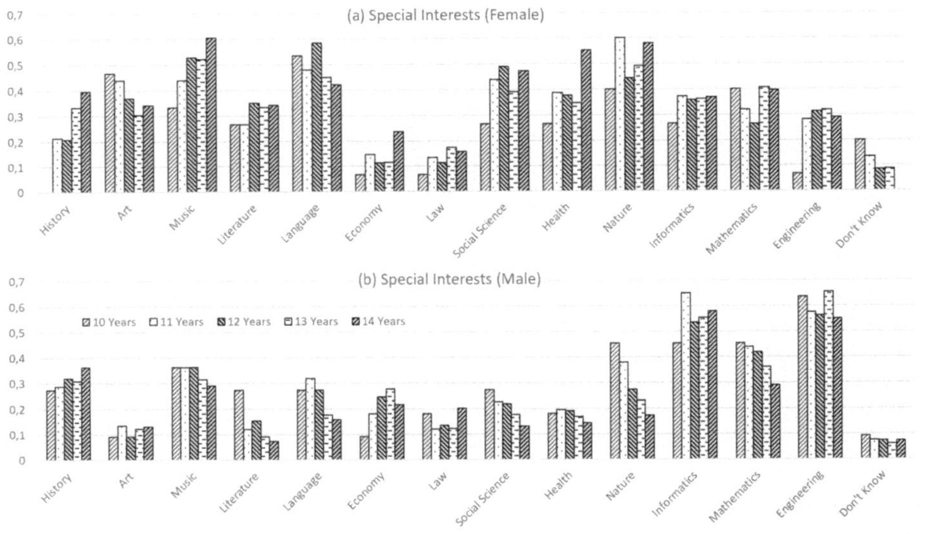

Fig. 5. Percentage of items reported for special interests for (a) female and (b) male pupils. $n_{Female} = \{15, 75, 106, 69, 38\}$, n_{Male} n = $\{11, 53, 110, 130, 69\}$)

5 Discussion

When pondering over the results of this study, one has to be careful as there are quite some threats to validity. Among them is the currently small size of the cohort of the 10-year-old pupils (26 in total). As at the current stage we are using descriptive analysis only, we decided to include them in the description to cover the full secondary I level. The good news is that, apart from the realistic and social RIASEC score and the interest in history, the results do not contradict findings in literature, e.g. higher results for Artistic and Social dimensions for girls [4].

Another issue is that the results form some kind of baseline for pupils in our region. It therefore cannot (and will not) be easily generalizable for other locations. On the other hand, the results are along with results of existing studies (which is valuable) and this also confirms the applicability of the KAUA survey to some extent.

One should also note that the "development over time" of interests, self-concept or personality is not the "development" of a single child - it is really just a baseline that is meant to be the starting point. Investigative, Artistic, Enterprising and Conventional are reported to be more stable over time [26]. As we are continuing to collect this data, by time we will be able to trace these measures back to an individual Level and can compare them to results in literature.

Additionally, there might have been problems with the honesty in filling out the questionnaire, but we had trained student assistants and the classroom teachers taking care of filling out the online survey and also explaining the importance of it. There might also be a bias in the interests and attitudes that we were not able to control as the teachers decided to make use of the offer of our Informatics-Lab by their own.

Apart from the above-mentioned threats, the results do have implications on the program that we offer at our Informatics-Lab. The overall assumption is that, according to the findings in literature and in order to achieve a lasting interest in computing science, self-concept, interests and personality should be considered when teaching. The most important recommendations, stemming from our observations above, are summarized hereinafter.

One insight is related to the fact that general interests (Fig. 1) are in a state of constant flow and can be influenced. Attractive materials and classroom interventions (appropriate to the current living environment) should stimulate realistic interests for girls and artistic interests for boys, and the investigative domain should always be included. This should reduce the gap reported in interests [4,10,19] as well as support interest that are important for the study interests.

Concerning personality development (Fig. 2), it is noticeable that especially girls tend to get less easy-going the older they are. Taking care of it and also reflecting on it when enacting teamwork in the classroom might be helpful. Apart of this, there are training tools like PlayBenno[2] that help developing personality.

Now let's not dwell on the regularly poor results of the Austrian school leaving exams in mathematics and German, but it is astonishing that the verbal and mathematical self-concept (Fig. 3) are at a really low level. We thus already started to include (and updated) interdisciplinary materials in our Informatics-Lab to train these skills but also to strengthen the pupils' self-confidence in these fields. Working together with teachers from other subjects also seems to be very beneficial here. These can be a factor to predict STEM persistence [1], especially for girls.

Concerning the interest in computing science in general (Fig. 4) and special interests (Fig. 5) it means that our teaching needs to be highly attractive to the learning brain [5]. Arousing a wide interest is one thing and can be done by working together in an interdisciplinary manner, but when e.g. the interest in music or languages is rising (as with girls), it is advisable to also touch these topics in ones' own classes. We already included such materials in our lab and a teacher education student is currently working on the relation between crocheting and computing science.

6 Conclusion

In order to make a maximum out of classroom interventions, every teacher should respond appropriately to the needs of her or his pupils. When trying to motivate for computing science, personality, interests, the verbal and mathematical self-concept and the gender gap do play an important role, but all too often these aspects are not looked at closer.

[2] https://inventures.eu/game-with-a-mission-wins-innovation-award/4539/.

In this paper we thus introduce a framework called KAUA that allows for collecting such measures from different age groups with just a small time-overhead (about 20 min) in the classroom setting. We then take a closer look at 676 girls and boys at the lower secondary school level and report on measurable similarities as well as differences.

In the context of our own teaching interventions, we then try to come up with recommendations and suggestions. Even though the results might not be generalizable to other locations, the work demonstrates that with not much effort, (secondary school) teachers are able to learn more about their pupils and might thus be able to support the interests of girls and boys in computing science appropriately.

The work presented here is ongoing work and in the winter term 2020 we will be able to roll out the survey more widely, reaching about several thousand pupils in Austria. For the next couple of years, we also plan to collect more data from University students (of different fields), and as we changed the rhythm of collecting the feedback from returning visitors we will soon be able to analyze changes in the scores on an individual level.

References

1. Ackerman, P., Kanfer, R., Beier, M.: Trait complex, cognitive ability, and domain knowledge predictors of baccalaureate success, stem persistence, and gender differences. J. Educ. Psychol. **105**, 911 (2013)
2. Aivaloglou, E., Hermans, F.: How is programming taught in code clubs? Exploring the experiences and gender perceptions of code club teachers. In: Proceedings of the 19th Koli Calling International Conference on Computing Education Research. Koli Calling 2019, Association for Computing Machinery, New York (2019). https://doi.org/10.1145/3364510.3364514
3. Bollin, A., Demarle-Meusel, H., Kesselbacher, M., Mößlacher, C., Rohrer, M., Sylle, J.: The Bebras contest in Austria – do personality, self-concept and general interests play an influential role? In: Pozdniakov, S.N., Dagienė, V. (eds.) ISSEP 2018. LNCS, vol. 11169, pp. 283–294. Springer, Cham (2018). https://doi.org/10.1007/978-3-030-02750-6_22
4. Babarović, T., Devic, I., Burusic, J.: Fitting the STEM interests of middle school children into RIASEC structural space. Int. J. Educ. Vocat. Guidance (2018). https://doi.org/10.1007/s10775-018-9371-8
5. Sabitzer, B., Stefan Pasterk, S.E.: Brain-based teaching in computer science - neurodidactical proposals for effective teaching. In: Proceedings of the 13th KOLI Calling Conference. ACM (2013)
6. Bergmann, C., Eder, F.: AIST-R. Allgemeiner Interessen-Struktur-Test mit Umwelt-Struktur-Test (UST-R) - Revision. Manual. Hogrefe, 1 edn. (2005)
7. Blum, L.: Women in computer science: the Carnegie Mellon experience (2001). http://www.cs.cmu.edu/lblum/papers/merged%20gh%20proposal2000.pdf
8. Cheryan, S., Ziegler, S., Montoya, A., Jiang, L.: Why are some stem fields more gender balanced than others? Psychol. Bull. **143** (2016). https://doi.org/10.1037/bul0000052

9. Dagienė, V., Futschek, G.: Bebras international contest on informatics and computer literacy: criteria for good tasks. In: Mittermeir, R.T., Sysło, M.M. (eds.) ISSEP 2008. LNCS, vol. 5090, pp. 19–30. Springer, Heidelberg (2008). https://doi.org/10.1007/978-3-540-69924-8_2
10. Dierks, P.O., Höffler, T.N., Blankenburg, J.S., Peters, H., Parchmann, I.: Interest in science: a RIASEC-based analysis of students' interests. Int. J. Sci. Educ. **38**(2), 238–258 (2016). https://doi.org/10.1080/09500693.2016.1138337
11. Ebner, M., Adams, S., Bollin, A., Kopp, M., Teufel, M.: Digital gestütztes Lehren mittels innovativem MOOC-Konzept (in German). journal für lehrerInnenbildung 20(1), 68–77 (2020). https://doi.org/10.35468/jlb-01-2020_05
12. Frenkel, K.A.: Women and computing. Commun. ACM **33**(11), 34–46 (1990). https://doi.org/10.1145/92755.92756
13. Grandl, M., Ebner, M.: Informatische Grundbildung - ein Ländervergleich. Medienimpulse **55**(2), 1–17 (2017). https://medienimpulse.at/article/view/mi1069
14. Holland, J.: Exploring careers with a typology - what we have learned and some new directions. Am. Psychol. **51**(4), 397–406 (1996)
15. Kelleher, C., Pausch, R., Kiesler, S.: Storytelling Alice motivates middle school girls to learn computer programming. In: Proceedings of the SIGCHI Conference on Human Factors in Computing Systems, CHI 2007, pp. 1455–1464. Association for Computing Machinery, New York (2007). https://doi.org/10.1145/1240624.1240844
16. Kunter, M., et al.: PISA 2000: Dokumentation der Erhebungsinstrumente. Materialien aus der Bildungsforschung, **72** (2002)
17. Mujkanovic, A., Bollin, A.: Improving learning outcomes through systematic group reformation - the role of skills and personality in software engineering education. In: 2016 IEEE First International Conference on Connected Health: Applications, Systems and Engineering Technologies (CHASE), pp. 97–103 (2016)
18. Pasterk, S., Bollin, A.: Digital literacy or computer science: where do information technology related primary education models focus on? In: 15th International Conference on Emerging eLearning Technologies and Applications (ICETA), Stary Smokovec, Slovakia (2017). IEEE. https://doi.org/10.1109/ICETA.2017.8102517
19. Proyer, R., Häusler, J.: Gender differences in vocational interests and their stability across different assessment methods. Swiss J. Psychol. **66** (2007). https://doi.org/10.1024/1421-0185.66.4.243
20. Resnick, M., et al.: Scratch: programming for all. Commun. ACM **52**(11), 60–67 (2009). https://doi.org/10.1145/1592761.1592779
21. Slany, W.: Pocket code: a scratch-like integrated development environment for your phone. In: Proceedings of the Companion Publication of the 2014 ACM SIGPLAN Conference on Systems, Programming, and Applications: Software for Humanity, SPLASH 2014, pp. 35–36. Association for Computing Machinery, New York (2014). https://doi.org/10.1145/2660252.2664662
22. Pasterk, S., Barbara Sabitzer, H.D.M.A.B.: Informatics-lab: attracting primary school pupils for computer science. In: Proceedings of the 14th LACCEI International Multi-Conference for Engineering, Education, and Technology, San José, Costa Rica, July 2016
23. Stoll, G., Rieger, S., Lüdtke, O., Nagengast, B., Trautwein, U., Roberts, B.: Vocational interests assessed at the end of high school predict life outcomes assessed 10 years later over and above IQ and big five personality traits. J. Pers. Soc. Psychol. **113** (2017). https://doi.org/10.1037/pspp0000117

24. Stout, J., Dasgupta, N., Hunsinger, M., McManus, M.: Steming the tide: using ingroup experts to inoculate women's self-concept in science, technology, engineering, and mathematics (STEM). J. Pers. Soc. Psychol. **100**, 255–270 (2011). https://doi.org/10.1037/a0021385
25. Wright, R.N., Nadler, S.J., Nguyen, T.D., Sanchez Gomez, C.N., Wright, H.M.: Living-learning community for women in computer science at Rutgers. In: Proceedings of the 50th ACM Technical Symposium on Computer Science Education, SIGCSE 2019, pp. 286–292. Association for Computing Machinery, New York (2019). https://doi.org/10.1145/3287324.3287449
26. Xu, H., Tracey, T.: Stability and change in interests: a longitudinal examination of grades 7 through college. J. Vocat. Behav. **93** (2016). https://doi.org/10.1016/j.jvb.2016.02.002
27. Yamada, Y., et al.: The impacts of personal characteristic on educational effectiveness in controlled-project based learning on software intensive systems development. In: 2014 IEEE 27th Conference on Software Engineering Education and Training (CSEE & T), pp. 119–128. IEEE, April 2014

Factors Influencing Lower Secondary School Pupils' Success in Programming Projects in Scratch

Miroslava Černochová[1](✉), Hasan Selcuk[2], and Ondřej Černý[3]

[1] Faculty of Education, Charles University, Magdalény Rettigové 4, Praha 1, Czech Republic
miroslava.cernochova@pedf.cuni.cz
[2] Faculty of Education, Psychology and Art, University of Latvia, Imantas 7. līnija–1, Riga, Latvia
[3] Gymnázium a SOŠ dr. V. Šmejkala, Ústí nad Labem, p. o., Stavbařů 5, Ústí nad Labem, Czech Republic

Abstract. In the Czech Republic, a radical change in the school curriculum is planned. Through a new, compulsory subject of "Informatics and ICT", the aim is to develop digital literacy across all school subjects, and computational thinking. Computational thinking will be implemented in the curriculum of pre-primary, primary, lower and upper secondary schools, and in teacher education at all faculties of education in the Czech Republic. To ensure readiness for the implementation of the new subject, it has been necessary to prepare and develop a set of learning materials for pupils and teaching guidelines for teachers. These textbooks focus on robotics, programming (Scratch, Python), and theoretical concepts from Informatics. This paper describes a qualitative study aimed at identifying key factors influencing lower secondary pupils' success in completing some activities related to programming in Scratch. Data were gathered from the feedback of five teachers and 121 pupils at five lower secondary schools, and from the researchers' observation reports from school visits. The key findings of the study showed that pupils' success programming in Scratch depends on their motivation to the theme of the Scratch activity, a positive climate in the learning environment, peer collaboration, and freedom in ways to learn new concepts and to find solutions to given problems. Programming in Scratch is promising in developing pupils' creativity and decision-making in problem-solving. Additionally, a stress-free, non-threatening, learning environment, where the teacher appreciates the enthusiasm, thinking process and effort of pupils to find an original solution has a positive influence on their success.

Keywords: Scratch · Lower secondary school · Programming · Peer collaboration · Motivation

1 Introduction

In accordance with the Government's Digital Education Strategy [13], the Ministry of Education, Youth and Sport of the Czech Republic is currently working on revisions

K. Kori and M. Laanpere (Eds.): ISSEP 2020, LNCS 12518, pp. 119–129, 2020.
https://doi.org/10.1007/978-3-030-63212-0_10

to its curricular document, the Framework Educational Programme, with two major changes: (1) improving pupils' digital literacy development at all educational stages, and (2) the implementation of a new compulsory subject of Informatics, instead of ICT. Informatics will centre on the development of computational thinking. Both changes are relatively radical and should be put into actual practice in pre-school, primary and secondary schools by 2021/22.

To achieve this goal, two three-year projects involving all faculties of education in the Czech Republic have been established: the project, "PRIM" (Support for computational thinking development [15]), and the project, "DG" (Support for the development of digital literacy [8]). Since October 2017, 14 textbooks and teaching guidelines for teaching Informatics as a new subject in primary and secondary schools and for the development of computational thinking in pre-school children have been produced from [15]. In the years 2018 to 2020, all these textbooks were verified at several kindergartens, primary and secondary schools and, based on the evaluation of experience with their use in teaching, modified into the final form. The final textbooks have been published since July 2020 on the website at imysleni.cz.

The didactic approach to all these 14 textbooks is based on Papert's constructionist idea, *learning-by-making*. Pupils can learn by experimenting and inquiring activities during solving interesting problems or their own ideas. Each textbook basically consists of two parts: one part (*learning material*) intended for pupils and the second part (*teaching guidelines*) dedicated to teachers.

Three textbooks are focused on computational thinking development at primary education (ISCED 1) and lower secondary school education (ISCED 2) using Scratch. Specifically, there is a textbook written by Kalas & Mikova [10] for school education level ISCED 1 and other textbooks written by Vanicek et al. [19] and by Cernochova et al. [6] for school education level ISCED 2.

This study presents some results from verification of the textbook by Cernochova et al. [7] at five Czech schools in 2019/20 with 121 pupils. This textbook brings ideas for eleven projects in Scratch; some projects are relatively simple and can be used as an exercise for the solving of more complex projects (games, animations, and stories), which are already more time-consuming, difficult and programming-intensive. This article is dedicated to two Scratch projects, 'Clock' and 'Interactive postcard'. The study is intended to reveal factors which determine pupils' success in completing the projects if they follow assignments formulated openly and based on questions for thinking, without any other strict guidelines.

2 Literature Review

Programming, which is one of the topics in the subject of informatics, has become a focus of attention for researchers to reveal new evidence about how to capture pupils' attention and catch their interest in undertaking programming tasks in a more effective and engaging way. As highlighted by Romero et al. [16, p. 2] "Programming is not only about writing code but also about the capacity to analyse a situation, identify its key components, model the data and processes, and create or refine a program through an agile design-thinking approach". Programming is generally not easy. "Beginners need to learn to identify the structure of a problem and the logic of a program to solve it - but they are simultaneously forced to deal with technical details of the programming environment that are not related to these core tasks" [17, p.764].

There are a lot of platforms to engage children in learning to program through the creation of computational artefacts, such as Logo, Karel, Blockly, Alice, Kodu etc. For many reasons, the most popular among them is currently a visual programming environment, Scratch. "Kids without much experience with computers and with no prior programming knowledge can quickly create interactive games or tell stories with Scratch" [17, p. 765].

Previous studies focusing on programming Scratch activities among secondary school pupils investigated the perceived cognitive load and its effects on the academic performance in Scratch-based programming activities (e.g., [5]), the use of Scratch environment for teaching computer science concepts (e.g., [1]), factors affecting Scratch-based coding on pupils' interest development in coding and in mathematics [9], the impact of introducing programming with Scratch at different stages at an early age in different school subjects [14], and the link between creative programming with Scratch and learner´s cognitive and metacognitive strategies [16].

As highlighted by Maloney et al. [11, p. 16.2] "Scratch added programmability to media-manipulation activities that are popular in youth culture, and it encouraged young people to learn through exploration and peer sharing, with less focus on direct instruction than other programming languages."

Baytak and Land [2, p. 765] discovered that 5th grade pupils were able to "design functional games in Scratch, following a learning-by-design process of planning, designing, testing, and sharing". In their exploratory case study with the 5th grade girls using Scratch, Baytak & Land also [3, p. 243] found "the potential role of game design as a vehicle to involve more girls in computer science". In the research based upon a novel combination of a revised Bloom's taxonomy and the SOLO taxonomy, Meerbaum-Salant et al. [12, p. 69] "showed that, in general, pupils could successfully learn important concepts of computer science, using new learning materials designed according to the constructionist philosophy of Scratch, although there were some problems with initialisation, variables and concurrency; these problems can be overcome by modifications to the teaching process".

Brennan conducted interviews with 30 pupils and 30 teachers working with Scratch in K-12 classroom and found that pupils working with Scratch value the freedom and open-endedness of Scratch the most because "it's more like real life". [4, p. 80]

3 The Study

3.1 Research Design

In our research, a qualitative methodology was used to collect and to analyse the data gathered from multiple sources, including online open-ended questionnaires for teachers and their pupils at five lower secondary schools, and from the researchers' observation reports from school visits.

Since the study intended to reveal the factors influencing lower secondary school pupils' success in completing Scratch-based programming tasks, two Scratch projects, which are 'Clock' and 'Interactive postcard', were undertaken by the N = 121 pupils with the guidance of five teachers during the school year of 2019–2020. Three lessons were allocated for each of these programming Scratch projects.

3.2 The Sample of Participants

The researchers collaborated with five teachers from five state schools in different regions of the Czech Republic (Table 1). These schools had the approval of the Ministry of Education, Youth and Sports to verify new learning and teaching materials. In this study, three criteria were determined to select the participants: (1) the school principal had to agree to implement these materials into teaching of Informatics in their school, (2) schools should provide education level 2 according to ISCED classification, and (3) the pupils should be previously introduced to basic features of Scratch.

Table 1. Characteristics of participants.

School	Population[a]	Geographic location	Type of school	Number of participants (pupils)	Pupils' age	Gender of Informatics teacher
School 1	93,000	Bohemia	Gymnasium	16	12–14	Male
School 2	1,200	Moravia	Basic school	60	13–14	Female
School 3	9,000	Bohemia	Gymnasium	16	13–14	Female
School 4	22,000	Moravia	Basic school	14	12–14	Female
School 5	1,300,000	Bohemia	Gymnasium	15	13–15	Female
			Total	121		

[a]Number of inhabitants in the town where the school is located.

3.3 Programming Scratch Projects

Two projects, 'Clock' and 'Interactive postcard', were chosen from 11 projects included in the textbook by [7]. One project, 'Clock', represents a project in which it is necessary to program a functional model that requires to formulate mathematical calculations to describe the motion of clock hands. The second one, 'Interactive postcard', requires not only pupils' creativity and stimulating ideas, but also understanding the use of blocks for clones.

Project 1 – 'Clock'

In the 'Clock' project, pupils are asked to design and create a functional model of a traditional clock with a second, a minute and an hour hand. The project can be divided into three phases, in which pupils solve partial problems related to the project. In the first phase, pupils design the graphical circle form of a clock and then they place in it the numbers from 1 to 12. Pupils are allowed either to program it or use a ready-made picture of a clock or draw it.

In the second phase, pupils place the long (minute), short (hour) and second hand of the clock and then set these three hands into circular motion. In the third phase, pupils adjust the clock to show the correct time. The specificity of the project is that it requires the application of some mathematical procedures to describe a circular motion of the hands and to adjust the clock.

When solving a task in the project, pupils follow self-directed, learning material, which contains some guidelines, instructions and questions prepared for pupils to undertake the project by themselves or with limited teacher guidance. The learning material does not contain any precise procedures or specific guidance about what to do and how to design the clock. In the material, pupils find only a few questions and recommendations on how to think about the process and find a solution to the task (Fig. 1).

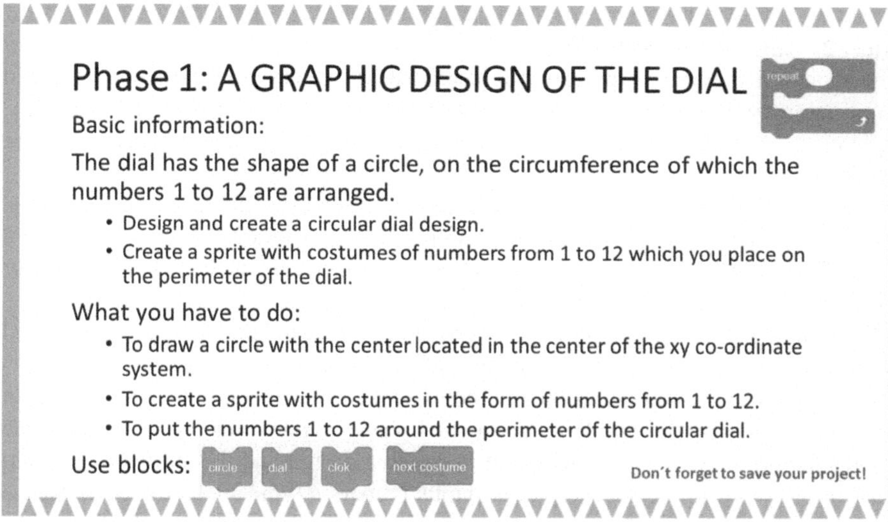

Fig. 1. Guidelines for pupils in the learning material for the Clock project

However, pupils do not have to program or to draw a shape of the dial in Scratch with its centre located in [0, 0] of the xy co-ordinate system, but they can use a picture of a circular dial downloaded from the Internet, or a scanned drawing of the dial, etc. Pupils use their creativity and imagination to create the graphic form of the dial.

Placing the clock hands in a circular motion and setting the correct time on the clock already requires knowledge of how to design a functional mathematical model and use mathematical blocks. Each hand moves at a different angular speed. Pupils can use blocks of the current hour, current minute and current second to set the clock (Fig. 2).

During the project, the teacher's role is to enable pupils to work independently on the project and to encourage pupils to work with their peers and help out each other by advising, explaining and sharing their ideas among themselves.

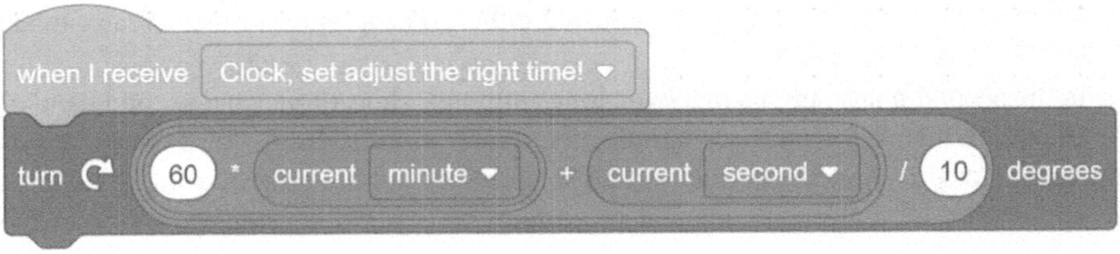

Fig. 2. Example of mathematical description of the circular motion of a big (Minute) hand clock

Even though, in our study, this project was completed practically by the majority of pupils, most of them did not show much enthusiasm because the solution required them to apply some mathematical calculations and an idea of circular motion studied in physics; its idea was not based on any story or principles of a game. Nevertheless, some boys found this task engaging and amusing.

Project 2 – Interactive Postcard

In the 'Interactive postcard' project, pupils are asked to create an interactive animated picture based on a simple story. When working on the project, the pupils' creativity, imagination, art skills, ability to invent and narrate a story play a key role in completing the task.

The most important thing is to choose a good and attractive theme as the core of the story on the postcard. The theme can be greetings from the holidays at grandma's, from a camp, from a stay by the sea, from a visit to the zoo, etc. It can also be a birthday or festive occasion wishes (Easter, Christmas, etc.).

The crucial part of the project is to implement the story in Scratch and to design and include a set of funny, interactive elements and striking effects in its scene.

With regard to the Christmas theme, the project can be divided into five phases, in which pupils solve partial problems. In the first phase, pupils think carefully about the story for the postcard. They contemplate its graphic design and the sprites that would appear in the story. In the second phase, pupils prepare a typical Christmas landscape scene (e.g., a house with a Christmas tree) and sprites (e.g., dog, cat, door, chimney, stars in the night sky). They then propose how selected sprites will be animated and which sprites, and how to interact with these sprites in the story. In the third phase, the pupils create a snowflake sprite and program how these snowflakes fall over the landscape. In the fourth phase, the pupils program how falling snowflakes step-by-step accumulate on the ground or on other surfaces of objects on the scene (trees, roof, etc.). In the fifth phase, if pupils have extra time, they can display on their interactive postcard a New Year's label, PF (*Pour féliciter*), with the relevant number for the incoming new year and add some sound effects, voices, or melodies.

Teachers can inspire pupils to work on an interactive postcard by explaining how to prepare the postcard as a present for small children or friends. The pupils can deal with interactions in Scratch in different ways (by clicking on the sprites, sending messages, meeting the logic conditions, etc.). They can complete the story with various sound recordings (the barking of a dog, creaking of the door, owl honking, cat meowing, etc.).

Teachers allow pupils to work independently, encourage the pupils to work together to advise or to explain to each other, and to exchange ideas.

In our study, this project was completed by practically the majority of highly interested pupils. Some pupils displayed the PF label very simply, inserting the label by using the "stamp" command in Scratch.

3.4 Data Collection Tools

The data that were collected for this study comprised of online open-ended questionnaires concerning programming projects in Scratch for teachers and for pupils. Furthermore, researchers' observation reports (elaborated after their school visits) were also included as one of the data collections tools.

The online questionnaires (A and B) with 28 open-ended questions for teachers were designed by the researchers and distributed to each teacher (N = 5) at the end of each project ('Clock' and 'Interactive postcard') in order to obtain information about pupils' understanding of the tasks in the projects and to identify the main problems which emerged during the course of projects, and also to find out how these problems were resolved.

Online questionnaires (C and D) with two or three open-ended questions for pupils were designed by their teachers to obtain feedback from pupils about what they have learnt and their views about programming in the projects. Pupils answered the questionnaires after they had completed all projects included in the textbook by [7].

During the programming projects in Scratch, researchers visited the schools and wrote eight observation reports. Researchers mainly observed how teachers were instructing pupils and how pupils were undertaking the programming projects. The Table 2 below illustrates the overview of data collection tools.

Table 2. Overview of data collection tools.

Data collection	Type of data set	Purpose
Two online open-ended questionnaires concerning programming projects in Scratch for teachers	Questionnaire A: 'Clock' project Questionnaire B: 'Interactive postcard' project	To obtain information about pupils' understanding the tasks in the projects and to identify the main problems concerning how to complete the projects
Two online open-ended questionnaires concerning programming projects in Scratch for pupils	Questionnaire C: 'Clock' project Questionnaire D: 'Interactive postcard' project	To obtain information from pupils about what they have learnt and their approach to programming the projects
Eight observation reports from the researchers	Reports from lessons observed during programming projects	To understand how teachers were instructing and how pupils were undertaking the projects

3.5 Data Analysis Procedure

Feedback from online open-ended questionnaires gained from teachers and pupils and taken from researchers' observation reports were all written data. Therefore, after researchers completed the data collection, all collected data were first transferred to one Word document. Second, to familiarise themselves with the content, researchers read all three datasets several times: teacher and pupil questionnaires and observation reports from researchers. Third, before moving to coding, researchers highlighted (with different colours) the key elements such as words, sentences or quotes, which appeared to be relevant to the topic under scrutiny and, hence, which would help to address the research question. Fourth, researchers started to carry out open coding in all three datasets, which involved assigning letters to meaningful codes for each segment in the transcripts and threads. This method enabled researchers to easily find statements that we wanted to check in transcripts and threads and identify the source of the statement. Fifth, in the three datasets, researchers undertook more detailed coding which involved clustering and organising the open codes into broader categories which describe the data. Sixth, researchers analysed the links/interconnections between the three datasets.

3.6 Findings

Project solution in Scratch using the textbook by [7] showed that the key factors affecting successful completion of project programmed in Scratch are (1) motivation, (2) a positive climate in the learning environment, (3) peer interaction and collaboration, (4) freedom in ways to learn new concepts and to find solutions to given problems, and (5) a constructionist teaching approach (Table 3).

Table 3. Some examples from datasets.

Factor	Pupils	Teachers	Researchers
(1) motivation	*"These projects motivated me to learn programming and at the same time aroused my interest in computers"*	*"Sometimes I had to explain some things a lot to the pupils, even though I think it's nicely explained. Pupils just do not want to read the learning materials carefully. I wanted to keep the pupils having fun and it was engaging for them"*	*"Teachers paid great attention to introducing pupils to the topic"*
(2) positive climate in the learning environment	*"Personally, I am not so interested in computers, but I have enjoyed programming in the projects and everything we did in class was great"*		*"When I entered the classroom, I felt like being in a beehive"*
(3) peer interaction and collaboration	*"I'm glad that we were able to help each other, because I probably wouldn't have enjoyed it very much"*	*"Pupils collaborated a lot, especially if the pupils were dealing with falling snowflakes (snowfall)"*	*"When solving a project, pupils could discuss and consult together and mutually help each other"*
(4) freedom in ways to learn new concepts and find solution to given problems	*"I have learned that Informatics is not just about boring information about the Internet, diacritics, and test writing, but it is also about practical things like programming"* *"But I really enjoyed the freedom we had when working with these tasks"*	*"Pupils came up with their own solution; they did not use 'costumes', but solved it as separate sprites that jumped on a given place. (interactive postcard)"*	*"One pupil, for example, designed a witch's house instead of a Christmas postcard"*

(*continued*)

Table 3. (*continued*)

Factor	Pupils	Teachers	Researchers
(5) constructionist teaching approach	*"It was fun in class, especially when we were given basic instructions, but everyone took it in their own way. Such works were the best"*	*"Learning material for Interactive postcard was understandable - pupils very quickly began to progress independently"*	*"Boys experimented with blocks more, embarked on unusual solutions, and took more risks whereas girls were more adhering to the instructions in the learning materials"*

4 Discussion

Our findings demonstrate that if pupils are given interesting issues to be solved (projects) and some questions that initiate their thinking about how to start to solve the problem, and if the teachers give them enough freedom to explore and experiment with a programming environment, they carry out these ideas with interest. At the same time, they learn new informatics' concepts and programming procedures. It corresponds with findings of [12] that children could successfully learn important concepts of computer science using learning materials which do not bring ready-made solutions, but which trigger their thinking and lead them to ask new questions.

The two projects selected, together with others in the learning material, were designed in accordance with a constructionist approach and based on Papert's idea of learning-by-making. The results confirmed that pupils following such type of learning materials are able to find ways to complete such projects themselves, especially when they work together with their classmates in a stress-free, non-threatening, learning environment, where their teacher appreciates their enthusiasm, thinking process and effort. This is evidenced by the teachers themselves, who stated that about 75% of pupils completed the 'Interactive postcard' project and 70% pupils programmed the project, 'Clock', in accord with the instructions in the learning material.

It appears that the teaching approach to programming employed in our study potentially corresponds with the third and fourth level of creative engagement in computer programming education introduced by [16].

5 Conclusions

The study findings have some implications for teachers and practitioners. For seamless integration of Scratch projects in school education, we recommend keeping pupils in close peer-collaboration and to encourage them to have the courage to take risks, to experiment with blocks and to look for original ideas. This does, however, require that teachers are thoroughly prepared to help pupils to program their bold ideas in Scratch. Teachers have to reckon on the fact that supporting pupils to go their own way, to learn-by-making and to learn from mistakes brings a lot of unexpected problems and need to help pupils to discover the resources of mistakes in their scripts; pupils will be impatient because they will want their Scratch program works as they intended. It is necessary to constantly maintain the interest of pupils in solving problems. Pupils' motivation disappears if a functional version of the Scratch program is not available for a long time.

In our study, we received a relatively large amount of feedback from pupils. We could observe how pupils proceeded in tackling projects. We still know very little about how pupils develop their key informatics concepts in Scratch and what are their misconceptions. Like Vanicek [18, p. 370], we are aware of the limitations of our research methods. In our future research, we plan to focus on identifying, in collaboration with teachers, these misconceptions and their causes.

In this study, we used only two projects out of the eleven in the textbook by [7]. For future research, we would like to include also other projects to investigate more deeply factors influencing pupils' success in their completion. There is a pressing need for closer investigation of this problem especially because, in 2021-22, Czech schools will include new curricula for Informatics education using the new 14 textbooks. In the Czech Republic, there will be great interest in detailed and comprehensive research of their impact on computer science learning, including programming.

Acknowledgement. This study is a result of the research funded by the PROGRES Q17 Příprava učitele a učitelská profese v kontextu vědy a výzkumu.

References

1. Armoni, M., Meerbaum-Salant, O., Ben-Ari, M.: From Scratch to "real" programming. ACM Trans. Comput. Educ. **14**(4), 25:1–25:15 (2015)
2. Baytak, A., Land, S.: An investigation of the artifacts and process of constructing computers games about environmental science in a fifth-grade classroom. Educ. Tech. Res. Dev. **59**(7), 765–782 (2011)
3. Baytak, A., Land, S.M.: Advancing elementary-school girls' programming through game design. Int. J. Gender Sci. Technol. **3**(1), 243–253 (2011)
4. Brennan, K.: Best of both worlds: issues of structure and agency in computational creation, in and out of school. Doctoral dissertation, MIT (2012). http://web.media.mit.edu/~kbrennan/files/dissertation/Brennan_Dissertation.pdf
5. Cakiroglu, U., Suicmez, S.S., Kurtoglu, Y.B., Sari, A., Yildiz, S., Ozturk, M.: Exploring perceived cognitive load in learning programming via Scratch. Res. Learn. Technol. **26**, 1–19 (2018)
6. Cernochova, M., Vankova, P., Stipek, J.: Programování ve Scratch pro pokročilé - projekty pro 2. stupeň základní školy. Pedagogická fakulta UK, Praha (2020). https://imysleni.cz/ucebnice/programovani-ve-scratchi-ii-projekty-pro-2-stupen-zakladni-skoly
7. Cernochova, M., Vankova, P., Stipek, J.: Programování ve Scratch II (projekty pro 2. stupeň základní školy). Beta version. PedF UK, Praha (2019)
8. DG. Podpora rozvoje digitální gramotnosti. DG. https://digigram.cz/
9. Dohn, N.B.: Students' interest in Scratch coding in lower secondary mathematics. Br. J. Edu. Technol. **50**(1), 71–83 (2019)
10. Kalas, I., Mikova, K.: Základy programování ve Scratch pro 5. ročník základní školy (2020). https://imysleni.cz/ucebnice/zaklady-programovani-ve-scratchi-pro-5-rocnik-zakladni-skoly
11. Maloney, J., Resnick, M., Rusk, N., Silverman, B., Eastmong, E.: The Scratch programming language and environment. ACM Trans. Comput. Educ. **10**(4), 1e15 (2010)
12. Meerbaum-Salant, O., Armoni, M., Ben-Ari, M.: Learning computer science concepts with scratch. In: Proceedings of the Sixth International Workshop on Computing Education Research, pp. 69–76 (2010)

13. MoEYS: Strategie digitálního vzdělávání do roku 2020 (2014). http://www.msmt.cz/uploads/DigiStrategie.pdf
14. Moreno-León, J., Robles, G., Román-González, M.: Code to learn: where does it belong in the K-12 curriculum? J. Inf. Technol. Educ. Res. **15**, 283–303 (2016)
15. PRIM: Podpora rozvíjení informatického myšlení. www.imysleni.cz
16. Romero, M., Lepage, A., Lille, B.: Computational thinking development through creative programming in higher education. Int. J. Educ. Technol. High. Educ. **14**(1), 1–15 (2017). https://doi.org/10.1186/s41239-017-0080-z
17. Tanrikulu, E., Schaefer, B.C.: The users who touched the ceiling of scratch. Procedia Soc. Behav. Sci. **28**, 764–769 (2011)
18. Vanicek, J.: Early programming education based on concept building. Constructivist Found. **14**(3), 360–372 (2019)
19. Vanicek, J., Nagyova, I., Tomscanyiova, M.: Programování ve Scratch pro 2. stupeň základní školy (2020). https://imysleni.cz/ucebnice/programovani-ve-scratchi-pro-2-stupen-zakladni-skoly

Informatics Teacher Education

Design- and Evaluation-Concept for Teaching and Learning Laboratories in Informatics Teacher Education

Bernhard Standl[1](✉), Anette Bentz[1], Mattias Ulbrich[2], Annika Vielsack[2], and Ingo Wagner[2]

[1] Karlsruhe University of Education, Karlsruhe, Germany
{bernhard.standl,anette.bentz}@ph-karlsruhe.de
[2] Karlsruhe Institute of Technology, Karlsruhe, Germany
{ulbrich,vielsack,ingo.wagner}@kit.edu

Abstract. The integration of practice-related aspects in pre-service informatics teacher education is an essential part in future teachers' qualifications. To further promote opportunities for teaching-practice into our teacher-preparation programs, we recently introduced a teaching-learning-laboratories (TLL) for informatics in Karlsruhe, Germany. This TLL not only offers pre-service informatics teachers students the opportunity to gain practical teaching experience, but we also promote competencies of secondary school pupils in workshops for school classes. In the laboratory, pre-service informatics teacher students can practice in micro-teaching learning scenarios both in seminars and in workshops with school classes. Based on this, we developed teaching-learning strategies as a combination of unplugged and plugged teaching-learning activities. In order to ensure the effectiveness of the workshops, they are also subject of an evaluation, examining the TLL from the perspective of the workshop concepts for pre-service informatics teacher students and the schools' pupils. From these two perspectives we investigate different fields of interest with the common goal to establish an effective TLL. In this paper we describe our approach of the TLL, our first experiences with workshops we have already conducted as well as the framework and the concept for evaluation.

Keywords: Teaching learning lab · Informatics teacher education · Evaluation of workshops

1 Introduction

Pupil laboratories are part of extracurricular out-of-school places of learning, where pupils themselves experiment and research. They learn about scientific work processes and methods but are accompanied in their (independent) experiments. In addition to this core definition, pupil laboratories should be oriented towards the principle of inquiry-based learning and strive for a high level of

K. Kori and M. Laanpere (Eds.): ISSEP 2020, LNCS 12518, pp. 133–145, 2020.
https://doi.org/10.1007/978-3-030-63212-0_11

authenticity, for example by using the premises for research projects or by bringing pupils into contact with doctoral students. In this sense, in a broad understanding of a pupil laboratory, the term "laboratory" can refer not only to a spatial laboratory, but also to a (artificial) situation specially created by humans, as well as to the research activity. A special form of a pupil laboratory, which is extremely relevant with regard to study and teaching, is the teaching-learning laboratory (TLL). In TLLs, groups of pupils are taught or supervised by pre-service teacher students. In some cases, the teacher students themselves develop and test the learning units or learning stations, for example within the framework of courses or final theses. When conducting teaching-learning labs, teacher students are usually responsible for a small group (3–5 pupils) at one learning station (similar to micro-teaching) and try out their teaching actions about 10–20 min with each group of pupils rotating through the lab. The personal responsibility and reduction of complexity can be adapted to the level of competence of the teacher students, for example with regard to moderation or the establishment of rules. In this way, teacher students gain early experience in dealing with pupils in a confined, less complex environment and can test their competencies in classroom situations during their teacher training and reflect on their actions in a guided manner [24]. Reflection in teaching-learning laboratories can take place in various ways, for example as peer feedback immediately after the training by fellow students or through expert feedback from the lecturers. In addition, self-awareness questionnaires are often used to support the reflection process and to identify individual learning needs. Furthermore, in the mode of research-based learning, empirical data can be collected independently to research the learning process.

In Germany, there are more than 400 laboratories for pupils related to different subjects at the beginning of 2020, which are mainly connected to universities as well as museums, industrial companies and science centres[1]. But only a couple of those laboratories are part of practice-related pre-service teacher programs and so far, only very few focus on informatics. Mostly, such laboratories in informatics were set up either as learning-labs for students, for outreach programs for schools or as research labs and practice space for pre-service teachers. In Austria some initiatives of teaching-learning laboratories emerged over the last decade as for instance the *COOL Lab* at the University of Linz. This is an interdisciplinary teaching-learning-lab aimed at addressing digital competencies of pre- and in-service teachers and private visitors with a focus on computational thinking [10]. Earlier, parts of this team introduced the so called *Informatikwerkstatt* (Informatics-Workshop) at the University of Klagenfurt, which is a teaching-learning lab also offering workshops for students, pupils and private visitors [23]. Similar formats have been introduced at the University of Paderborn, Germany [18]. At the University of Oldenburg, Germany, a lab was introduced, which sets its focus on workshops for teachers with pupil-groups[2]. The RWTH Aachen University in Germany, offers a Student-Lab called *InfoSphere* [7]. At the FU

[1] https://www.lernortlabor.de.
[2] https://uol.de/lernlabor-informatik.

Berlin, high-school classes can visit workshops designed by pre-service informatics teacher students in a teaching-learning-lab [4].

To further promote opportunities in integrating teaching practice into our teacher-preparation programs, we recently started a new TLL for pre-service informatics teacher education in Karlsruhe, Germany[3]. This TLL has two sites at the Karlsruhe University of Education (PHKA) and the Karlsruhe Institute of Technology (KIT). The two sites are located in close proximity and since the universities target different student groups (becoming teachers at different school types), the two sites complement each other ideally. On the one hand, the new TLL aim at motivating students to engage in informatics or even to become future university students in informatics. On the other hand, the TLL also offers future informatics teachers practical teaching experience. Therefore, parts of the TLL activities are carried out by pre-service informatics teacher students as part of their studies with supervision by university lecturers. Our TLL is accompanied by a research-oriented approach that examines the teaching-learning lab along the workshop concepts considering different research objectives aimed at the pupils and the future informatics-teachers. In this way we aim at a well-concepted integration of the TLL in the development of activities in the context of informatics education.

The remainder of this paper is structured as follows. First, we describe the concept of our TLL and then we give three examples of our workshops. Then we describe the evaluation concept and first experiences. We conclude with a short outlook on future activities.

2 Description of the Teaching-Learning Lab

The TLL pursues the approach of creating an integrative structure that allows to apply concepts from informatics in practice and it is designed in a way to achieve a sustainable effect for informatics education through the interaction of practical experience, and research. The underlying theoretical pedagogical concept is based on the constructivistic learning theory, whereby students construct knowledge rather than just receive knowledge from the teacher [6]. Based on constructivism, the constructionist learning theory by Papert [22] has a long tradition in informatics education for hands-on activities [9]. For the TLL a designated room was set up at both locations, which is designed in such a way that many forms of teaching-learning concepts can be applied. The spectrum of teaching/learning materials ranges from mini-computers such as Arduino or mBot to tasks and materials developed by us that are processed "unplugged" without the use of computers. On a conceptual level, the overall approach of the TLL is aimed at two goals: The integration of practical experience for pre-service informatics teachers into seminars and the promotion of informatics among school-pupils. Although the students try out teaching-learning sequences and develop materials within seminars in the TLL even in the absence of pupils, they are also actively

[3] http://www.lehr-lern-labor.info.

involved in the design and implementation of workshops for pupils. The advantage in contrast to existing practical phases at school locations is, that teaching sequences can be applied, observed and evaluated on a small scale directly in the TLL. Hence, the practical relevance promotes the professionalisation process of the prospective informatics teachers. Workshops for pupils are also designed, conducted and evaluated by academic staff, who also accompany the evaluation of the workshops. As a consequence, we are also able to explore pupils' learning processes and interest in informatics based on the workshops we offer (see Sect. 4). A further characteristic of the TLL with its two locations at the Karlsruhe Institute of Technology and the Karlsruhe University of Education is that we intentionally combine the competencies of both institutions (technical science and didactics) in close cooperation and thus obtain an added value in quality. This means that we take the opportunity to incorporate the expertise of the Karlsruhe Institute of Technology and the pedagogical-didactical expertise of the Karlsruhe University of Education into the operation of the TLL.

2.1 Workshop-Examples

In order to provide an idea of our activities in the TLL, we will describe three of our workshops briefly. They are aimed at pupils in 7th till 9th grade of secondary schools and have a duration of 90–120 min.

Workshop 1: Schokomat ("Choc-Machine"). This workshop is an introductory exercise in algorithmic thinking. While programming is an important element of the curriculum in informatics[4], the concept of *automata* (a.k.a. *finite state machines* or *state charts*) is not introduced. In this workshop we want to give pupils the possibility to approach the subject of (reactive) algorithms very playfully, and to build up an intuition on how machines (or computers) make decisions and how decision-making rules can be formulated in form of automata.

The workshop itself is divided into two parts, an unplugged and a plugged one: (1) After a short introduction the pupils work together in groups of four. In each group two pupils simulate the inside of a chocolate machine using a cardboard mockup with a coin slot, a button and an output slot (Fig. 1(a)). They have to control the output of the chocolate machine according to a given state chart. The other two pupils have to figure out how this specific chocolate machine is working. Therefore, they have to try different inputs and write down their conclusions in form of a state chart. When finished, they can compare the original and the recreated state chart, check their results and flip roles. The pupils work independently and in their own pace. They learn and personally experience the concepts of "state", "event" and "state transition" which are central for (reactive) algorithms. (2) In the *plugged* part of the workshop, the pupils use a desktop computer program developed for this purpose (Fig. 1(b)) to design automata on their own and to interact with them. The application has the benefit of obeying the automata rules rigorously which allows pupils to

[4] In our state, a course of informatics is compulsory in grade 7.

explore what automata can do in general and to experiment and probe their understanding of the concept. A physical chocolate machine that can be driven by the software is currently under development.

Conducted Workshops have shown that the playful introduction allows pupils an easy and intuitive access to state charts and the concept of automata. Especially younger pupils enjoy playing with the mock-ups. This leads to ongoing motivation during the whole workshop.

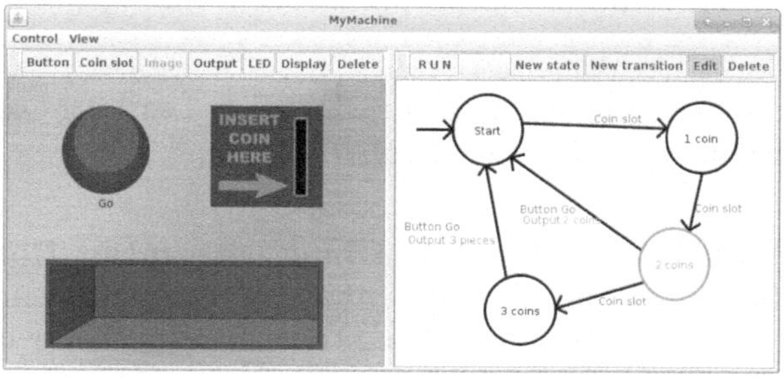

(a) **(b)**

Fig. 1. Material for the "Schokomat" workshop: (a) the unplugged setup, (b) screenshots of the Desktop app to design and run automata

Workshop 2: Interactive Coding for Beginners. This workshop focuses on teaching pupils the concept of algorithms and the ability to develop them. Using self-regulated learning methods, the pupils develop either a basic idea of algorithmic thinking or may dive deeper in and experiment with variables and functions. The workshop has two distinct parts: programming with analog technique and programming of a robot. The duration of each part can easily shift from not existing to very extensive and the impact of analog techniques on motivation and learning success can be investigated in detail. To arouse the interest of the pupils, we introduce robots in socially relevant topics and draw comparison with playful robots. In the unplugged programming part, one pupil plays the part of the programmer by lining up commands, while the other pupil plays the part of the robot, by executing these commands, for example walking around the room or drawing simple pictures. The programming is performed by arranging magnetic programming blocks on small boards as depicted in Fig. 2.

Commands may be "go one step" or "draw one line". Using the blocks, the pupils are introduced to the basics of block programming and debugging in a haptic and social way, without being distracted by the advanced functionality of a real development environment. Subsequently a simple robot and its development environment are introduced. After the pupils get used to controlling the robot, they are asked to proceed with challenges in which the robot fulfils various tasks. Different missions, from 'easy' to 'advanced', are provided and the pupils are free

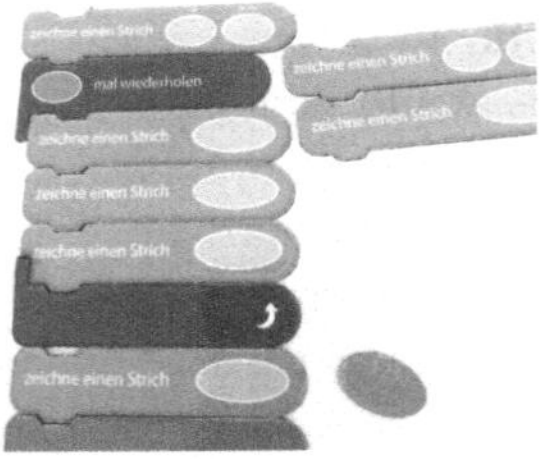

Fig. 2. Prototypes of self-developed magnetic programming blocks

to select an assignment of their choice. Learning guides are available to support the pupils in their self-regulated learning.

Workshop 3: Follow the Line with mBot Robots. The mBot Workshop also aims to promote algorithmic thinking through the programming of mBot robots and was prepared and carried out by future informatics teacher students. The workshop focuses on the integration of haptic experiences in order to motivate students to engage with algorithmic thinking. The educational robots mBot were used to perform the classical "Hello World" task from robotics, the following of a line. Before the workshop took place, we consulted the responsible teacher of this school class. We knew that the students already had some previous experience with block languages. The concept was hence designed in such a way that the pupils could build on their previous knowledge in block-based programming. Therefore, a quick introduction into the use and control of the robot with the block-based programming language was given at the beginning of the workshop. Then we worked out how to follow a straight line together.

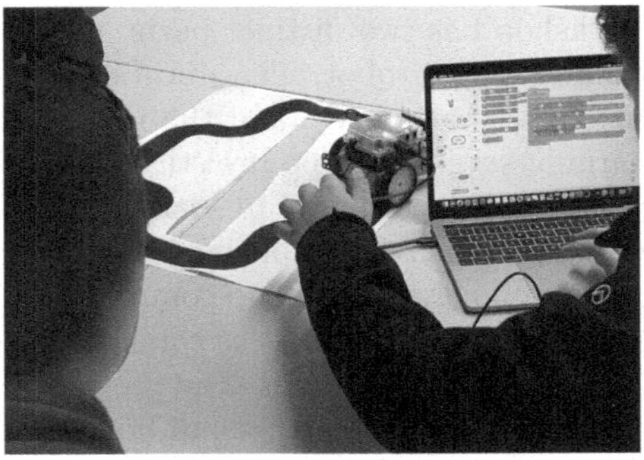

Fig. 3. Pupils developing an algorithm for the mBot following the black line

Afterwards, the challenge to program the robot for a given race track followed in groups as shown in Fig. 3. It turned out, that on the one hand the haptic experience with the robot seemed to have very positive effects on the motivation of the students. On the other hand, however, some of basic structures of algorithms would have been necessary for the development of the algorithm in the group work. We conclude that an introduction to algorithmic thinking in relation to robot control in the future must be considered at the beginning of the workshop.

3 Method of Evaluation

Subject of our evaluation are the workshops conducted in TLL. The goal of the evaluation is to establish an effective TLL in informatics education for both, pupils and pre-service teacher students. We define an effective TLL along our research objectives (RO): optimized learning processes (RO1), higher self-efficacy and interpersonal-attitudes (RO2) and a higher interest in informatics (RO3). This is based on the assumption that learning is most effective when it takes place holistically, i.e. involves all three levels of development: the intellect (RO1), the (social) skills and the intuitions and feelings (RO2/3) [20]. Therefore, we accompany the activities with an evaluation concept, which focuses on the workshops with pupils. However, the evaluation does not focus on content-related research topics as e.g.. *coding* but rather emphasizes on evaluating the impact of our workshop concepts on students and pupils attitudes in the fields such as problem-solving, attitudes and awareness for informatics. From the perspective of research methodology, the workshops (as intervention) can therefore be considered as independent variables the research objectives (as response) can again be described as dependent variables.

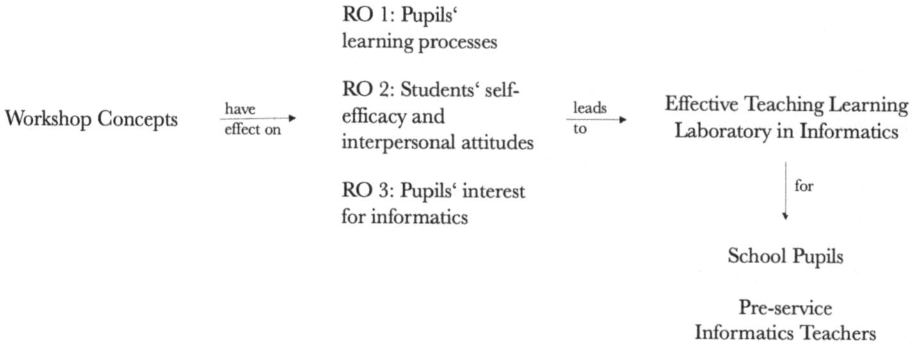

Fig. 4. Research setting

As it is shown in Fig. 4, the process of evaluation hence aims to improve the quality of the TLL based on the workshop concepts on different research objectives. In Subsect. 3.2 we will show that this is represented in a cyclic refinement process.

3.1 Research Objectives

We have divided the research into three objectives: The first relates to learning processes, the second to students' attitudes and the last to pupils' interest in informatics.

Objective 1: Pupils' Learning Processes: In this objective, we are in particular interested in *critical decision points* in the transition from unplugged-activities to the integration of the computer as plugged-activities. We will take a close look at so called intended learning trajectories, which is an approach for a systematic design and evaluation of an intended progression and has its roots in mathematics education research [11]. As problem-solving processes in informatics (education) have commonly ambiguities in their solving path [19], it will therefore be particularly interesting to model these processes. We assume, that we will be able to identify and optimize typical learning paths. *Overall research question:* When is the right time during a learning process to advance from unplugged to plugged teaching-learning activities?

Objective 2: Students' Self-efficacy and Interpersonal Attitudes: In our TLL students co-design workshops for pupils and carry out self-planned micro-teaching-learning settings within seminars. In order to support this development, seminars and workshops are embedded in a trustful student-centered climate. As the teachers' self-efficacy [2,3] can affect student achievement [13], we are also interested in investigating the impact of the TLL on future teacher students' self-efficacy in relation to informatics. Based on scales developed and tested for informatics-teacher further education [15], we will evaluate the changes in students' self-efficacy as a consequence of the TLL integration into the studies. Moreover, future teachers' interpersonal attitudes and the nature of the teacher–student relationships [14] can be considered as essential for inspiring pupils for a subject [21]. The quality of a student-teacher relationship can be identified along attitudes as authenticity, acceptance and empathy [1], which are also a requirement for student-centered teaching [8]. *Overall research question:* To what degree does students' self-efficacy change and to what degree develop students their student-centered teaching qualities?

Objective 3: Pupils' Interest for Informatics: Since our TLL not only serves as an experimental room for pre-service informatics teacher students in the context of lectures, but also offers workshops to school classes, we are also interested in the effects of the workshops on pupils. It has been shown, that outreach programs for pupils can increase interest in informatics [12]. Moreover, unplugged activities can lead to an increased level of interest in informatics [5]. The goal is to find out if the workshops have an impact on the pupils' interest in informatics. *Overall research question:* Has the participation in a workshop impact on pupils' interest for informatics and does the pupils' knowledge about informatics change through the workshop participation?

3.2 Research Process

In order to investigate the research objectives, we chose the action research approach as overall procedure. Introduced in 1946 [17], this approach has a long tradition in education and is refined into a cyclical process of diagnosing, action planning, action taking, evaluation and specifying learning [25]. We interpret a cycle as the implementation of a workshop in the TLL, in which we address one or more of the research objectives mentioned above, depending on the workshop format. We are aware that a cycle could also extend over several workshops. The reason for the short step-by-step cycle approach is that we look at each individual workshop to develop appropriate measures for improvement. Our experience has shown that the density of events valuable for data collection can be sufficient even within 90-min workshops. As the action-research approach provides an overall procedure for conducting research, we additionally integrate a more specific approach for evaluating workshops with *case studies*. The case study approach as suggested by Yin [26] enables a detailed documentation of the planning, implementation and analysis of the collected data. In such mixed research field this is particularly necessary to ensure quality criteria of validity, reliability and objectivity [27]. As part of the case study process, a case study protocol is also created, which not only stores the collected data, but also describes the entire research process, including the research objectives, research methods, approach and methods of analysis. The case study protocol is again stored in a case study database. The more workshops have been conducted and researched, the more data will have been collected, which will enable further methods of analysis on a statistical basis. However, for direct quality measures during the first phase of the TLL it is important that workshops receive immediate and direct feedback for improvement.

As it is shown in Fig. 5, the outer circle represents the action research process (diagnosing, action taking, evaluating, specifying learning) and the inner one the corresponding steps of the case study approach (design, collect, analyze, share). To keep the two circles symmetrical, we have combined the first two steps in action research. In the first step of the action research cycle, the diagnosis, we establish links from the research objectives to the existing workshop concept. This means, that in the case of the research objectives, we first examine the workshop concept and then determine which parts of it can be addressed by the research objectives. In the second stage of the action research cycle, data will be collected during workshops using mixed methods. Depending on which research objective a workshop focuses on, we use different research instruments for data collection. On the one hand, existing and proven instruments are used, but also new ones will be developed. For our research, we will use instruments as questionnaires, feedback sheets, documentation of self-reflection and video recordings.

In the third step, the collected data is evaluated and interpreted. We will mainly use the technique of explanation building, where a phenomenon is explained by an analysis of the collected data and the research questions [26]. In qualitative social research, this is also described using a hermeneutic procedure

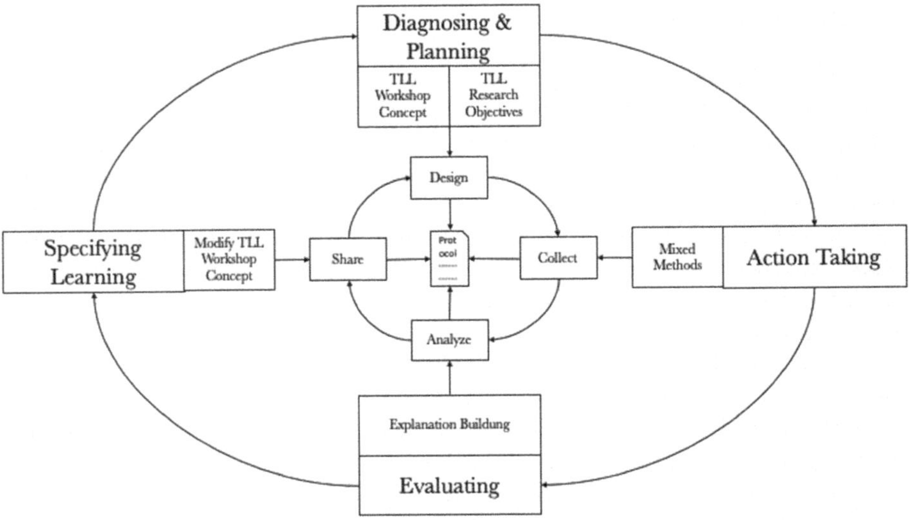

Fig. 5. Research process

or content analysis. In the latter case, the reduction of data to their essential aspects also enables ways to an objective analysis [16]. In the final step of the action research cycle, the results of the analysis will lead to a refinement of the workshop concept, which will again be considered in future action research cycles of future workshops.

Example. To illustrate the research process, we briefly outline how the research plan is implemented with research objective 2 ("Students' self-efficacy and interpersonal attitudes") with a workshop, organized by pre-service teachers within a didactical seminar. Considering the first part of the question: *To what degree does students' self-efficacy change?*, we assume as a precondition, that the students' self-efficacy expectations change due to the practical experiences in TLL during the term. In order to determine a change, we use questionnaires at the beginning of the semester, before the workshop, after the workshop and at the end of the semester to determine the students' self-efficacy. In addition we develop questions based on the questionnaire with the possibility of free text answers. These will be filled in immediately after the workshop. This gives us a qualitative impression of the students' immediate experience and also indications of where to find phases in the workshop that hinder the development of self-efficacy. From the statistical analysis of the questionnaires and the qualitative evaluation of text answers, we derive an overall picture for the revision of the workshop and adaptation of the seminar organization with regard to the self-efficacy of the students. However, the results will not only be used for immediate exploitation as described in this example. As they have been saved in the case-study database, they are also used in an accumulated form for higher-level analyses.

4 First Results and Experiences

Even tough our TLL has only existed for a short period of time and we also were slowed down by the Covid-19 crisis in conducting and researching our workshops, we can already report first experiences from the first pilot workshops. As we can only present selected results in this paper, we chose to focus on our research objective 1, the transition from unplugged-activities to the integration of the computer as plugged-activities. Regarding this, we observed in our workshops the importance of unplugged, haptic experience. In both, the Schokomat-workshop and in the workshop with mBot robots, it was evident that the haptic component of the workshop (the cardbox chocolate machine and the driving robot mBot) visibly increased the pupils' motivation for their learning engagement. The pupils' use of haptic elements during discussions of the newly introduced concepts with each other suggests that such items help particularly during short workshops. From this we have recognized the high relevance of the observation of the transition from analog to digital components.

In general, the school subject informatics has a special relationship with digitisation: Since informatics in the large is the driving scientific and economic force behind digitisation, the use of computing or media devices is – for informatics – not only a matter of choice of the teaching medium, but inherently also an integral part of the subject itself. Informatics is not the subject of "how to use a computer", but its concepts in many cases only receive a meaning when brought together with a computing device of some sort or other. Hence, it goes without saying that informatics as a subject is taught in digitised environments. It is rather the opposite question which is interesting in this special case: Can digitisation in Informatics education be overemphasized? This threat is real with many visualisations and learning tools available (in particular for programming). Therefore, it is a goal of the TLL to assess the right timing during a teaching-learning activity when it is beneficial to use adequate digitised tools, and when it is beneficial to remain in the "analog" world with unplugged contents. The unplugged world has the advantage that it allows pupils to apply concepts which are part of their experience onto newly arising questions. On the other hand, this may cause improper analogies to arise. Plugged (media-supported, computerised) content allows for more realistic application scenarios to be used in teaching that connects the addressed topics with the pupils' everyday experience in our digitised world, but they are less flexible and due to complexity have the potential of being overwhelming if used to early in the learning process.

The research questions that arise here and that we want to address in our future research are: What are the main contributing factors for the ideal transition point from unplugged to plugged teaching/learning methods? How can we devise experiments to investigate that point? How individual is this transition, and in particular, how much would the learning effect of an entire class benefit if every pupil made the transition at their respective ideal time? As a first step, we are currently designing an experiment how to set up the Workshop "Schokomat" from Sect. 2.1, which has a distinct unplugged and a distinct plugged phase, with different transition points and various intended learning trajectories to gather further experimental data.

5 Summary and Further Work

In this paper we described our concept of a TLL, which fosters opportunities to integrate teaching practices into teacher-preparation programs and offers special learning experiences for school pupils. To illustrate our concept, we added examples describing our workshops. To ensure the effectiveness of the workshops, they are evaluated. Key aspects of our evaluation are the conceptual framework (with special focus on the transition from unplugged to plugged activities), teacher students' self-efficiency and teaching qualities, and pupils' interest regarding informatics. At the moment we are developing further workshop concepts and due to the corona-pandemic we are adapting our workshop scenarios to be applicable as online-courses supported by video-conference-calls between teacher students and pupils. As next steps we plan to wider spread our ideas and thereby foster the founding of further TLL at other locations. This publication is an essential part to contribute to this aim.

Acknowledgement. This work was supported by the Vector Foundation.

References

1. Aspy, D., Roebuck, F.: Kids Don't Learn from People They Don't Like. Human Resource Development Press, Champaign (1977)
2. Bandura, A.: Self-efficacy: toward a unifying theory of behavioral change. Psychol. Rev. **84**(2), 191–215 (1977)
3. Bandura, A., Freeman, W., Lightsey, R.: Self-efficacy: the exercise of control (1999)
4. Barendsen, E., Dagiene, V., Saeli, M., Schulte, C.: Eliciting computing science teachers' PCK using the content representation format. ISSEP 2014 p. 71 (2014)
5. Bell, T., Alexander, J., Freeman, I., Grimley, M.: Computer science unplugged: school students doing real computing without computers. N. Z. J. Appl. Comput. Inf. Technol. **13**(1), 20–29 (2009)
6. Ben-Ari, M.: Constructivism in computer science education. J. Comput. Math. Sci. Teach. **20**(1), 45–73 (2001)
7. Bergner, N., Schroeder, U., Schulte, C.: Konzeption eines informatik-schülerlabors und erforschung dessen effekte auf das bild der informatik bei kindern und jugendlichen. Technical report, Fachgruppe Informatik (2016)
8. Cornelius-White, J., Harbaugh, A.P.: Learner-Centered Instruction: Building Relationships for Student Success. Sage Publications Inc., London (2009)
9. Csizmadia, A., Standl, B., Waite, J.: Integrating the constructionist learning theory with computational thinking classroom activities. Inform. Educ. **18**(1), 41–67 (2019)
10. Demarle-Meusel, H., Sabitzer, B., Sylle, J.: The teaching-learning-lab-digital literacy and computational thinking for everyone. In: International Conference on Computer Supported Education, vol. 2, pp. 166–170. SCITEPRESS (2017)

11. Duschl, R., Maeng, S., Sezen, A.: Learning progressions and teaching sequences: a review and analysis. Stud. Sci. Educ. **47**(2), 123–182 (2011)
12. Franklin, D., et al.: Assessment of computer science learning in a scratch-based outreach program. In: Proceeding of the 44th ACM Technical Symposium on Computer Science Education, pp. 371–376 (2013)
13. Gibson, S., Dembo, M.H.: Teacher efficacy: a construct validation. J. Educ. Psychol. **76**(4), 569 (1984)
14. Hattie, J.: Visible Learning: A Synthesis of Over 800 Meta-Analyses Relating to Achievement. Routledge (2009). https://doi.org/10.4324/9780203887332
15. Hildebrandt, C.: Mit dem Glauben Berge versetzen ... - Die Selbstwirksamkeitserwartung von Informatiklehrkräaften. In: Informatische Bildung zum Verstehen und Gestalten der digitalen Welt (2017)
16. Lamnek, S.: Qualitative Sozialforschung: Lehrbuch. Beltz, PVU, Weinheim und Basel (2005)
17. Lewin, K.: Action research and minority problems. J. Soc. Issues **2**(4), 34–46 (1946)
18. Magenheim, J.: Informatik lernlabor-systemorientierte didaktik in der praxis. Informatische Fachkonzepte im Unterricht, INFOS 2003, 10. GI-Fachtagung Informatik und Schule (2003)
19. Moreno-León, J., Robles, G., Román-González, M.: Towards data-driven learning paths to develop computational thinking with scratch. IEEE Trans. Emerg. Top. Comput. (2017)
20. Motschnig-Pitrik, R.: Effectiveness of person-centered learning in the age of the internet. In: Lytras, M.D., Ruan, D., Tennyson, R.D., Ordonez De Pablos, P., García Peñalvo, F.J., Rusu, L. (eds.) WSKS 2011. CCIS, vol. 278, pp. 494–499. Springer, Heidelberg (2013). https://doi.org/10.1007/978-3-642-35879-1_61
21. Motschnig, R., Mallich, K.: Effects of person-centered attitudes on professional and social competence in a blended learning paradigm. J. Educ. Technol. Soc. **4**(7), 176–192 (2004)
22. Papert, S.: Children, computers and powerful ideas (1990)
23. Pasterk, S., Demarle-Meusel, H., Sabitzer, B., Bollin, A.: Informatik-werkstatt: Entwicklungen und erfahrungen einer lern-und lehrwerkstatt für informatik. Informatik 2016 (2016)
24. Priemer, B., Roth, J. (eds.): Lehr-Lern-Labore: Konzepte und deren Wirksamkeit in der MINT-Lehrpersonenbildung. Springer, Heidelberg (2020). https://doi.org/10.1007/978-3-662-58913-7
25. Susman, G.I., Evered, R.D.: An assessment of the scientific merits of action research. Adm. Sci. Q., 582–603 (1978)
26. Yin, R.K.: Case Study Research: Design and Methods. Sage Publications, London (2008)
27. Zohrabi, M.: Mixed method research: instruments, validity, reliability and reporting findings. Theory Pract. Lang. Stud. **3**(2), 254–262 (2013). https://doi.org/10.4304/tpls.3.2.254-262

A Case of Teaching Practice Founded on a Theoretical Model

Sylvia da Rosa(✉), Marcos Viera, and Juan García-Garland

Instituto de Computación, Facultad de Ingeniería, Universidad de la República, Montevideo, Uruguay
{darosa,mviera,jpgarcia}@fing.edu.uy

Abstract. This paper tries to clarify the way in which our theoretical model relates to teaching practice in response to questions about how the model could potentially be applied. The theoretical model introduces an extension of Jean Piaget's general law of cognition to explaining the difference between algorithmic thinking and computational thinking by adequately locating the latter in the specificities of the subject instructing a computer. The teaching practice consists on activities introducing programming in high school mathematics courses. These are organised in a functional programming course to high school mathematics teachers and didactic instances in which the teachers teach their students to program solutions to mathematics problems.

Through examples we explain how the model helps teachers in finding a meaning of the popular and controversial expression "computational thinking". The goal of the didactic instances is to educate students in thinking algorithmically and computationally.

1 Introduction

This paper tries to clarify the way in which a theoretical model relates to teaching practice in order to response to question of how the model could potentially be applied.

The theoretical model introduces an extension of Jean Piaget's general law of cognition, that explains how conceptual knowledge is constructed when an individual solves a problem [10]. We have applied Piaget's general law of cognition to investigate the construction of knowledge of algorithms and data structures. In the case of knowledge of programs, the research led us to extend Piaget's general law of cognition, because the goal is to know how to help students learning *how to program*, not just to know how to help them learning *how to write program texts* (algorithms). The ontological approach of our programming didactics considers that a program is in some sense a synthesis between a text (an algorithm) and a machine that executes it. That means that knowledge about the text becomes necessary but not sufficient to deal with programming problems. The research of the construction of knowledge about programs has two main results: it offers a theoretical model that explains the relationship between conceptual knowledge of algorithms and of programs [13], and gives a clear definition of the

K. Kori and M. Laanpere (Eds.): ISSEP 2020, LNCS 12518, pp. 146–157, 2020.
https://doi.org/10.1007/978-3-030-63212-0_12

controversial expression "Computational Thinking" (hereinafter CT) [12]. In this paper we describe how and why teachers activities introducing programming in high school mathematics courses are an example of the application of the theoretical model. At the same time, the experience describes a way of introducing CT into school, contributing to educators' concern since CT became popular in educational settings [5,9].

The rest of the paper is organised into the following sections: in Sect. 2 we describe the theoretical model, while in Subsect. 2.1 we introduce the extended law of general cognition; in Sect. 3 we describe a teaching experience with mathematics teachers and explain how and why it relates to the theoretical model, and contributes to clarify teachers and students ideas of CT. Finally, we include conclusions and references.

2 The Theoretical Model

In Piaget's theory, human knowledge is considered essentially active, that is, knowing means acting on objects and reality, and constructing a system of transformations that can be carried out on or with them [11].

The problem of determining the role of experience and operational structures of the individual in the development of knowledge **before** the formalisation was studied in depth by Piaget in his experiments about genetic psychology. From these he formulated a *general law of cognition* [10], governing the relationship between know-how and conceptualisation, generated in the interaction between the subject and the objects that he/she has to deal with to solve problems or perform tasks. It is a dialectic relationship, in which sometimes the action guides the thought, and sometimes the thought guides the actions.

Piaget represented the general law of cognition by the following diagram:

$$C \leftarrow P \rightarrow C'$$

where P represents the periphery, that is to say, the more immediate and exterior reaction of the subject confronting the objects to solve a problem or perform a task. This reaction is associated to pursuing a goal and achieving results, without awareness neither of actions nor of the reasons for success or failure. The arrows represent the internal mechanism of the (algorithmic) thinking process. By that process the subject becomes aware of the coordination of the actions -a method- that she/he has employed to solve the problem (P → C in the diagram) and of the modifications that these actions impose to objects, as well as of objects' intrinsic properties (P → C' in the diagram). C and C' represent awareness of the actions (maybe mental) encapsulated in the algorithm and of the data structures, respectively. The process of the grasp of consciousness described by the general law of cognition constitutes a first step towards the construction of concepts.

2.1 The Extended Law of General Cognition

The construction of knowledge about algorithms and data structures is a process regulated by the general law of cognition. Over the years we have investigated the construction of knowledge by novice learners of algorithms and data structures (for instance sorting, counting, searching elements) basically by applying Piaget's law. A synthesis of previous work can be found in [14].

However, in the cases where the subject must instruct an action to a computer, the thought processes and methods involved in such cases differ from those in which the subject instructs another subject, or performs the action him/herself. In order to program a computer to solve a problem, the learners have to establish a causal relationship between the algorithm (he/she acting on objects), and the elements relevant to the execution of the program (the computer acting on states). By way of analogy with Piaget's law we describe that causal relationship by the following diagram:

$$\underbrace{C \leftarrow P \rightarrow C'}_{newC \longleftarrow newP \longrightarrow newC'}$$

where newP is characterised by a periphery centred on the actions of the subject and the objects he/she acts on. The centres newC and newC' represent awareness of what happens inside the computer: newC of the execution of the program instructions and newC' of the undergone modifications of the representation of data structures. The causal relationship between the first row and the second row is the key of the knowledge of a machine executing a program. It is indicated with the brace in the diagram above. The diagram describes the situation in which the subject reflecting on his/her role as problem solver becomes aware of how to do to make the computer solve the problem [16].

According to Piaget, we identify that the construction of knowledge of methods (algorithms) and objects (data structures) occurs in the interaction between C, P and C'. Likewise, we claim that the construction of knowledge of *a program as an executable object* takes place in the internal mechanisms of the thinking process; marked by the arrows between newC, newP and newC'. In other words, the general law of cognition remains applicable to the thinking process represented by the arrows; in both lines of the diagram pictured above. In [13] we describe an empirical study in which we introduce the extended law of cognition (hereinafter extended law). In [12] we explain that our extension of Piaget's law introduces a clear definition of the notion of CT (represented by the second line of the above diagram). Further, this new definition is adequately located in relation to the notion of algorithmic thinking (represented by the first line of the above diagram). The above diagram represents the theoretical model of the construction of knowledge of algorithms, data structures and programs.

In the next section we describe a teaching experience and explain how and why it relates to the theoretical model and contributes to clarify ideas of CT in educational settings. It consists of activities that provide teachers with a clear description of CT according to our theoretical definition. The teachers become trained to help the students learning to program, in a way that respects the process of learning how to think algorithmically and computationally.

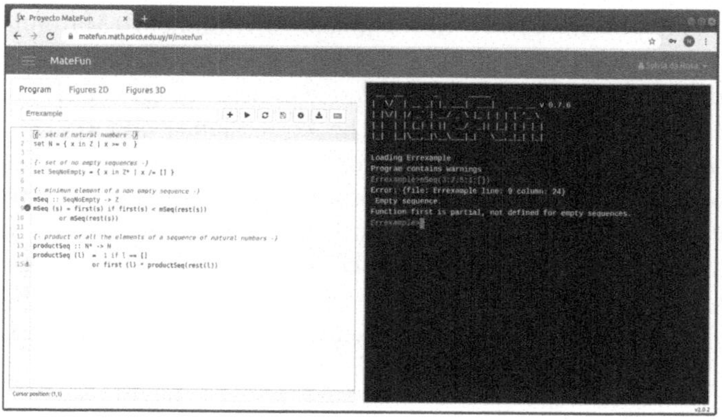

Fig. 1. MateFun IDE

3 CT in Educational Settings

The activities were developed in 2019 and consisted of a six weeks programming course for high school mathematics teachers and the supervision of six weeks activities that these teachers carried out with their students after taking the course. The teachers teach in diverse educational centres in different regions of Uruguay. They also teach in different high school years, and most of them teach to more than one group of students.

The main objective of the activities is the integration of mathematics and programming as a way to facilitate understanding and learning of mathematical concepts and at the same time to provide basic programming knowledge to high school students (see [15] for more details).

The guiding idea of the experience comes from [8] (p. 327), in the sense that programming a solution to a problem exposes aspects of the resolution process that are otherwise hidden. Some examples are the need of formulating algorithmic problems as such; the role of programming for the training of abstraction; the possibility of comparing algorithms and choosing those that are more efficient; and the introduction of a method of proof of equivalence between algorithms (see Sect. 3.2, first, second, third and fourth example respectively).

The functional language MateFun, briefly described in the next subsection, was used in the experience (see [15] for more details).

3.1 The Language MateFun

The language MateFun [3,4] is a functional programming language designed with the specific purpose of being a tool to support mathematical learning, especially in high school.

MateFun is purely functional, meaning that functions do not introduce side effects and they only depend on their arguments. To be easily approachable it is available as a web integrated development environment (Matefun IDE[1]), as shown in Fig. 1. The left frame is a text editor, where the program is written, and the right frame is a shell with a read-eval-print-loop, where the programs can be loaded (if they are correct) and the expressions evaluated.

Syntax and semantics of MateFun are both influenced by the seek to be a tool to express mathematics. The syntax is minimal and close to the usual mathematical notation. Semantically, it has the peculiarity of being strongly typed, while having no type inference. The skill to specify the domain and range of a function is part of the learning process when learning about functions. In MateFun type information must be given by users, and types in MateFun are called sets.

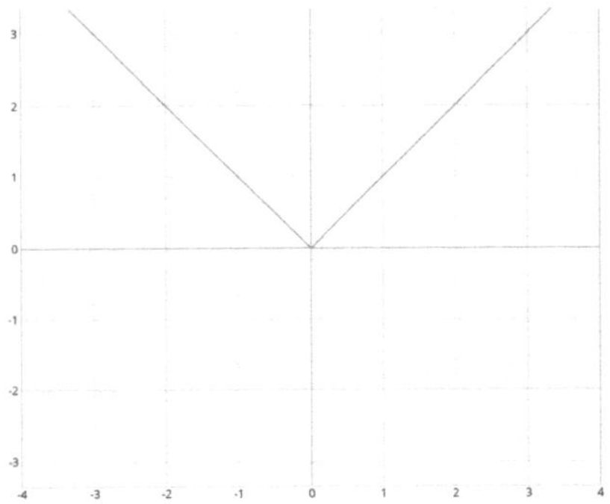

Fig. 2. Function plot: `?plot abs`

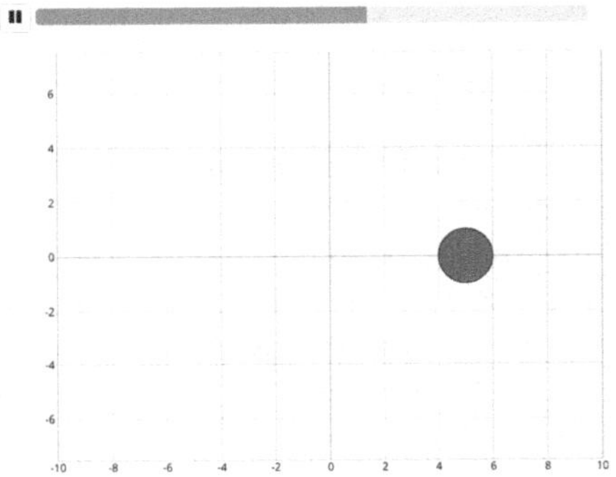

Fig. 3. `moveRight(redCirc(1),10)`

A MateFun script is a list of definitions of *sets* and *functions* over such sets. Predefined sets such as `R` (representing real numbers) or `Z` (representing integer numbers) are available as built-in constructs.

The user can define new sets either by comprehension or by extension, just as usually presented in mathematics courses. In the following example we define the sets of natural numbers (`N`), non-zero real numbers (`Rno0`), days of the week (`Day`) and (`Bool`):

```
set N    = { x in Z | x >= 0 }
set Rno0 = { x in R | x /= 0 }
set Day  = { Mon , Tue , Wed , Thu , Fri , Sat , Sun }
set Bool = {True , False}
```

Sets such as `Rno0`, defined by comprehension, take a base set (`R` in this case) and refine it with a predicate. Predicates can be built by relational operators and from other predicates by conjunctions.

Functions are defined giving a signature and a proper definition. For example, one could define the inverse function over the non-null real numbers:

[1] https://matefun.math.psico.edu.uy.

```
inv :: Rno0 -> R
inv (x) = 1/x
```

MateFun supports some of the idioms used to define functions in mathematics. For instance, piece-wise functions can be defined, while, unlike most functional languages, it does not support pattern matching or conditional expressions. The following MateFun definition specifies the absolute value function over the real numbers:

```
abs :: R -> R
abs (x) =    x if x >= 0
          or -x
```

This program resembles the definition in the usual mathematical notation:

$$abs : \mathbb{R} \rightarrow \mathbb{R}$$

$$abs(x) = \begin{cases} x & \text{if } x \geq 0 \\ -x & \text{otherwise} \end{cases}$$

Then, if we load the program in the interpreter, we can ask to compute the absolute value of the number `-10` by typing the expression:

```
Example>abs(-10)
10
```

The interpreter evaluates expressions and interprets special commands. For instance, we can graph a (one-variable) function using the command `?plot`. The result of plotting `abs` is shown in Fig. 2.

```
Example>?plot abs
```

To emphasise that not all functions are numeric, MateFun allows to define non-numeric sets (eg. `Day` and `Bool`) and functions between those sets, such as `holiDay`:

```
holiDay :: Day -> Bool
holiDay (d) =  True if  d == Sun
            or True if  d == Sat
            or False
```

We can also define *sequences* of elements of a given set; usually called *lists* in programming. The sequence set `A*` is defined inductively as:

- `[]`, the empty sequence
- `a:as`, a sequence composed by an element `a` belonging to `A` and a sequence `as` belonging to `A*`.

For instance, `N*` is the set of sequences of natural numbers.

There exist some primitive functions to operate with sequences: `first(s)` returns the first element of the sequence `s`, `rest(s)` returns the sequence `s` without its first element, and `range(n,m,k)` returns a sequence of numbers

$(n, n+k, n+2k, ...)$ from n to m with step k. With range, combined with a function to sum the elements of a sequence, we can for instance implement the summatory $\sum_{i=m}^{n} i$.

```
summatory :: N X N -> N
summatory (m, n) = sum(range(m, n, 1))

sum :: R* -> R
sum (xs) =  0 if xs == []
            or first(xs) + sum(rest(xs))
```

Notice the use of recursion in the implementation of sum and the domain using two variables. Domains with multiple variables can be defined using *n-tuples* (the generalisation of Cartesian products).

The language includes the primitive sets Figure and Color, and a set of primitive functions to create and transform *figures*. For example, the following function returns a red-coloured circle of a given radius, centred in the $(0, 0)$ point of a Cartesian plane.

```
redCirc :: R -> Fig
redCirc (r) = color(circ(r), Red)
```

In MateFun, *animations* are sequences of figures. The following function takes a figure fig and a number n of steps, and returns an animation in which the figure is moved n times one step to the right on the x-axis:

```
moveRight :: Fig X Z -> Fig*
moveRight (fig, n)
  = [] if n == 0
  or fig : moveRight(move(fig, (1, 0)), n - 1)
```

The expression move(fig, (1, 0)) moves fig to the point obtained adding 1 and 0 to the abscissa and the ordinate of the centre of fig respectively. Figure 3 shows the sixth frame of the following animation:

```
Example>moveRight(redCirc(1),10)
```

3.2 Teachers and Students Activities

The first part of the experience is a MateFun programming course to mathematics teachers and the second part consists of activities that teachers do with their students. A complete description of teachers and students activities can be found in [15], as well as teachers' reasons of their choices of problems and comments about students work. Here some activities are selected to describe how those relate to our theoretical model and offer a way of introducing CT in classrooms.

In educational settings, the starting point for developing a program is usually the design of the program's text, that is, an algorithm. In other words, the first step in getting the computer to solve a problem is to have an algorithm that allows an individual to solve specific cases of the problem. The construction of knowledge in this first step is regulated by Piaget's general law of cognition (see Sect. 2). Many of the problems covered in the course, are contributed by the teachers themselves and they know the solutions. In the course they are trained to program these solutions in MateFun, that is, to teach a computer to solve the problems, a process regulated by the extended law (see Sect. 2.1). Facing this challenge teachers' thinking starts from the new periphery (newP), since they manage to elaborate an algorithm to solve the problem, and it has to move towards the elements of program execution (newC and newC'). However, the process is dialectical and often, the transition of the thought from the algorithm and data structures, (C and C') to elements of program execution (newC and newC'), shows the need to modify the algorithm, and even the formulation of the problem. In the examples below, part of that dialectical process is described.

First Example: Computability. A theme introduced by the teachers in a group of third-year high school students (aged 13–14) is related to the problem of finding the multiples of a natural number. The accumulated experience[2] has taught us that often mathematics teachers are not used to rigorously formulate problems; many times they formulate problems forgetting details that are unconsciously interpreted, as in this case. The result could be expressed as "0, 3, 6, 9, ..." or "0, 3, 6, 9, and so on". However, if the question is to write the solution in a rigorous language, such as a programming language, and executing the program, neither the dots nor "and so on" are acceptable. That means that the problem has to be reformulated in terms of input-output [7], to explicitly including the natural number *and a bound* as input. This is an example of going from algorithmic to computational thinking, or in terms of the extended law, from newP to newC and newC', because thinking on program execution requires new knowledge about the input (newC') and the actions (newC).

It is worth mentioning that MateFun is a more powerful tool than other languages (Python, C), since being strongly typed, it requires to write the signature of the function as part of its definition (in this case, forcing to express the input as a pair of natural numbers). The solution in MateFun can be found in [15].

Simple examples like this give teachers the opportunity to introduce computing problems such as computability, in an understandable way by the students.

Second Example: Abstraction. Although a solution of a general problem has to be expressed as an algorithm, the power of abstracting is revealed in all its magnitude when the algorithm is transformed into a program that can be executed for several cases. The process has a greater impact in the case of novice learners, for whom the possibilities of experimenting their solutions in action is a reason of high motivation, as teachers comment in [15]. We illustrate the case using the following example.

[2] We have taught the course for about twelve years using other languages [15].

Teachers asked the students to program a function that makes a circle move n steps through the points of multiples of three on the x axis. A solution is presented below, in which the students adapted the function `moveRight` (see 3.1) to program a function `move3` that moves a figure n steps through points corresponding to multiples of three on the x axis. They also programmed `move3cir` in which the parameter `fig` of `move3` is instantiated to a red circle previously defined. Notice that adapting `moveRight` induced the students to write `move3`, abstracting the figure in the parameter `fig` as in `moveRight`.

```
circle :: R X Color -> Fig
circle (r, c) = color(circ(r), c)

move3 :: Fig X Z -> Fig*
move3(fig,n) =  [] if n < 0
                or fig : move3(move(fig, (3, 0)), n-1)

move3cir :: N -> Fig*
move3cir (n) = move3(circle(0.5, Red), n-1)
```

Since the problem asks for the multiples of three, the students used the concrete case of the point `(3,0)` in the function `move3`. When the teachers presented this solution in our course they were asked how to generalise it to the multiples of *any natural number*, that is, abstracting the point (3,0) to `(num,0)`. To construct a general solution they observed that `move(fig,(num, 0))` moves the figure `fig` through the multiples of any natural number -represented by `num`- on x axis. The point discussed was how to define a single function that also performs the movement n times. Observe that in terms of the general law of cognition that means that the thought advances towards newC' (the parameters) and newC (the action of moving), respectively. Finally, teachers introduced the definition of `moveMultiples` below.

```
moveMultiples :: Fig X Z X N -> Fig*
moveMultiples(fig, n, num)
  = [] if n == 0
  or fig : moveMultiples (move(fig,(num, 0)),n-1, num)
```

For instance, moving the red circle through the multiples of three, five times, is obtained with `moveMultiples(circle(0.5, Red), 5, 3)`.

The point is to always start from teachers or students solutions to construct new ones. In this type of exercises not only the abstraction is trained but also the skill of getting better programs by composing and combining other functions (predefined or not).

Third Example: Complexity. In our course the teachers are asked to solve many problems involving programming of functions over sequences, using recursion and/or composition of functions. The example below shows a MateFun program for the factorial function (`fact`). This is a well known definition by the teachers and all of them succeed in solving this problem.

```
fact :: N -> N
fact (n) =  1 if n == 0
         or n * fact(n-1)
```

Then the teachers are asked to write another program (`factorial`) for the same function using two functions: `productSeq` that returns the product of the elements of a sequence (see below), and `range` introduced in Sect. 3.1.

```
productSeq :: Z* -> Z
productSeq (l)  =  1 if l == []
                or first (l) * productSeq(rest(l))
```

Most of the teachers arrived to a solution similar to:

```
1 factorial :: N -> N
2 factorial (n) =  1 if n == 0
3               or productSeq(range(1, n, 1))
```

It can be observed that the definition has a redundant equation in line 2, induced by the recursive definition of `fact`. The equation in line 2 is used for a case that is actually encompassed by the definitions of functions `range` (case b < a) and `productSeq` (`productSeq([]) = 1`). This kind of errors in which edge cases are mishandled are frequently made by both teachers and students. Several lessons are learnt from solving that kind of exercises. One of the most important is that a program perhaps gives the correct result (teachers' solution of `factorial` does), but has errors anyway. From the point of view of programming it is an error to make the computer do things that are not necessary or are redundant. Understanding why the redundant equation is an extra effort for a computer is a clear example of transiting from algorithmic to computational thinking. In terms of the general law of cognition that means understanding how the computer performs the actions (newC) on the objects (newC'). One could argue that the redundant equation can be noted even in the algorithm and this is true, especially to more experienced programmers. In early stages of learning, however, to experience the need of a concept is the first step of constructing the concept [10] (in this case the need of efficiency). This training gives teachers the opportunity of introducing their students into topics such as programs complexity, inducing them to think computationally.

Fourth Example: Program Correctness. Programming more than one solution to a problem gives us the opportunity of introducing teachers to a topic that brings mathematics and functional programming even closer: the use of the principle of *structural induction* to prove properties of programs. For instance, one can prove that the two above definitions of the function factorial are equivalent in the sense that both give the same result when applied to the same value. The property is:

Property 1. $\forall$ n $\in$ N, `fact(n) = factorial(n)`.

and is proved using the principle of structural induction. For space reasons it is not included here, but can be found in [15].

Although the proofs are done with pen and paper, it is possible to do them using equational reasoning (substituting equals for equals where every step has to be well founded) since MateFun is a pure functional language (without side effects).

It is worth saying that traditionally, the principle of induction is used in a very restricted way in high school education, usually making no sense for students. Teachers could teach this method as a way of verifying program correctness, in other words, thinking about the correctness of the computer's actions (newC) on the objects (newC'). At the same time, the students would learn the basis of a topic of mayor relevance for understanding computer science.

4 Conclusions

The absence of clear definitions and substantiated claims about CT, "... leave teachers in the awkward position of not knowing exactly what they supposed to teach or how to assess whether they are successful". Those are P. Denning's words in [5]. In fact, the application of a concept that is theoretically weak can even be counterproductive. As L. Paulson notes in [9]: "Unless somebody can come up with a more insightful definition, it is indeed time to retire 'computational thinking"'.

Taking principles of Jean Piaget's theory, Genetic Epistemology [12], our theoretical model offers an insightful definition for CT adequately located in relation to the notion of algorithmic thinking. Therefore, our definition leaves teachers in a position of knowing ideas of CT in educational settings and being able to decide how to apply them.

Our claim is that any learning process is built stepwise and is governed by the general law of cognition. In the specific case of learning to program, the process is governed by the new law of cognition as we have formulated it on Sect. 2.1. Teachers activities presented in this paper show how our theoretical model of CT relates to teaching practices. Particularly, these activities help teachers to understand what CT means and how introduce the students in learning to program, in a way that respects their teaching practices. As a consequence teachers and students are educated to think algorithmically and computationally.

Furthermore, our contribution satisfies Denning and Matti Tedre definition (Chap. 1 of [6]) in the sense that not only the activities show how "to get computers to do jobs for us", but introduce teachers and students in some of the relevant problems of computer science, that make "the world a complex of information processes" [6]. For instance, the examples show how computability and complexity of programs could be discussed at high school level. The examples also reveal the power of abstraction in all its magnitude when putting into practice one of the main contributions of CT: to make the computer to solve general problems. Abstracting from concrete cases to obtain generic elements is not a trivial issue, and learning to program plays a fundamental role in training of abstraction from early stages, as several authors indicate [1,2,16,17].

Our theoretical model explains -in the framework of Piaget's theory of construction of knowledge- the relationship between logic, definitions, properties and proofs (algorithmic thinking), and the elaboration and execution of programs (computational thinking). The presented examples constitute examples of a didactic application of the model insofar as they show how the model supports teaching practice.

References

1. Aho, A.V.: Computation and computational thinking. Comput. J. **55**, 832–835 (2012)
2. Ambrosio, A.P., da Silva, L., Macedo, J., Franco, A.: Exploring core cognitive skills of computational thinking. In: Proceedings of the 25th Annual Psychology of Programming Interest Group Workshop, University of Sussex (2014)
3. Cameto, G., et al.: Using functional programming to promote math learning. In: 2019 XIV Latin American Conference on Learning Technologies (LACLO), pp. 306–313 (2019)
4. Carboni, A., Koleszar, V., Tejera, G., Viera, M., Wagner, J.: MateFun: functional programming and math with adolescents. In: Conferencia Latinoamericana de Informática (CLEI 2018) - SIESC (2018)
5. Denning, P.J.: Remaining Trouble Spots with Computational Thinking. Communications of the ACM **60**, (2017)
6. Ferragina, P., Luccio, F.: Search Engines. Computational Thinking, pp. 111–127. Springer, Cham (2018). https://doi.org/10.1007/978-3-319-97940-3_9
7. Harel, D., Feldman, Y.: Algorithmics the Spirit of Computing. Addison-Wesley, Boston (2004). An imprint of Pearson Education Limited
8. Knuth, D.: Computer Science and Its Relation to Mathematics. Basic Books Inc., Publishers, New York (1974)
9. Paulson, L.C.: Computational Thinking is not Necessarily Computational. Commun. ACM **60**, 8–9 (2017)
10. Piaget, J.: La Prise de Conscience. Presses Universitaires de France (1964)
11. Piaget, J.: Genetic Epistemology, A Series of Lectures Delivered by Piaget at Columbia University, Translated by Eleanor Duckworth. Columbia University Press, New York (1977)
12. da Rosa, S.: Piaget and computational thinking. In: CSERC 2018: Proceedings of the 7th Computer Science Education Research Conference, pp. 44–50 (2018)
13. da Rosa Zipitría, S., Dorelo, A.A.: Students Teach a Computer How to Play a Game. In: Pozdniakov, S.N., Dagienė, V. (eds.) ISSEP 2018. LNCS, vol. 11169, pp. 55–67. Springer, Cham (2018). https://doi.org/10.1007/978-3-030-02750-6_5
14. da Rosa, S., Gómez, F.: Towards a research model in programming didactics. In: Proceedings of 2019 XLV Latin American Computing Conference (CLEI), pp. 1–8 (2019). https://doi.org/10.1109/CLEI47609.2019
15. da Rosa, S., Viera, M., García-Garland, J.: Mathematics and MateFun, a natural way to introduce programming into school. https://hdl.handle.net/20.500.12008/25233. Accessed Sept 2020
16. Papert, S.: Mindstorms: Children, Computers, and Powerful Ideas. Basic Books, New York (1980)
17. Wing, J.: Computational thinking and thinking about computing. Philos. Trans. Roy. Soc. A **366**, 3717–3725 (2008)

In-Service Teacher Training and Self-efficacy

Jørgen Thorsnes, Majid Rouhani, and Monica Divitini(✉)

Department of Information and Computer Science, NTNU, Trondheim, Norway
{jorgen.thorsnes,majid.rouhani,monica.divitini}@ntnu.no

Abstract. Programming is increasingly introduced in secondary schools, both as a stand-alone subject or integrated into other subjects, leading to growing attention to the training of in-service teachers. Teachers need to learn both (a) how to program and (b) how to teach programming, often in the context of different disciplines. The paper explores the impact of a university-level training program offered to in-service teachers, with a focus on teachers' self-efficacy in teaching programming. The paper reports the interviews with ten teachers after about one year they have completed the program. The results indicate that the training has improved teachers' self-efficacy, and the impact is lasting in time. Also, some teachers expressed concerns about their skill level in programming, but this does not necessarily associate with lower self-efficacy in teaching programming. The paper presents the results from the study and some implications for the design of training of in-service programming teachers.

Keywords: In-service teacher training · Self-efficacy · Programming

1 Introduction

In a recent report on the status of Informatics education in Europe, it is recommended that all pupils must have access to ongoing education in Informatics, and the teaching must be undertaken only by teachers who have formal education in Informatics [1]. However, there are several challenges to meet this recommendation and a growing demand for teacher training, in particular for the re-skilling of in-service teachers. In this context, it is essential to understand in-service teacher training to define relevant and effective training. In this paper, we focus on how formal training of in-service teachers impacts self-efficacy, with a focus on long-term impact. Self-efficacy refers to the belief in one's capabilities to organize and execute the courses of action required to produce a given result [2]. In terms of teaching a specific subject, the teacher's self-efficacy refers to their belief in their capabilities to teach the subject, such that pupils achieve the desired learning outcomes. Positive self-efficacy is connected to increased student and teacher outcomes, and it has a positive influence on teachers' psychological well-being [3]. However, several studies identify challenges with self-efficacy connected to programming education. For example, in two recent Swedish studies on teachers' attitudes and self-efficacy towards programming, the researchers found that many Swedish teachers lack confidence in teaching programming [4, 5]. Similar results were reported in UK

K. Kori and M. Laanpere (Eds.): ISSEP 2020, LNCS 12518, pp. 158–169, 2020.
https://doi.org/10.1007/978-3-030-63212-0_13

schools, with many teachers worried that they miss practical and theoretical knowledge of computing [6]. Given this background, we investigate how formal education at the university level for in-service programming teachers affects their self-efficacy. The main research question explored in this paper is: *How do in-service teachers perceive the lasting effect of programming education concerning their self-efficacy in programming and teaching programming?* To answer this question, we interviewed ten teachers who attended a university-level program on programming and programming education. Interviews were conducted almost one year after the completion of the course.

2 Case and Method

Case Description. Our study is connected to the in-service teacher training program at our university. The program consists of two courses of 7,5 ECTS each, the first with a focus on basic programming and the second on teaching programming. In the first course, teachers get an introduction to Python. The second course is more flexible, and teachers can select programming languages and topics on which to specialize based on their interests and needs [7]. Though there are no requirements for teachers to follow both of the courses, most do. The study program is aimed at in-service teachers in grades 8–13 (Lower and Upper Secondary School). The program is an online study, with web-based lectures and weekly activities such as online lectures and regular compulsory work exercises. Students participate in the course with the support of their school, which is committing to provide some free time to teachers to complete the course, though they continue their primary duties during the two semesters. The additional costs for the schools are partly covered by a national program of the Ministry of Education. This support leads to a very high completion rate. A survey distributed at the end of the program indicates high levels of satisfaction with the course. With this follow up study, we investigate how the training has contributed to teachers' self-efficacy and the long-term impact of the educational program.

Overall Method. This study is based on interviews with teachers that participated in the continuing education program in 2018-19. The study uses semi-structured interviews to explore the research questions by capturing teachers' reflections on their self-efficacy towards teaching programming.

Interview Guide. The interview guide was constructed based on three main elements: (a) Attitudes towards programming in school; (b) Self-efficacy in teaching programming; (c) Self-efficacy in programming. Since we are interested in understanding the impact of the program, for each element, we added questions connected to the perceived impact of the program and changes since its completion.

For Attitude (a), we asked teachers their opinion about the ongoing introduction of programming in different subjects and, specifically, in the subjects that they teach. The questions related to Self-Efficacy in Programming (b) are inspired by the Teachers' Sense of Efficacy Scale (TSES) [8], with a focus on Efficacy for instructional strategies. Concerning teachers' programming skills (c), which is also relevant to teachers' ability to teach programming [9], questions were created to investigate how the teachers feel towards their own programming skills.

The questions were tested through test-interviews with three pre-service math teachers. The interviews were conducted during the COVID-19 pandemic. Schools were closed, with all the teaching taking place online and some elective subjects being postponed. We, therefore, added a final question on COVID-19. Our goal with this question was not to investigate its broader impact, but simply to check the validity of our study.

Participants. An invitation letter was sent to all the participants of the 2018/2019 cohort. An interview was then planned with the ones who expressed interest in participating in the study. Table 1 provides an overview of the participants.

Table 1. Overview of interviewees with Gender (M/F), school level (Upper Secondary School, USS, or Lower Secondary School, LSS), Subjects they are teaching (in italics the ones where they are *not* expected to use programming); Type of school (General, G, or Vocational, V)

ID	G	Level	Subject(s)	Type
1	F	USS	Economics	V
2	M	USS	Math, physics	G
3	F	USS	Math, natural science	V
4	M	LSS	Math, natural science, programming	G
5	F	LSS	*English, social studies, gymnastics*, programming	G
6	M	USS	Math, physics	G
7	F	USS	Math, *computer and electronics*	V
8	F	LSS	Math, natural science, *religion*, programming, *work-related training*	G
9	F	USS	*Physics*, math, programming, natural science, *technology and research*	G
10	F	USS	Construction - and control technique	V

Interviews were conducted via Zoom, using the service offered internally by our university for GDPR-compliance. The interviews were recorded with an external recorder and then transcribed by the interviewer. The relevant national agency approved the research. All the participants have been informed about the study, their rights and have been explicitly given their consent.

Analysis. After the transcription of the interviews, a thematic analysis [10] was performed by one of the authors using themes connected to the Teachers' Sense of Efficacy scale. The coding process was done with NVivo (QSR International, 2018). The final categories are: Attitudes towards programming in school; Teaching programming self-efficacy; Programming skill; Impact of programming education; Impact of time after programming education; COVID-19.

3 Results

3.1 Attitudes Towards Programming in School

The interviewees are generally positive towards teaching programming in school. They also express that they are positive towards using programming in an interdisciplinary context and underline the relevance for future jobs.

However, they also expressed some concerns that the inclusion of programming will be a long process, without a quick fix, especially considering the number of teachers who do not have any competence or education in programming. One of the issues that emerged from the analysis is the importance of teachers' community and collaboration. Four of the teachers expressed that they found collaboration with colleagues important when dealing with programming in school. Those who had someone to collaborate with reported that it was beneficial. Some other teachers indicated that they do not have colleagues to work within programming and that they would like to have that. Also, some teachers reported to have colleagues who are rather hostile to programming in school:

> *... Colleagues? They can be absolutely cruel! ... I heard the lecturers talk about programming in school as the future... You know, I was standing talking to one of my younger colleagues in the hallway in front of the coffee machine, and a colleague came past me, jumping out of the neighboring room and scolding me! So, it's like that, and it shouldn't even be mentioned at work.... (Teacher 3-Female-Math-USS)*

Some teachers also talked about gender differences related to programming. Particularly worrying is the resistance of gender stereotypes. One male teacher expressed that male teachers were more interested in programming than female teachers. One female teacher experienced that male teachers got much of the responsibility of programming related tasks in school, even if she is the only teacher with programming education:

> *...But I notice at work, that when being a woman – "no, you have almost no clue," they put the men to take those jobs.... (Teacher 3-Female-Math-USS)*

3.2 Teaching Programming and Self-efficacy

In general, all ten teachers responded that they could teach programming, even if this is mostly connected to a specific subject or school level, for example:

> *...I can't teach block programming, I can't make a lesson in game programming, I can't make a lesson in micro:bit ... But I think I can make good lessons and exercises that are relevant to my subjects, such as solving differential equations, solving equations with numerical methods, etc..... (Teacher 2-Male-Math-USS)*

Adapted Teaching. All of the teachers expressed that they could provide suitable challenges to capable pupils in programming, for example:

… I am very focused on giving open assignments because I have pupils on the whole scale … I really feel that with open assignments, I can differentiate to different levels, yes. (Teacher 7-Female-Math-HS)

Some teachers explained that even though some pupils might be better than them in programming, this is not a major challenge. Teachers could usually find suitable assignments together with the pupils, or the capable pupils could get appropriate challenges through open tasks or freely choosing what they work with. In a recent study [11], US K-12 computer science teachers reported that it was challenging to meet all pupils' needs on an individual level. However, in our study, only one of the teachers indicated a lower sense of self-efficacy in adapting her teaching to her pupils. Despite this, she still felt that she could provide appropriate challenges for highly skilled pupils by giving them freedom in what they were doing.

Assessment. The data analysis reveals that the teachers had a more varied sense of self-efficacy when it comes to assessment in programming. Four of the teachers expressed that they find assessment in programming difficult, for example because it is easy to find solutions online for the pupils and that they need strategies and tools for assessment. As a teacher explains:

…I think I need a strategy or tools for this. I think it is difficult. It's a little bit like putting your finger in the air when you think about the assessment of the pupils. I've had some assignments where they have to program something, and it's hard to know if they have copied the solution or whether it is their own, one must actually observe the whole process, and that is simply incredibly difficult…. (Teacher 4-Male-Math-SS)

Other teachers, however, are confident that they can assess their pupils, and some suggested oral presentations as a useful method, also to unveil whether the pupils understand their solutions or if they have copied it. One of the teachers that finds assessment challenging feels that it was little focus on this in the program.

Motivation. In general, the teachers seemed to have a relatively high sense of self-efficacy in motivating their pupils in programming. Nine of the teachers expressed that they felt they could motivate their pupils to learn to program. Some also thought that it was easier to motivate than in other subjects. For example:

…Yes. … they [pupils] get to try something new. And those who have some prior knowledge get to do something they master. So yes, I think it is easier to motivate them in programming than in accounting, for example…(Teacher 1-Female-Economics-USS)

However, one of the teachers reported challenges with motivating students in elective courses:

… It's about how you meet the students. And in discussing with them, attempt to find angles of attack that motivate them. I feel that I manage that with some

pupils, but then there is a problem in that not all pupils in elective programming are necessarily motivated to learn to program. ... Some of the pupils are there just because they did not get into the elective they wanted... that's a challenge... (Teacher 4-Male-Math-SS)

Explaining and Conveying Programming Knowledge. Of the ten teachers, eight of them believe that, to some extent, they can explain programming concepts and come up with alternative explanations when pupils do not fully understand. Two of the teachers expressed that they could explain some programming concepts, but probably not all. Six of the teachers believed that they would not be able to answer difficult programming questions from the more capable pupils. The other four thought they could answer some difficult questions, but not all. However, nine of the teachers believed that they could either come back to the pupil with the answer later or find the answer together:

... the pupils are also quite understanding when you say, "I can't do this very well, but I find it very fun! And I want to show you, and then we can figure it out together". They understand that, kind of. (Teacher 1-Female-Economics-HS)

The teachers seemed to have a moderately high sense of self-efficacy in this theme, but the main challenge is that the teachers do not perceive their programming competence as very advanced.

Developing Teaching Material. Eight of the teachers expressed that they can create good lesson plans and exercises, though it might be time-consuming, and that it would be beneficial with more time for planning lessons. Two of the teachers stated that they could not create suitable lessons from scratch, but they could by adapting existing teaching resources:

... I'm probably more about finding and adapting than making them myself. I don't feel I have enough expertise for that.... (Teacher 5-Female-English-SS)

Most of the teachers state that they are using and finding teaching material online and adapt it to their classes. Four of the teachers expressed that they would like more relevant teaching material resources available. In general, the teachers indicated that they had a relatively high sense of self-efficacy in designing lessons in or with programming when there is relevant teaching material that they can adapt to their teaching. However, the willingness of experimenting with new lesson plans might be limited:

...I don't know if I'm going to make that much varied, and I'm not so secure in the coding that I just toss myself into it and just try everything possible, so I limit it to something that I see will work, or something I've experienced that worked earlier... (Teacher 9-Female- Math-HS)

Challenges in Teaching Programming. When the teachers were asked what they perceived as the biggest challenge in teaching programming, two themes were prominent: Pupils' digital competences and technical issues. Three of the teachers talked about pupils' computer skills as a challenge. For example:

... Several of them name their files "one" "two" "three" and such, they do not have any system. So it will be difficult when you need to help them find a structure in programming when they can't even structure other things, so I think that might be most challenging...(Teacher 1-Female-Economics-USS)

Three of the teachers also talked about technical challenges. One of the teachers answered that some computer programs are challenging to use and cause technical problems and that she would like more user-friendly programs. Two other teachers explained that there are many technical issues, for example:

...The biggest challenge is technical. For example, when we code in Python, there are a lot of libraries and stuff that one needs, and then the pupils may have different versions, and different modules and libraries, and nothing matches ... so we end up turning the computer off and on again, restarting, get frustrated because something that works, or code that works on one PC doesn't work on another PC. And that is by far the most frustrating, and what we spend the most time on - unnecessary time. Sometimes we also give up ... And there I have no competence to find out what the problem is.... (Teacher 9-Female- Math-USS)

3.3 Programming Skill

The teachers were asked how they perceive their own programming skills. Eight of the teachers expressed that their programming skills were sufficiently good for teaching in their subjects and grades. However, six of the teachers indicated that their programming skill was relatively low, as one teacher states:

...For example, it is when we have embarked on slightly larger projects, which I may not have complete control over the development in. But so far, I have not been on extremely thin ice, but I have felt that "oh, I have to go home and pick up the book and read some more" I have had some of those rounds with myself.... Teacher 5-Female-English-LSS)

In general, the answers indicate that the teachers did not have a very high sense of self-efficacy towards programming, but that this did not severely impact their self-efficacy towards teaching programming. It also seems that even when their programming skills are relatively low, teachers perceive that they can increase this skill. Three of the teachers explained that they would like to have more follow-up in term of exercises or a local programming group to get better at programming:

...Yes, that it becomes just like an anonymous alcoholics group, that you have a follow-up group, "anonymous coders" who need some follow-up. Get some challenges and keep up .... (Teacher 4-Male-Math-LSS)

Previous research suggests that it is essential for teachers of programming to attain skills in programming [9]. This is also found in this study. However, even when the teachers perceive their own programming skills as not very high, they still feel capable of teaching programming in their grades and subjects. Many of the teachers also report that they feel capable of increasing their programming skills on their own or with colleagues and that they will get better with experience. This result indicates high self-efficacy towards getting better in programming.

3.4 Impact of Programming Education on Self-efficacy in Teaching Programming

Six of the teachers expressed that they could not teach programming before the courses, but that they felt they were able to teach it in their subjects and grades after the program. This result indicates a very positive impact on the teacher's self- efficacy towards teaching programming. Three of the teachers felt they could have taught programming before the courses, but express that they felt more secure in their teaching afterward. One teacher thought that the first course had a negative impact on her ability to teach programming because of the demanding workload and difficult exercises made her more confused than competent. However, this improved during the second course. Five of the teachers also stated that programming education had a positive impact on their attitudes towards programming in school, especially in terms of why programming in school can be relevant and beneficial in other subjects.

Some of the teachers felt that the learning curve in the first course was very steep. That programming can be hard to learn is often reported in the literature, e.g., [12]. Most of the teachers still felt that they learned a lot from the first course, and most were happy with both the learning outcome and the workload in the second course. Two of the teachers, however, reported that they thought the introductory programming course was very good, while they felt the second course was either too easy or had little impact on their competence.

3.5 Impact of Time After Course

The interviews were conducted close to one year after the teachers finished their programming studies. Therefore, they were also asked how the time that had passed since the completion of the program had impacted on their teaching. Most teachers perceived their programming skills lowered over time, when not used actively:

> *…I don't have it as much in my fingers anymore, since I work less on it myself… I notice that programming is something I should keep a lot more maintained. It's like programming is a skill that you have to practice, to a much greater extent than math and physics, where you basically have it…. (Teacher 9-Female-Math-HS)*

At the same time, these teachers expressed that they could "refresh" their programming skills and knowledge with little trouble. Also, a lower self-efficacy towards programming does not seem to relate to lower self-efficacy for teaching it.

The teachers that have taught or used programming in their classes in the last year explained that they also feel more capable of teaching programming due to the experience, for example:

> *…I have used programming more in teaching this year than I did the year before. So I feel that I am more secure in the role, and promote it more, and want more people to use it…. (Teacher 7-Female-Math-USS)*

Only one of the teachers felt less competent in pedagogical aspects of programming because he has not been teaching programming in the last year, but he also states that it will come back when he starts planning for it:

> *…I feel less ready now because I haven't practiced it in a year. No, that's not entirely true, I'm lying, but if you had me sit down with an exam in coding now, I would have been better off a year ago than now. Pedagogically as well. But it will return when I start planning a bit again, and I've looked a bit on it, I've discussed a bit with some colleagues, and worked a little with coding …(Teacher 2-Male-Math-USS)*

Some of the teachers stated that they would have liked more follow up exercises or a community of teachers to help in maintaining programming skills after the courses. This suggestion can be seen in relation to the fact that many programming teachers work in schools without other teachers in their content area [11].

3.6 Impact of COVID-19

Five of the teachers stated that the COVID-19 situation might have impacted their answers. Interesting is, for example, that two of the teachers reported that they had found new teaching methods. For example, one stated:

> *…Maybe towards differentiation in that I discovered that TinkerCad had some functions similar to Scratch because I have never used TinkerCad before. I have been very focused on the pupils working with it physically, which we now could not … But when I used it now, I saw that it was easier to differentiate for the students because I could use block programming … So yeah, so that's how it probably affected because I've discovered new things during this period because I had to make way for another way of teaching… (Teacher 7-Female-Math-USS)*

One teacher reported that the answers might have been affected by insecurity about how to continue teaching programming in the current situation. Other teachers reported the lack of contact with colleagues and general concerns for the future, considering that many other teachers have not been able to follow planned training in the Spring. Interesting is also to see that the situation might have increased concerns about the general digital competence of other teachers:

> *…I am one of those who are positive towards programming. But of course, I see big challenges in including it in the subjects. Because now, when we are teaching through Teams, we have employees that struggle with technical stuff there, right. I don't think this will be done quickly…. (Teacher 8-Female-Math-LSS)*

4 Discussion and Implications

The results of our study indicate that the teachers perceive that the education that they received had a positive impact on their self-efficacy towards teaching programming. Some of the teachers report that the studies also had a positive effect on their attitudes towards programming. The teachers say that their self-efficacy in teaching programming increases with experience in teaching programming, and does not significantly decrease without experience over time. The teachers report that their programming skills lower over time when not used, but that they can quickly refresh their programming skills when needed. This can be seen as a positive trend in relation to other studies where teachers showed a low level of self-efficacy in teaching programming [4–6]. Based on the results from the interviews, we identify some issues that need attention when designing training for in-service programming teachers.

Profiling and Flexible Paths. The evaluation of the two courses is rather varied. For some, the first course was too demanding, for others appropriate. The same holds for the second course. Though there is a space for improvement of the actual course content, we think that these differences are strongly connected with the nature itself of the program. Participating teachers have different competence levels and different needs since they teach different subjects to different students. One could advocate for more specific courses, focusing on specific needs or requiring defined competencies for admittance. However, this is a model that is difficult to implement for economic reasons, and with pedagogical limitations, caging teachers in a specific subject and level. The alternative is then to create modular courses that support different learning trajectories, as in the program of our study [7]. However, this requires identifying ways of profiling participants and scaffolding their participation in the course.

Mini-courses/Continuous Education. One introductive course on programming and teaching is not enough to meet the challenges that teachers meet every day and to stay updated. Teacher training should be seen as a continuous process, with the possibility to follow up a more formal and structured training with shorter training activities in the form of, e.g., seminars and workshops on specific programming and pedagogical issues. This training requires a commitment from the providers of training to design their courses as a continuous process that looks at long term opportunities.

Importance to Promote Community. Collaboration among programming teachers is useful, both to increase and maintain programming skills and to share and discuss the teaching of programming. Some teachers also experience that their colleagues are negative towards programming in school. There is a need to develop and strengthen communities of practice in the domain of teaching programming. This can be done at different levels. Many countries have nation-wide communities to support programming teachers, as the CAS network in the UK [13]. These constitute an essential model, but it might be equally important to create a landscape of communities, locally at the teachers' school and around specific training courses. In this perspective, it is essential during a course to promote a sense of community among the teachers attending the courses and nurturing this community after the course is completed as a form of continuous education.

Re-use of Resources. In our study, most of the teachers expressed that they can develop and adapt varied teaching material in programming and seem to have a relatively high sense of self-efficacy towards developing and adapting teaching material. However, some express that it can be difficult to find the most suitable teaching resources in the abundance of teaching resources in programming found online. A similar result is also found in the interview study of US K-12 computer science teachers [11]. Some teachers express that they would like more teaching resources in programming, as also indicated by the teachers in the study reported in [14]. The results also suggest that the teachers have a relatively high sense of self-efficacy towards motivating their pupils in programming, but that it can be difficult to create exercises that engage the lesser capable pupils in programming, while also giving them a sense of mastery. This indicates the need to create resources that can be adapted at different levels and to different national contexts, considering both language and study plan. As part of the training, it is important to include information about available resources and how to adapt them.

Assessment. Our respondents identify assessment as challenging, mirroring other studies that pointed out the need for quality assessment tools in computer science and coding education [11]. Though we do not have conclusive evidence, it also seems that assessment in programming is a more significant challenge than the teachers without experience perceive. It is, therefore, important that any teacher training program explicitly addresses this issue and challenges teachers to address assessment as an integrated part of the definition of their lesson plan.

Programming Skills. The results in this study can help ease the minds of future programming teachers that are concerned about their programming skills. Many of the teachers in this study perceived their programming skill as relatively low, but also sufficient for their teaching of programming, and they had a relatively high sense of self-efficacy in teaching programming. In other words, teachers do not necessarily need to be expert programmers to feel capable of teaching programming to their pupils, and it seems possible to attain sufficient programming skills for teaching programming through continuing education in programming over two semesters.

5 Conclusions

In this paper, we presented the results from interviews conducted with ten teachers, one year after they completed formal university-level training in programming. The teachers express high self-efficacy about teaching programming, though some of them are reporting low skills in programming. The study shows that teachers perceive formal training at the university level as having a positive and long-lasting impact.

The interviewees differ in terms of subjects they teach and school type. Therefore, the study covers different perspectives. However, we are fully aware that they are all connected to the same course, and it might be difficult to generalize the results. More studies are necessary. Considering that this type of training requires a heavy investment, both at the individual and the school level, we claim it is crucial to investigate which types of training have the highest impact, not only in terms of acquired knowledge but also in terms of attitudes and self-efficacy. From our study, formal training at the university level seems a promising option.

Acknowledgments. We thank the teachers who participated in the interviews. The work is partly funded by Excited, The Norwegian Center for Excellent IT Education (https://www.ntnu.edu/excited).

References

1. The Committee on European Computing Education (CECE): Informatics Education in Europe: Are We All In The Same Boat? Association for Computing Machinery, New York (2017)
2. Bandura, A.: Self-efficacy: toward a unifying theory of behavioral change. Psychol. Rev. **84**, 191–215 (1977). https://doi.org/10.1037/0033-295X.84.2.191
3. Zee, M., Koomen, H.M.Y.: Teacher self-efficacy and its effects on classroom processes, student academic adjustment, and teacher well-being: a synthesis of 40 years of research. Rev. Educ. Res. **86**, 981–1015 (2016). https://doi.org/10.3102/0034654315626801
4. Hartell, E., Doyle, A., Gumaelius, L.: Teachers' attitudes towards teaching programming in Swedish Technology education. Presented at the PATT 37, Pupils Attitudes Towards Technology (2019)
5. Mannila, L., Nordén, L.-Å., Pears, A.: Digital competence, teacher self-efficacy and training needs. In: Proceedings of the 2018 ACM Conference on International Computing Education Research. pp. 78–85. Association for Computing Machinery, New York (2018). https://doi.org/10.1145/3230977.3230993
6. The Royal Society: After the reboot: computing education in UK schools. The Royal Society, November 2017
7. Rouhani, M., Divitini, M., Vujosevic, V., Stai, S., Olstad, H.A.: Design of a programming course for teachers supporting flexible learning trajectories. In: Proceedings of the 8th Computer Science Education Research Conference, pp. 33–38. Association for Computing Machinery, New York (2019). https://doi.org/10.1145/3375258.3375263
8. Tschannen-Moran, M., Hoy, A.W.: Teacher efficacy: capturing an elusive construct. Teach. Teach. Educ. **17**, 783–805 (2001). https://doi.org/10.1016/S0742-051X(01)00036-1
9. Korkmaz, O.: Prospective CITE teachers' self-efficacy perceptions on programming. Procedia Soc. Behav. Sci. **83**, 639–643 (2013). https://doi.org/10.1016/j.sbspro.2013.06.121
10. Braun, V., Clarke, V.: Using thematic analysis in psychology. Qual. Res. Psychol. **3**, 77–101 (2006). https://doi.org/10.1191/1478088706qp063oa
11. Yadav, A., Gretter, S., Hambrusch, S., Sands, P.: Expanding computer science education in schools: understanding teacher experiences and challenges. Comput. Sci. Educ. **26**, 235–254 (2016). https://doi.org/10.1080/08993408.2016.1257418
12. Guzdial, M.: Learner-Centered Design of Computing Education: Research on Computing for Everyone. Synthesis Lectures on Human-Centered Informatics, vol. 8, pp. 1–165 (2015). https://doi.org/10.2200/S00684ED1V01Y201511HCI033
13. Brown, N.C.C., Sentance, S., Crick, T., Humphreys, S.: Restart: the resurgence of computer science in UK schools. ACM Trans. Comput. Educ. **14**, 9:1–9:22 (2014). https://doi.org/10.1145/2602484
14. Kadirhan, Z., Gül, A., Battal, A.: Self-efficacy to teach coding in K-12 education. In: Hodges, C.B. (ed.) Self-Efficacy in Instructional Technology Contexts, pp. 205–226. Springer, Cham (2018). https://doi.org/10.1007/978-3-319-99858-9_12

Computational Thinking in Small Packages

Dennis Komm[1,2](✉), Ulrich Hauser[3], Bernhard Matter[1], Jacqueline Staub[1,2], and Nicole Trachsler[2]

[1] PH Graubünden, Chur, Switzerland
{dennis.komm,bernhard.matter,jacqueline.staub}@phgr.ch
[2] Department of Computer Science, ETH Zürich, Zürich, Switzerland
nicole.trachsler@inf.ethz.ch
[3] FH Graubünden, Chur, Switzerland
ulrich.hauser@fhgr.ch

Abstract. This article describes an approach to foster computational thinking in different school subjects. Our approach includes several teaching units (packages) that are self-contained and have been designed for university courses attended by prospective and graduate primary and secondary school teachers. Around 30 packages have been designed so far and together cover eight aspects of computational thinking in six different subjects. In this report, some examples are sketched out together with the experiences gathered.

Keywords: Computational thinking · K-12 · Primary school · Interdisciplinarity

1 Introduction

Computational thinking is regarded as one of the main contributions of informatics to general education. The term was introduced by Seymour Papert [10] and further popularized by, for instance, Jeanette Wing [11]. It is obvious that many aspects of computational thinking are not endemic to informatics, but can also be found in other disciplines. Computational thinking marks itself by the aim not just to solve a single instance of a problem, but to create a general strategy to solve *any* problem instance of the problem class at hand. The description of this general strategy in a formal language is called an *algorithm*. The design of an algorithm is a process which requires creativity, but its (automatic) execution requires no creativity at all.

While virtually all experts agree that computational thinking is important, there is no general formal definition. As a consequence, we focus on the following eight aspects as its core: *Abstraction*, *Algorithm Design*, *Evaluation*, *Generalization*, *Iterative Improvement*, *Information Representation*, *Precise Communication*, and *Problem Decomposition*. Five of these aspects have been inspired by

K. Kori and M. Laanpere (Eds.): ISSEP 2020, LNCS 12518, pp. 170–181, 2020.
https://doi.org/10.1007/978-3-030-63212-0_14

Selby and Woolard [15], three have been added to stress the aspect of interdisciplinarity in the context of this project.

This report describes an approach to foster computational thinking interdisciplinarily by creating small teaching units (referred to as *packages*) for lecturers of universities for teacher education. These units are intended to be used with students in their education towards being a primary or secondary school teacher. Our approach is in contrast to many other projects which mainly concentrate on the direct training of students. All packages will be published as a collection and made available to the public through an online platform.

Several related projects aim in the same direction and produce contents for fostering computational thinking in diverse contexts. Bebras tasks, for instance, offer learning opportunities in domains which, at first glance, often are not directly anchored in computer science [14]. However, these tasks typically aim at students aged 6 to 18. In contrast, our materials aim at lecturers rather than students. A second example can be found in CS Unplugged, which tackles central aspects of computational thinking in a diverse context, too [13]. While this project aims at making computer science "experienceable" mainly without computers, we want to show that computational thinking does not only exist in computer science but also in other disciplines. Whether or not a computer is used for this purpose is not relevant in our context.

In order to design the packages, we visited university courses for future teachers, and made ourselves familiar with the respective curricula. Then, together with the lecturers, packages have been designed (and are still designed as this report is written) in order to build a bridge between the respective subject and computational thinking. After that, these packages have been tested as part of workshops.

The main part of this report brings forward examples of designed packages and describes our experiences during workshops. The ultimate goal is to have the packages implemented as parts of the courses of teacher education, and thus sensitize (future) teachers about the matter.

2 Project Context

According to the Swiss curriculum *"Lehrplan 21,"* all fifth and sixth graders who live in one of the 21 German-speaking cantons enjoy one hour per week that is partly dedicated to informatics. This somewhat scarce endowment for computer science as a separate subject fortunately is connected to a requirement that the corresponding competencies are also to be promoted in an interdisciplinary way. Concretely, computational thinking should be promoted not only in computer science but in all subjects. Furthermore, the interdisciplinary embedding of computational thinking starts considerably earlier, namely from Kindergarten age onwards.

Our project *Computational Thinking in Primary School* is a collaboration of two Swiss universities: (i) PHGR, a university of teacher education and (ii) FHGR, a university of applied sciences. The goal of this collaboration is to spread computational thinking to various courses taught at PHGR. The main target are primary school teachers, but some secondary school topics are covered as well.

The work presented in this article is part of an even larger collaboration project with multiple Swiss universities. The overall goal is to strengthen STEM subjects in Swiss education [8]. Our work is only one of two projects at PHGR that involve teaching informatics interdisciplinarily; the other project focuses on specific informatics competencies that are defined within the "Lehrplan 21" curriculum, having students in the vocational semester as target group [7].

PHGR contains the six departments *Design*, *Language*, *Mathematics*, *Music-Rhythm-Theater*, *Nature-Human-Society*, and *Sports*, which are responsible for teacher education with regard to the respective subjects. For each of them, different packages have been created as part of the project. While there are obvious connections between, say, mathematics and computational thinking, quite surprising links to other subjects have been discovered as well.

It needs to be noted that the project is currently work in progress. In particular, the findings have not yet been completely evaluated, which is why our experiences are mostly anecdotal. Moreover, much of the content presented is not entirely new, but the algorithmic aspects needed to be made more visible, which lead to an *algorithmic enhancement* of a given topic taught in a given subject. In many cases, computational thinking made objects that were studied theoretically more tangible by actively *constructing* them (for instance, geometric objects).

3 Example Packages

All packages are documented in written form, specifying which subjects they can be used for, and which of the above aspects of computational thinking they cover. Furthermore, we supply an estimate of how much time is needed to implement the package.

The packages are primarily designed for lecturers teaching at universities of teacher education. The underlying idea is that some lecturers will integrate packages into their courses, which allows future teachers to cover computational thinking later as part of their respective teaching at school.

Each package starts with an introduction for the lecturer, describing the main topic and how computational thinking is applied. The main part is then usually an example session that exemplifies how the topic can be introduced to university students. For each exercise, there is a solution at the end of the material, and all exercises slowly increase in complexity. A package always concludes with didactic remarks, possibilities for advanced exercises, and a thorough explanation of what different aspects of computational thinking are covered, and why.

Language

We designed several packages that deal with formal languages, for instance, using simplified *finite automata* or *context-free grammars* in order to describe simple words or sentences with some specific structure in a playful way. Another package deals with *Braille encodings* of words.

Fig. 1. An example construction as used in the package aiming to train precise communication. It counts seven bricks, none of which are identical.

Here, we want to use yet another package as an example of how to train a very important aspect of algorithm design – *exhaustive and unambiguous communication*. We have tested the package several times as part of a workshop, which is why subsequently we will be speaking of "the participants." The participants are given a small construction, say, a *tower*, built of some brick system, for instance, Lego Duplo. There should not be more than a maximum of seven bricks used, and those bricks should at least partly be distinguishable by, for instance, their color or size. Figure 1 shows an example of such a construction.

The participants now work in groups of two. Each participant is presented with a construction and the task to give a precise written description of it within ten minutes – it is not allowed to use any kind of drawing, only language. The two members of a team prepare their respective description such that they cannot see the other construction. A photograph of the construction is taken and then it is disassembled. The two members of a group now try to use their peer's description in order to recreate the exact same construction within five minutes. An evaluation of how well the reconstruction went, followed by a reflection and discussion, concludes the workshop.

Our experience shows that workshop participants perceive the package very positively. It is not surprising, however, that a large fraction does not succeed to rebuild the construction – despite of initial enthusiasm as they are only "playing with toys for children." We have often observed that only while writing down the description, one starts to realize how imprecise and ambiguous everyday language is. Simply stating "place the big blue brick on the small red one" usually does not work.

Precise Communication is the central aspect of this package, while the description of how to rebuild the tower is ideally at least close to an algorithm, that is, it can be carried out without interpretation and only following the given steps systematically.

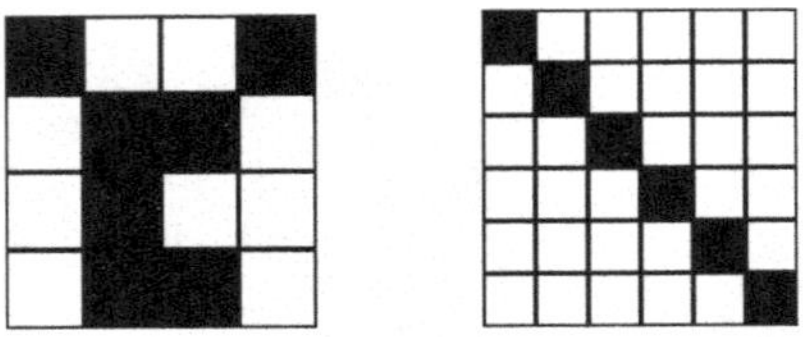

(a) (b)

Fig. 2. Two black and white pixel graphics.

Design

For a package that can be applied within *Design* classes, we decided for the topic of pixel graphics. We only give a short summary. The participants are presented the idea of representing a black and white picture as a string of Bs and Ws (representing black and white pixels, respectively). For instance, the picture in Fig. 2a can be encoded as the string $BWWBWBBWWBWWWBBW$.

After some conversions back and forth between a given image and the respective encoding, the participants face the question of how such pixel graphics can be compressed. As an example, in the picture shown in Fig. 2b, there are large sequences of white pixels. The obvious way of encoding this figure as

$$BWWWWWWBWWWWWWBWWWWWWBWWWWWWBWWWWWWB$$

can be shortened quite straightforwardly by writing

$$1B6W1B6W1B6W1B6W1B6W1B$$

instead, where a number indicates that the following letter should be repeated the respective number of times. An even better compression using parentheses would result in

$$1B5(6W1B).$$

Another topic deals with *palindroms* in pixel graphics (the same topic may be revisited when speaking about context-free grammars). Graphics which encode palindromes possess central symmetries, which are explored by the participants.

The major aspect covered in this package is *Information Representation*, in particular, how to present information efficiently.

Mathematics

The overlap between mathematics and informatics is large [2–4], and many of the aspects that make up computational thinking are just part of *systematic problem solving*, which is at the core of mathematics.

Some members of the project team are active in teaching with turtle graphics, for instance, using dedicated Logo or Python environments [5,6,17–19]. Although the majority of our packages follows an *unplugged* approach, we additionally designed some packages that make use of Logo.

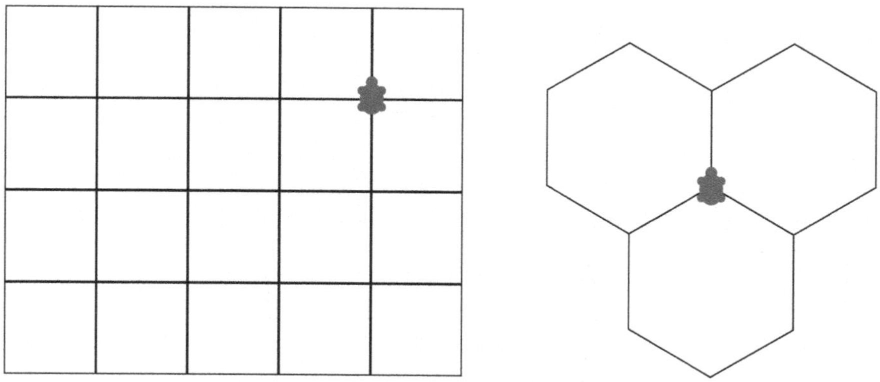

(a) Placing 20 squares. (b) Placing three hexagons.

Fig. 3. Filling the plane with squares and hexagons with Logo. The green Turtle marks the turtle's final position. (Color figure online)

Using the turtle, some topics of geometry can be made more tangible than when just using pen and paper. More specifically, we decided for an advanced topic, namely filling the Euclidean plane with (identical) regular polygons. It is well known that this is only possible with equilateral triangles, squares, and hexagons. Constructing regular polygons with the turtle means to perceive them somewhat locally, not with global coordinates, but with reasoning about how (that is, at what angles) the different lines should be connected.

For this package, we assume that the students and lecturers have some basic knowledge about Logo. Recall that there are four essential commands that let the programmer navigate the turtle over the screen – `fd` x moves the turtle x pixels in the direction it currently looks, `bk` x moves the turtle x pixels in the opposite direction. The turtle rotates by a degrees to the left with `lt` a and to the right using `rt` a. As advanced concepts, we assume that the students are familiar with simple `repeat`-loops and defining programs with parameters. For the details of Logo, we refer to the literature [1,12].

The first task is to fill the screen with squares such that no two squares overlap and no gaps exist between them as in Fig. 3a. Then the notion of a square can be generalized to that of an n-gon. The important thing is that the rotation angle $360/n$ of the turtle is elaborated together with the students. They discover that the internal angels of a given n-gon always equal $180–360/n$. This insight comes in particularly handy when filling the plane with hexagons (which have internal angles of 120 degrees); placing three hexagons such that there is no gap in between and they do not overlap is shown in Fig. 3b. Clearly, the single point where all of them overlap (and where the turtle is placed in the figure) induces an angle of 360 degrees and therefore no gap appears. Advanced exercises ask about filling the plane with triangles where the internal angles can also be deduced easily from the turtle's movements. Trying to fill the plane with

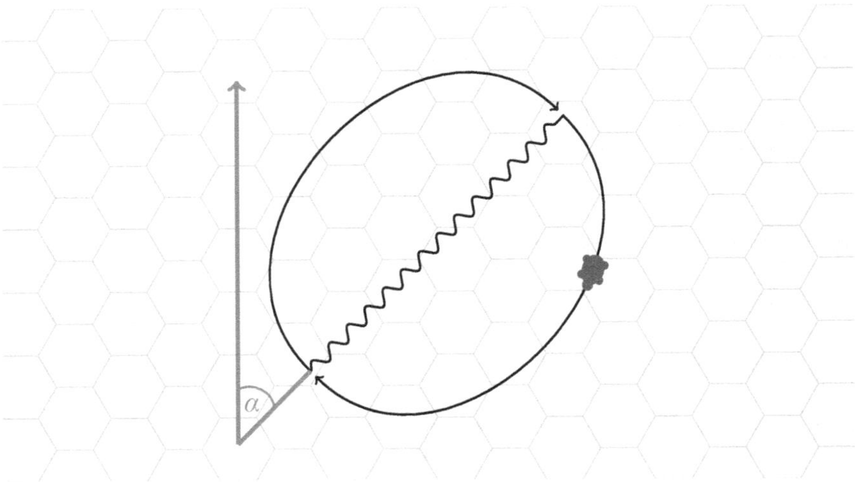

Fig. 4. The turtle dancing the bee's waggle dance.

pentagons or any regular polygons with more than six edges, the participants realize, is doomed to fail.

A major aspect that is used to develop the algorithms is *Problem Decomposition*; for instance, first strategies to draw squares are designed, which are then combined to draw rows of squares etc. In this package, programming with turtle graphics is used to dig deep into regular polygons and constructing them in order to understand why most of them cannot be used to fill the plane. Filling the plane with hexagons lends itself for an excellent transition to the next subsection.

Nature-Human-Society

As the name indicates, many different topics are part of the subject Nature-Human-Society. We use the *Nature* part to demonstrate that algorithms are indeed omnipresent, independent of programming languages, and not per se human-made. As an example, we take the honey bee's *waggle dance* [9], which we mimic with Papert's turtle.

The dance is used by bees to communicate the position of nutritional sources – we consider a simplified version that captures the basic idea. There are essentially two parameters that need to be communicated in order to locate the food source, namely the direction and the distance to the food. The former is specified by the angle α between the sun and the source; the bee positions itself such that it is rotated by α degrees with respect to the vertical axis on the honeycomb – which means that the bees mastered the abstraction of the "global direction towards the sun" to the "local vertical direction on the comb." The waggle dance is composed of three parts. In the middle part, the bee runs from a point x to a point y while describing a wavy line; then it describes a semicircle and returns back to x. The distance d to the source is communicated by how long the bee takes to perform the middle part of the dance, that is, the wavy line – the longer it takes, the further away the food source. After returning to x, it repeats the procedure, alternatingly describing a semicircle to the left or to the right.

To implement the algorithm, we again assume a basic knowledge about Logo as in the previous subsection. The idea behind the algorithm is shown in Fig. 4. It is important to understand that the waggle dance can indeed be regarded as an algorithm. The input consists of two parameters, namely the angle α and the distance d, and the execution is the movement of the bee (turtle) depending on these parameters.

The major aspect of this package is of course *Algorithm Design*, but due to the modular design of the resulting algorithm (as in the previous subsection), also *Problem Decomposition* plays an important role.

Music-Rhythm-Theater

For the above examples of *Mathematics* and *Nature-Human-Society*, we showed how to use turtle graphics to both revisit important programming concepts and at the same time study topics rooted in the respective subjects.

Conversely, after visiting a lesson on *Rhythm*, the project team found a somewhat unexpected link to turtle graphics as the students were asked to move according to a specific rule system. Inspired by this, we designed a package, which we again tried out with some of the lecturers at PHGR as part of a workshop. The tasks are carried out in teams of two where one person acts as a robot (just like the turtle) and one person acts as a programmer. The following rules need to be followed.

- The robot moves straight ahead one step at a time.
- The robot always starts its path with the right foot.
- If the programmer *claps*, the robot immediately rotates by 90 degrees and then makes the step into the new direction. Depending on which leg is on the move, the robot either turns to the left or to the right; the rotation is always into the direction of that leg.

As an example, consider Fig. 5, where the orange tones denote positions at which the programmer claps – actually, she should clap some short time before, just after the respective foot has been lifted. The robot starts with its right foot and makes a step. Then it lifts its left foot and the programmer claps, which results in a 90-degree turn to the left and then making the step. Next, the right foot is lifted again, and so on. In Fig. 6a, we have sketched the result on checkered paper. We say the corresponding pattern is "clappable" by the programmer.

Fig. 5. An example of clapping to specific tones.

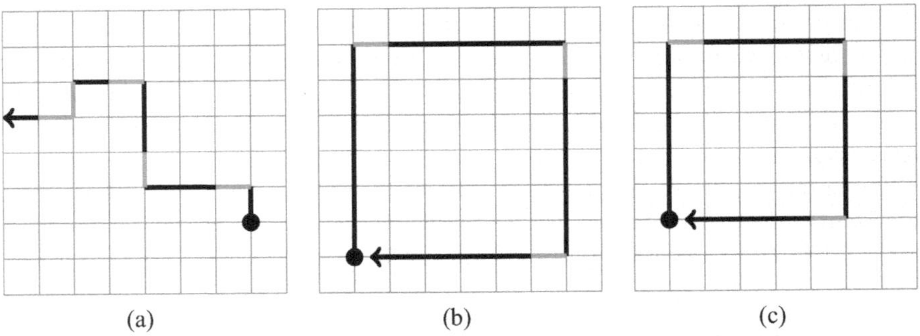

Fig. 6. Three patterns, two of which are possible results of robot walks. The dot marks the starting position, and the robot starts with lifting its right foot. Figure (a) corresponds to Fig. 5; (b) can be clapped, while (c) cannot.

There are then some exercises about clapping certain patterns. In particular, the above rule system is quite restrictive, because the feet are lifted alternatingly, and the rotation direction is determined by the foot that is currently not touching the ground. This makes some patterns impossible to be clapped; for instance, the square in Fig. 6b can be clapped, because it corresponds to a square with even side length; Fig. 6c cannot be clapped, because the side length is odd. There are similar observations to be made about other patterns that allow to systematically explore the rule system under consideration.

A central aspect of computational thinking, which is covered here, is *Evaluation.* A given rule system may be too restrictive for certain tasks, but powerful enough for others.

Sports

Official rules in sports are mostly given as written text, often supported by sketches or photographs. A good example is given by the international volleyball rules[16] covering about 90 pages of text. In this package, an alternative way of displaying or even defining rules in sports is introduced, using *state diagrams* like the one in Fig. 7 to describe the states of a game and transitions between them.

Each game corresponds to a specific sequence of states, each of which is represented by an ellipse. The system can stay in such a state for any time. The arcs leaving and entering the states each represent a state transition from one state to the next which we assume to happen instantly. In Fig. 7, the transitions

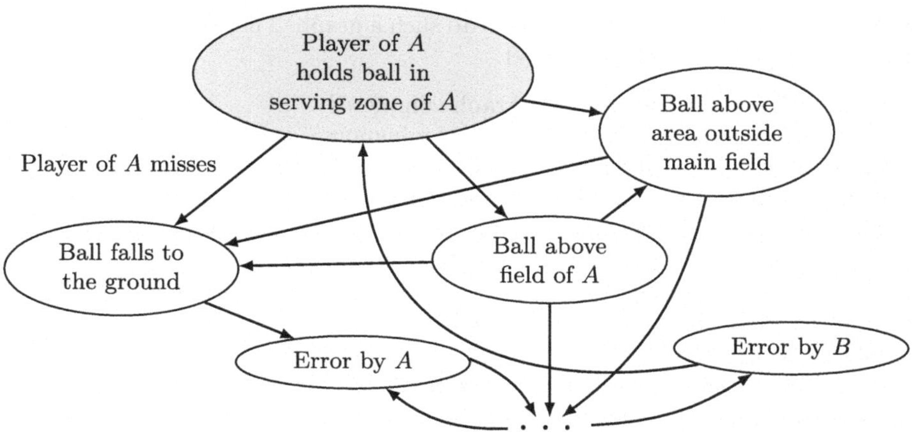

Fig. 7. An example graph depicting states and transitions emerging at the beginning of a volleyball move.

are not labeled with text to increase readability; an exception is the arc labeled "*Player of A misses.*"

The initial state corresponds to a serving situation, when a player of team A holds the ball to perform the service. The corresponding ellipse has a light gray background. The player may miss the ball. The ball then will fall to the ground, represented by a state on the left side of the graph. When the ball touches the ground, this event leads to team A being given an error situation, again indicated by a state.

The usual scenario of a service is described in the center of the graph. The serving player of team A hits the ball. Following this event, the ball will soar across the area of team A, over the net into the area of team B. Subsequently, a normal move, first under the control of team B, continues.

Only the first transitions of a move are given in the graph, hiding the remainder in the "... " part. In case of the service, this is the part up to the ball crossing over the field of team A.

While playing, the students are requested to follow the sequence of states and think about questions such as the following:

- What possible events might happen next?
- Which events will lead to our team getting a point just now?
- Which events will lead to the opposing team getting a point just now?
- What are the individual consequences of the events I found?
- How could the states be named according to the consequences of the events?

The questions and events given above are exemplary and do not specify a real time instant during a game. The outcome of the student's analysis is transformed into a graph like the one given in Fig. 7.

It can be seen that such a graph develops a remarkable degree of complexity quite quickly, which may oppose people to this way of depicting sports rules.

It needs some scrutiny to set up or to read such a graph. Therefore, an evaluation of the developed graph is performed.

- Is the information given by the graph complete?
- Is the information given by the graph ambiguous?
- Can this graph be understood by a computer? (All state diagrams can be transformed into executable code automatically.)
- The rules for volleyball cover many pages of text. May this text be transformed completely into a number of diagrams?
- May the resulting diagrams be more concise than the written rules?
- May the graph be – once one is used to reading it – be superior to written rules in some ways?
- If the graph and the written rules are both describing the rules exhaustingly and unambiguously, may they be exchangeable as equivalent?
- Is it possible to test the written rules for ambiguity? How does the graph compare here?
- If the two representations of rules are equivalent and a graph can be converted into code (which then essentially is an algorithm), is the written version of the rules an algorithm as well?

By answering the above questions, the students will be guided towards the conclusion that the graph is a representation of an algorithm. Algorithms or their representation can be found in many places, even unexpected ones. A recipe for cooking a meal (for an arbitrary number of people), advice on how to tend a garden (of arbitrary size), the well-planned execution of a series of (arbitrarily scalable) experiments – all are instances of algorithms.

The representation shown here as a graph normally can be tested more easily for exhaustion and ambiguities than the associated set of written rules. This is quite obvious if one puts oneself in the position of a state and imagines all possible events and their consequences, forking from one state to a whole set of possible following states. This is extremely difficult to represent in a linear text.

This last package is based on the concepts of *Information Representation* and *Algorithm Design*.

4 Conclusion

We introduced an approach of implementing computational thinking in subjects other than computer science. As mentioned before, much of the work is about sensitizing lecturers and teachers, as many of the aspects that make up computational thinking are already present implicitly. Most of the time, what we newly introduced was the explicit design of an algorithm rather than teaching problem solving skills in order to solve concrete problem instances. This results in our packages being not too invasive, which is why we hope to have them applied by a larger number of lecturers and consequently motivate (future) teachers to integrate computational thinking in their own teaching at school.

It should be noted that, while we received very positive feedback so far, only a test of time will tell whether the project was really successful.

References

1. Gebauer, H., Hromkovič, J., Keller, L., Kosírová, I., Serafini, G., Steffen, B.: Programming in LOGO. http://abz.inf.ethz.ch. Accessed 20 Oct 2020
2. Hauser, U., Komm, D.: Interdisciplinary education in mathematics and informatics at Swiss high schools. Bull. EATCS (126) (2018). The Education Column
3. Hauser, U., Komm, D., Serafini, G.: Wie Mathematik und Informatik voneinander profitieren können - Teil 1: Abstraktionsfähigkeit. Informatik Spektrum **42**(2), 118–123 (2019)
4. Hauser, U., Komm, D., Serafini, G.: Wie Mathematik und Informatik voneinander profitieren können - Teil 2: Variation der Problemstellung und Modularisierung. Informatik Spektrum **42**(2), 124–129 (2019)
5. Hromkovič, J., Kohn, T., Komm, D., Serafini, G.: Combining the power of Python with the simplicity of logo for a sustainable computer science education. In: Brodnik, A., Tort, F. (eds.) ISSEP 2016. LNCS, vol. 9973, pp. 155–166. Springer, Cham (2016). https://doi.org/10.1007/978-3-319-46747-4_13
6. Kohn, T., Komm, D.: Teaching programming and algorithmic complexity with tangible machines. In: Pozdniakov, S.N., Dagienė, V. (eds.) ISSEP 2018. LNCS, vol. 11169, pp. 68–83. Springer, Cham (2018). https://doi.org/10.1007/978-3-030-02750-6_6
7. Komm, D., Matter, B.: Informatics in Swiss primary schools - a case for interdisciplinarity. Bull. EATCS (130) (2020). The Education Column
8. Nationales Netzwerk MINT-Bildung. https://www.fhnw.ch/de/die-fhnw/hochschulen/ht/mint-bildung. Accessed 20 Oct 2020
9. Waggle Dance. https://en.wikipedia.org/wiki/Waggle_dance. Accessed 20 Oct 2020
10. Papert, S.: Mindstorms. Basic Books, 2nd edn. (1993)
11. Wing, J.M.: Computational thinking. Commun. ACM **49**(3), 33 (2006)
12. XLogo Online. https://xlogo.inf.ethz.ch. Accessed 20 Oct 2020
13. Bell, T., Lodi, M.: Constructing computational thinking without using computers. Constructivist Found. **14**(3), 342–351 (2019)
14. Dagienė, V., Sentance, S., Stupurienė, G.: Developing a two-dimensional categorization system for educational tasks in informatics. Informatica **28**(1), 23–44 (2017)
15. Selby, C., Woollard, J.: Computational thinking: the developing definition. University of Southampton (E-prints) (2013)
16. Official Volleyball Rules. http://www.fivb.org/EN/Refereeing-Rules/documents/FIVB-Volleyball_Rules_2017-2020-EN-v06.pdf. Accessed 20 Oct 2020
17. Staub, J., Barnett, M., Trachsler, N.: Programmierunterricht von Kindergarten bis zur Matura in einem Spiralcurriculum. Informatik Spektrum **42**(2), 102–111 (2019). https://doi.org/10.1007/s00287-019-01161-6
18. Hromkovič, J., Serafini, G., Staub, J.: XLogoOnline: a single-page, browser-based programming environment for schools aiming at reducing cognitive load on pupils. In: Dagiene, V., Hellas, A. (eds.) ISSEP 2017. LNCS, vol. 10696, pp. 219–231. Springer, Cham (2017). https://doi.org/10.1007/978-3-319-71483-7_18
19. Trachsler, N.: WebTigerJython - a browser-based programming IDE for education. Master's thesis, ETH Zurich (2018)

Curriculum and Pedagogical Issues

Identification of Dependencies Between Learning Outcomes in Computing Science Curricula for Primary and Secondary Education – On the Way to Personalized Learning Paths

Yelyzaveta Chystopolova, Stefan Pasterk(✉), Andreas Bollin, and Max Kesselbacher

University of Klagenfurt, 9020 Klagenfurt, Austria
{Yelyzaveta.Chystopolova,Stefan.Pasterk,Andreas.Bollin, Max.Kesselbacher}@aau.at
https://www.aau.at/en/informatics-didactics

Abstract. The multitude of curricula and competency models poses great challenges for primary and secondary teachers due to the wealth of descriptions. Defining optimal (or personalized) learning paths is thus impeded. This paper now takes a closer look at 7 curricula from 6 different countries and presents an approach for the identification of learning outcomes and dependencies (requires and expands) between them in order to support the identification of learning paths. The approach includes different strategies from natural language processing, but it also makes use of a refined and simplified version of Bloom's Taxonomy to identify dependencies between the learning outcomes. It is shown that the identification of similar learning outcomes works very well compared to expert opinions. The identification of dependencies, however, only works well for detecting learning outcomes that refine other learning outcomes (expands dependency). The detection of learning outcomes which build on each other (requires dependency) is, on the other hand, still heavily dependent on the definition of dictionaries and a computing science topics ontology.

Keywords: Primary and secondary education · Learning outcomes · Computing science · Natural language processing

1 Introduction

Every year the field of Computer Science becomes a bigger part of everyday life not only of scientists but also of all the people. Schools pay more attention to teaching the basics of Computer Science starting already from primary school. However, teachers often face the problem of choosing the optimal learning path, which will be the most suitable for every exact group of students. There are lots

K. Kori and M. Laanpere (Eds.): ISSEP 2020, LNCS 12518, pp. 185–196, 2020.
https://doi.org/10.1007/978-3-030-63212-0_15

of curricula, which describe different standards, and different options of achieving a certain learning goal. In some aspects they differ, but also similarities can be found. Using the collected knowledge from some of them can help to improve the level of Computer Science education in general and be more flexible to the current needs of students as well as to new improvements in the field. Merging of Computer Science curricula rises the question: "How to represent the collected knowledge from several curricula?".

Pasterk and Bollin present a graph-based approach for analysis of Computer Science curricula, where they map the Learning Outcomes (LO) to a graph by connecting them via dependency relations which can be of two types "EXPANDS" and "REQUIRES" [10]. Relation type "EXPANDS" shows that 2 LO share same main topic extending each other, while the relation of the type "REQUIRES" assume that in the pair of 2 LO (LO1 and LO2), LO1 cannot be reached without LO2 and at the same time they do not form a pair, with the relation type "EXPANDS" [9]. Showing a wide range of new possibilities, this model requires considerable effort for dependencies identification between LO.

To identify all the dependencies, the experts need to work with curricula, which are presented in PDF files. Some of them store LO in the form of a table, however, in most cases, they are presented as lists or plain text. Even looking for dependencies inside one curriculum, the experts need to keep in mind dozens of LO. Adding new curricula makes the situation even more complicated. Besides the identification of dependencies inside one curriculum, the experts need to find relations between LO from different curricula. Thus the number of LO to work with rapidly increases to hundreds, which makes the task too complicated for human experts.

The goal of this paper is to describe a semiautomatic approach for dependencies identification between LO among Computer Science curricula for primary and secondary education. We also describe a possibility to transfer the available curricula, which are stored in PDF files, to a directed graph, and also to simplify the addition of new LO in the future.

To introduce the approach, this paper gives answers to the following questions:

- To which extent is it possible to identify dependency relations of the type "EXPANDS" between learning outcomes?
- To which extent is it possible to identify dependency relations of the type "REQUIRES" between learning outcomes?
- To which extent is it possible to identify directions for dependencies between learning outcomes?
- How similar is the semiautomatic approach for dependencies identification to the experts' opinion?

In order to answer these questions we use seven curricula from six countries. This way, we have a diverse set of learning outcomes concentrating on the Primary and Secondary education.

This paper is structured as follows. After a motivation and an overview of related work in first two sections, two approaches for determination of dependencies of two types, together with the approach for direction determination are presented. Section 4 shows first results from the comparison of semi-automatic determination to the precision of experts. The paper concludes with the section for discussion and future work.

2 Related Work

With the rise of the research interest for computer science education, the amount of published literature also increases. More and more papers discuss the analysis of curricula content in different options (e.g. relevance of the topics [4]). Different approaches using graph representations of curricula for analysis and comparison can be found as well (see e.g. [7]). Pasterk and Bollin also propose to present curricula as graphs [10] which opens new opportunities for further analysis. LO in such graphs are presented as nodes, and dependencies as edges between these nodes. Dependent relations can be of two types: "EXPANDS" and "REQUIRES" [9]. Those mentioned approaches are based on expert opinions who add relations between courses, knowledge areas, or LO.

Sekiya, Matsuda, and Yamaguchi [13] use statistical methods from natural language processing (NLP) and text analysis to identify relations between topics and to generate maps of curricula. With the method called *latent Dirichlet allocation (LDA)* topics from curricula are extracted and their relations are calculated. The results from this process using *LDA* are interpreted as coordinates for the generation of maps of curricula. Similar techniques are used by Badawy, El-Aziz, and Hefny [2] to analyze textbooks for higher education based on included LO. They follow their aim to identify important chapters in these textbooks according to intended LO of a curriculum. The steps they take in their research are comparable to a standard process in NLP which includes *data preparation*, *synonym identification*, *data preprocessing*, and the analysis of LO based on *frequency of the occurring words* [2].

Pasterk, Kesselbacher, and Bollin present an approach to semi-automatically categorize LO into *computer science* or *digital literacy* which is also based on NLP [11]. Asking experts to also categorize the LO to produce a validation corpus, they found out that experts focus on keywords, especially on nouns, during categorization, and that the experts' opinions are often diverse. In the best cases the semi-automated system matched in 70% of the LO categorization with the data from the experts [11].

Based on the approach of Pasterk and Bollin [10] the present contribution describes different approaches to semi-automatically determine dependencies of different types between LO and the directions of the dependencies. These approaches are based on the textual analysis of the LO and NLP techniques, and are described in the following section.

3 Methodology

3.1 Background and Process Description

As already mentioned Pasterk and Bollin define the two types of dependencies "EXPANDS" and "REQUIRES" [10]. Each of these types needs its own approach for relation determination. Relations of the type "EXPANDS" connect learning outcomes on the same topic, those which share some similar context. As every learning outcome is presented by a short sentence, we can use sentence similarity measures [1].

In this paper we concentrate on Jaccard Similarity Coefficient. In its original version this measure compares the size of the intersection of the words occurring in two sentences (A, B) to its union (Eq. 1).

$$J(A, B) = \frac{|A \cap B|}{|A \cup B|} \quad (1)$$

Being rather simple, compared to other Natural Language Processing methods for similarity determination between sentences, the Jaccard Similarity Coefficient includes all the needed features for identifying relations of the type "EXPANDS". It is not only easy to implement but can also serve as a good basis for different modifications. Hamedani and Kim propose a few ways of using unweighted and weighted options for link-based similarity measure in graphs [12].

Identification of dependent relations of the type "REQUIRES" is a more complicated task. Pairs of learning outcomes, which have a connection of this type, can belong to different topics. They mostly do not share common lexis, thus similarity metrics are not suitable for their determination. Nevertheless, even without common lexis, they do have a connection, which can be found by human experts based on knowledge of the field.

Such a knowledge base can be created with the help of relation extraction (RE) technics which give a possibility not only to extract dependent pairs of keywords, but also some background knowledge [5]. It is obvious that for such knowledge extraction we need to have data, where dependencies between LO will be already defined. With such a goal a group of experts was working with 7 curricula from 6 countries to create a validation corpus (VC). As a result of their work, we got a document, which includes identified dependencies of two types ("EXPANDS" and "REQUIRES") including directions between LO withing one or several curricula.

Together with identifying pairs of dependent LO and type of relations, we need also to identify directions. It will be easy if we know the level of each LO in the pair. It is a well-known approach in the field of education to use Bloom's Taxonomy for such goals. A revised version of Bloom's Taxonomy [8] is popular nowadays, and for computer science a 2-dimensional version is suggested by Fuller et al. [3]. Both taxonomies are based on action verbs which are separated in levels. In the case of revised Bloom's taxonomy, there are 6 cognitive levels: remembering, understanding, applying, analyzing, evaluating, creating.

In the case of two-dimensional Bloom's Taxonomy, the same categories got transferred into two dimensions [3]: the ability to understand and interpret the existing product, and the ability to design and build a new product.

Even though Bloom's Taxonomy is very popular, Johnson and Fuller showed that it is not perfect for Computer Science education [6]. In the course of our study, we noticed that it includes only about 36% of action verbs, which we met in LO from Computer Science curricula for primary and secondary education. Nevertheless, Bloom's Taxonomy served as a ground base for our own approach for direction determination.

3.2 Preprocessing and Standardization

The task of dependencies identification is complex and requires a few preprocessing steps. Besides manual transferring of the curricula that were stored in PDF to CSV files, it includes cleaning and standardization. Firstly we remove all the irrelevant information, such as punctuation, stop words, and also irrelevant phrases such as text in brackets and the phrase "The students are able to..." (or its equivalents). This step finishes with lemmatization, which helps to present all the words in their base (dictionary) form.

Working with a variety of Curricula we found out that many concepts are presented by different synonyms and it influences the relation determination. Thus the Standardization step aims to reduce the number of diverse synonyms in learning outcomes saving the semantic context. As an example, we met four synonyms for the term **"algorithm"**: *"sequence of events"*, *"sequence of instructions"*, *"sequence of steps"*, and *"set of step-by-step instructions"*.

Figure 1 shows how a learning outcome changes during the preprocessing phase.

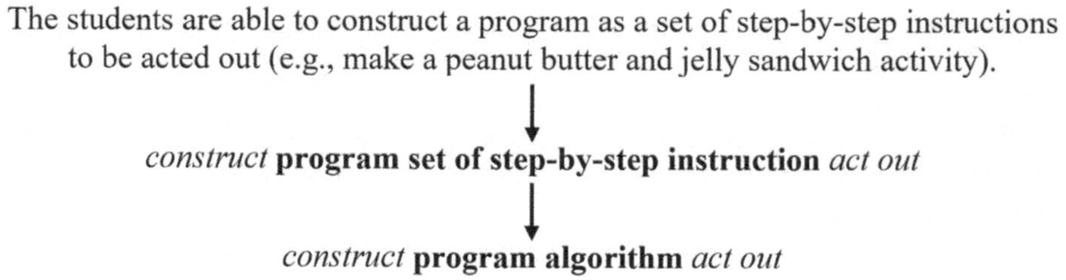

Fig. 1. Preprocessing of the learning outcome.

3.3 Weighted Jaccard Similarity

For relation identification of the type "EXPANDS" we use modified Jaccard Similarity Coefficient. The main difference compared to the original method is that words with different parts of speech have different levels of influence on the result.

If we take a deeper look on the pair of learning outcomes, which are connected, we will see that nouns play the most important role in similarity determination. They show the object (what exactly the student should learn). The next level of importance goes to action verbs. They show what exactly the student should do with the object. Most learning outcomes include also auxiliary words (adjectives, adverbs, prepositions), which are not as important as nouns and verbs, but still have influence on calculations, helping to calculate similarity more precisely.

Modifying the original Jaccard Similarity Coefficient we add weights to it. It means that instead of contributing equally, some parts of speech contribute more than others. The default weight distribution is: nouns - 50%, verbs - 30%, and auxiliary words - 20%.

However, it can change, depending on the presence of different parts of speech in LO. Thus, if LO does not contain any adverbs, adjectives or prepositions, the weight of auxiliary words will be equally distributed between Nouns and Verbs.

3.4 Relation Extraction Between Keywords

As mentioned earlier, nouns are the most meaningful for relation determination. Even though nouns in the pairs of learning outcomes connected with the type "REQUIRES" in most cases belong to different categories, we can still see the connection between them.

With the validation corpus, it was possible to create a knowledge base, which shows related pairs of keywords. Based on the expert evaluation, we extracted pairs of keywords from the pairs of LO with the relation type "REQUIRES". Thus we got pairs of keywords (which include nouns and verbs) in the form *requires(K1, K2)*, where the term *K1* requires *K2*.

The problem of such an approach was that automatic extraction gave us not only words which are relevant for Computer Science, thus we needed to edit the table manually.

Having such knowledge as a basis, we can use it for dependency identification between LO. If two LO contain an extracted earlier pair of related keywords, we can preliminary see that such LO might be connected. However, to check it more precisely, we need to look for the percentage of keywords, which have a pair in the opposite LO. If the result is more than 37%, it is most likely that LO we are currently checking are connected, otherwise, they are not.

3.5 Action Verbs Triples

In the field of education, Bloom's taxonomy is a very popular tool for level determination of learning outcomes. Knowing the level we can easily determine the direction of relation for the connected pair of LO. Nevertheless, our try to apply it on praxis did not show satisfying results. Less than 5% of directions were determined. The problem was, that having a variety of action verbs divided in 6 levels (in the revised Bloom's Taxonomy), it is still missing most action verbs specific for the field of Computer Science.

Giving better results in those cases, when action verbs were included, the Revised Bloom's Taxonomy served as a basis for the next idea: using triples of Action Verbs, extracted from the Validation Corpus (Fig. 2).

The first step in this process is to extract all the action verbs (AV) and to add them into the middle column of the three-column table. It is known from VC, that directions between LO go from lower to higher levels. Applying this knowledge for AV, two other columns can be added. For each AV in the middle column, we extracted possible AV of lower and higher levels by investigating the pairs of related LO. For a pair of related LO (LO1, LO2), with LO1 being of a lower level compared to LO2, the AV of LO1 can be added to the left column of the respective AV of LO2. On the other hand, the AV of LO2 can be added to the right column of the respective AV of LO1. To avoid cases when the same AV appear in one row in the left and right column, we use a count (how many times the AV was met in this position). If the count of the AV from the left column is higher, it stays there, otherwise in the right one.

-	arrange	understand
arrange	understand	control, identify, discuss
understand	control	construct, accomplish, develop
recognize, control	construct	implement
construct	implement	-

Fig. 2. Automatically extracted triples of action verbs.

The table shows action verbs from easier to harder levels (left to right). With its help we know that for example before being able to *"control"* something, the student should *"understand"* it.

With the help of such a table, we cannot identify the exact level of the LO, however, we can check which of two LO to compare are of the higher level. Thus if LO1 includes the action verb *"understand"* while LO2 includes *"discuss"*, we can see that LO2 is of a higher level than LO1.

Applying it for relation determination, we increase the percentage of determined directions between pairs of learning outcome to 83%. However there were still not-determined directions. The problem was that in some pairs both learning outcomes had the same action verb. An improvement of the identification of the dependency direction between such LO is difficult using Action Verb Triples, or Bloom's Taxonomy. The possible solutions of this problem are to be discussed in Sect. 5.

In the following section the results of applying the methodology are presented.

4 Trial Results

4.1 Relation Determination

Each of two types of relations between LO needs its own approach for dependency identification:

- for the type "EXPANDS" we use weighted Jaccard Similarity Coefficient, where weights are distributed depending on part of speech,
- for the type "REQUIRES" we use extracted pairs of keywords *requires(K1, K2)*, where the term K2 requires the understanding or knowledge of the term K1.

As we are using a weighted Jaccard Similarity Coefficient (the metric, which gives us a probability of how close are two sentences) for relation identification of the type "EXPANDS", the results depend on the probability boundary (Fig. 3).

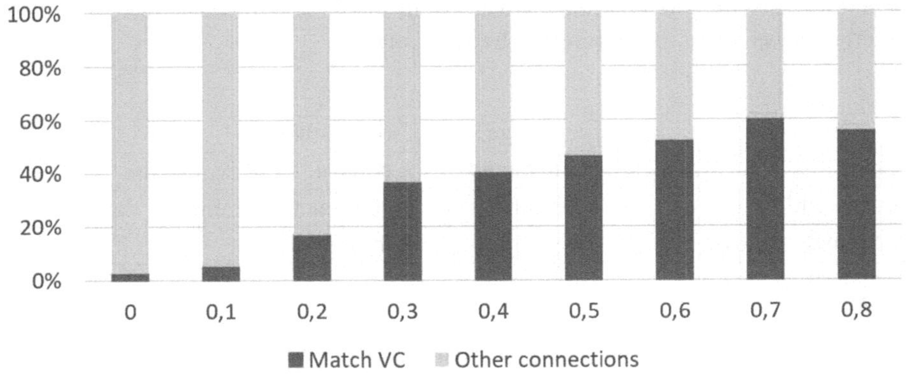

Fig. 3. Automatically determined relations of the type "EXPANDS". (Color figure online)

The x-axis shows the probability of how close the LO are in the range from 0 to 1. The closer the value is to 1, the more similar are the LO. The y-axis shows with the green color percentage of determined relations which match VC comparing to all the determined dependencies (yellow color) of the type "EXPANDS".

We can see, that the higher the probability is, the higher is the percentage of identified dependencies that match VC. However, Fig. 4 shows us, that the higher the probability is, the lower is the percentage of identified dependencies from VC.

Analyzing the results, presented on the Figs. 3 and 4, we choose the boundary of 0.4, as it maximally reduces the percentage of noise (which is now 54.02% compared to the lower probability boundaries) and at the same time helps us to identify 62.5% of dependencies from VC.

Besides comparing the gained results to VC we asked experts for a new evaluation. The goal was to check whether all the pairs of LO which were not met

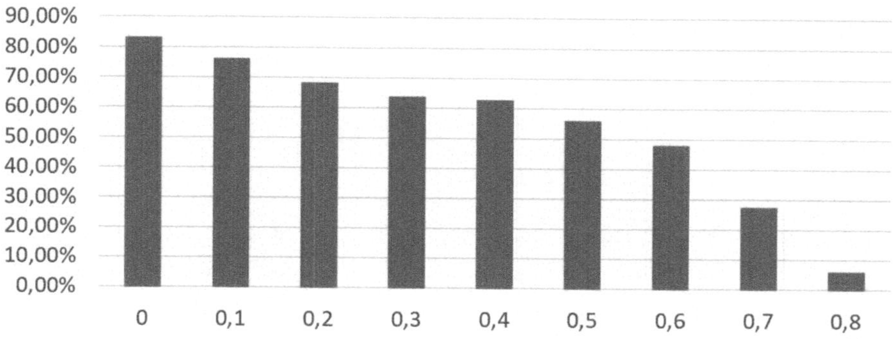

Fig. 4. Automatically determined relations of the type "EXPANDS" which match VC.

in VC were really identified wrongly, or if they were simply missed by experts during the first evaluation. The results of Precision and Recall for dependency identification of the type "EXPANDS" showed that the actual level of noise is much lower (Fig. 5). Having identified 41% (recall) of dependencies from VC, the second evaluation done by experts showed that 96.4% (precision) of automatically determined relations of the type "EXPANDS" were identified correctly.

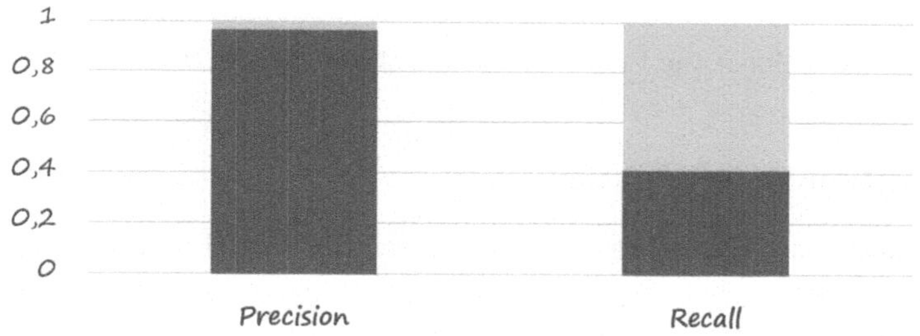

Fig. 5. Results of the Precision and Recall for "EXPANDS" relations

As for dependencies identification of the type "REQUIRES", the results were less satisfying. Related pairs of keywords gave us a chance to identify a high amount of dependencies from VC, but at the same time, the level of noise was too high even after excluding pairs of keywords that are irrelevant for Computer Science (Fig. 6).

Together with reducing the level of noise (Fig. 6), also the percentage of identified relations from VC was cut in half.

Asking experts for reevaluation, we found out, that our approach helped to identify dependencies of the type "'REQUIRES" with a precision of 52.7% (which includes related pairs of LO which were missed by experts during the first evaluation) and a recall of 10.3% (Fig. 7). It shows that, in order to identify relations missed by experts, our approach needs improvement, as the level of noise is too high.

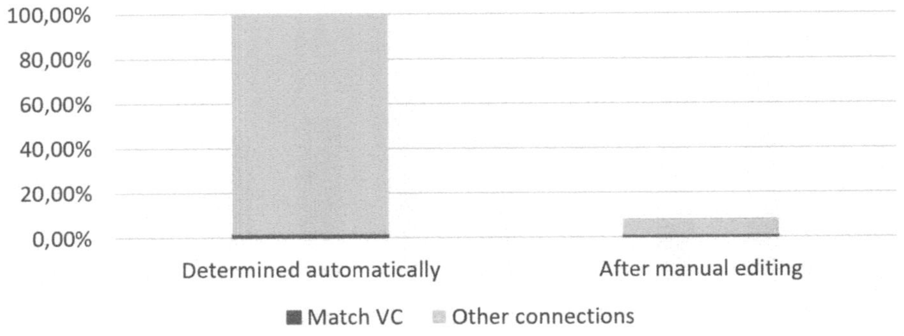

Fig. 6. Automatically determined relations of the type "REQUIRES".

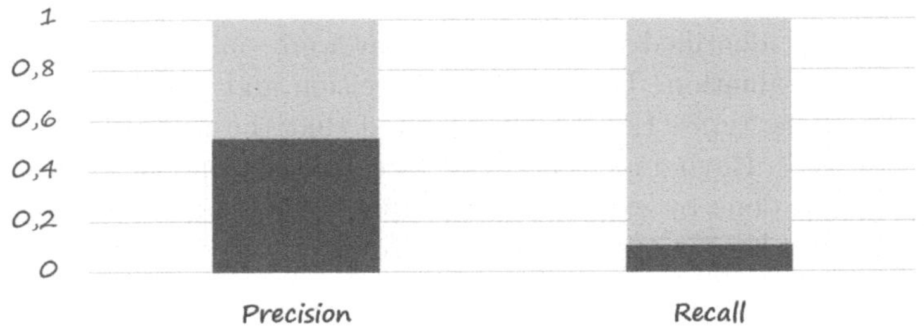

Fig. 7. Results of the Precision and Recall for "REQUIRES" relations.

4.2 Direction Determination

Direction determination is needed for the relations of the type "EXPANDS". Jaccard Coefficient shows us that Learning Outcomes are connected, but does not show the order. That is why we are using Triples of Action Verbs, to identify the relative level between two LO which have a dependency of the type "EXPANDS".

In the case of direction determination, we were able to get satisfying results using triples of Action Verbs. This approach gave us 88.5% of correctly determined directions.

The main problem of such an approach is, that it is impossible to identify the direction, if both LO from the pair share the same Action Verb. That is why we still get 11.5% of not identified directions.

5 Discussion of Findings

Dependency identification between LO which are presented as short sentences is a rather complicated task. While dependency as well as direction identification of relations of the type "EXPANDS" works quite well, it is still pretty weak for relations identification of the type "REQUIRES".

It is easier to identify relations of the type "EXPANDS" as they share similar topics. Nevertheless, some related LO share terms, which belong to the same topic, but are not synonyms or that obviously connected.

The approach for dependencies identification of the type "REQUIRES" still needs improvement. While a high percentage of dependent LO from VC can be identified, the level of noise still has to be reduced. Nevertheless, it can serve as a good basis for example for developing a Computer Science Ontology of key terms. Such an ontology might be helpful both for the identification of relations of the type "EXPANDS" and direction identification.

Triples of action verbs show positive results for direction determination (88.5%). As Bloom's Taxonomy served as a basis of our approach, the range of action verbs can be extended. The problem of defining directions between those LO which share the same action verb still remains a problem which we also hope to solve in the future with the help of ontology.

6 Conclusion

In the current paper, we show the approach, which will serve as a helping instrument for experts in dependencies identification between LO from Computer Science curricula. It includes relation identification of two types: "EXPANDS" and "REQUIRES". We can identify the relations of the type "EXPANDS" with the precision of 96.4%. As the weighted Jaccard Similarity Coefficient, the method for relation identification of the type "EXPANDS" gives us results only on the probability of how close are the two LO, we use also triples of action verbs for direction identification. Such an approach gives us a possibility to identify directions with the precision of 88.5%.

The task of dependency identification of the type "REQUIRES" is more complicated. It requires a knowledge base, which includes dependencies between key terms. With such knowledge, we were able to identify relations of this type with a precision of 52.7%. Our approach gives a high level of noise, which we plan to decrease by developing and using an ontology of Computer Science terms.

Approaches for dependency identification of both types still can be improved, however already on this point they showed, that human experts miss the radical amount of relations. For example, only half of the relations of the type "EXPANDS" was identified by experts during primary evaluation.

The presented approach, for now, cannot serve as an independent tool for dependency identification, nevertheless, it is a helping hand for experts. It makes a process of relation identification faster and easier, showing related pairs of LO, it gives an opportunity for experts to work with a bigger amount of computer science curricula, and simplify the task of adding new ones.

References

1. Achananuparp, P., Hu, X., Shen, X.: The evaluation of sentence similarity measures. In: Song, I.-Y., Eder, J., Nguyen, T.M. (eds.) DaWaK 2008. LNCS, vol. 5182, pp. 305–316. Springer, Heidelberg (2008). https://doi.org/10.1007/978-3-540-85836-2_29
2. Badawy, M., El-Aziz, A.A.A., Hefny, H.A.: Analysis of learning objectives for higher education textbooks using text mining. In: 2016 12th International Computer Engineering Conference (ICENCO), pp. 202–207 (2016)
3. Fuller, U., et al.: Developing a computer science-specific learning taxonomy. ACM SIGCSE Bull. **39**, 152–170 (2007)
4. Gupta, S., Dutta, P.K.: Topic objective and outcome: performance indicators in knowledge transfer through in-depth curriculum content analysis. Procedia Comput. Sci. **172**, 331–336 (2020). 9th World Engineering Education Forum (WEEF 2019) Proceedings
5. Ji, G., Liu, K., He, S., Zhao, J.: Distant supervision for relation extraction with sentence-level attention and entity descriptions. In: Thirty-First AAAI Conference on Artificial Intelligence (2017)
6. Johnson, C.G., Fuller, U.: Is Bloom's taxonomy appropriate for computer science? In: Proceedings of the 6th Baltic Sea Conference on Computing Education Research: Koli Calling 2006, pp. 120–123 (2006)
7. Lightfoot, J.M.: A graph-theoretic approach to improved curriculum structure and assessment placement. Commun. IIMA **10**(2), 59–73 (2010)
8. Anderson, L.W., et al.: A taxonomy for learning, teaching, and assessing: a revision of Bloom's taxonomy of educational objectives (2001)
9. Pasterk, S.: Competency-based informatics education in primary and lower secondary schools. Ph.D. thesis, University of Klagenfurt - Department of Informatics Didactics (2020)
10. Pasterk, S., Bollin, A.: Graph-based analysis of computer science curricula for primary education. In: 2017 IEEE Frontiers in Education Conference, pp. 1–9 (2017)
11. Pasterk, S., Kesselbacher, M., Bollin, A.: A semi-automated approach to categorise learning outcomes into digital literacy or computer science. In: Passey, D., Bottino, R., Lewin, C., Sanchez, E. (eds.) OCCE 2018. IAICT, vol. 524, pp. 77–87. Springer, Cham (2019). https://doi.org/10.1007/978-3-030-23513-0_8
12. Reyhani Hamedani, M., Kim, S.W.: JacSim: an accurate and efficient link-based similarity measure in graphs. Inf. Sci. **414**, 203–224 (2017)
13. Sekiya, T., Matsuda, Y., Yamaguchi, K.: Analysis of computer science related curriculum on LDA and Isomap. In: Proceedings of the Fifteenth Annual Conference on Innovation and Technology in Computer Science Education, pp. 48–52. ITiCSE 2010, ACM, New York, NY, USA (2010)

Computing in Pre-primary Education

Daniela Bezáková(✉), Andrea Hrušecká, and Roman Hrušecký

Comenius University, 842 48 Bratislava, Slovakia
{bezakova,hrusecka,hrusecky}@fmph.uniba.sk

Abstract. In this paper we present our approach to study whether and how some basic computational pre-constructs (like agent, instruction, sequence, program, record, order) can be developed with preschool children (aged 5 to 6).

In many kindergartens Bee-Bots are used to introduce programming. But Bee-Bots themselves do not offer any visual representation of a program which we think a little bit limiting. To conduct our research, we wanted to use a tool that would enable *direct control of an agent* and *a visual representation of a program as a record*. Being inspired by the former work of our colleagues, educational programming environments for lower primary years and research within the Emil project we have designed an educational microworld for pre-school children – *Circus.*

In *Circus* environment children control a main character (an acrobat) in order to train it a performance. Instructions for the acrobat are interpreted immediately and a record of given instructions is being made simultaneously. *Circus* is aimed to be used with an interactive whiteboard by a small group of children and by a teacher moderating the activities of children with the software. The microworld itself is open, it doesn't present any tasks to be solved.

In the paper we document an iterative process of designing, developing, using, evaluating and analysing a) *Circus microworld*, b) *activities* to be done by children *in the microworld* and related *unplugged activities* c) *methodology for teachers* d) *worksheets for children* in the cooperation with two kindergartens and present some findings.

Keywords: Programming in preschool age · Direct control · Program as record

1 Background

In last two decades several tools to support learning of computing for kindergarten children in a developmentally appropriate way have been developed and also several studies about introducing computing to kindergarten children or developing other competencies through computing were conducted, e.g. using Bee-Bots [1, 2], ScratchJr [3, 4] or KIBO [4, 5]. **Bee-Bots** are simple programmable floor robots with four instruction buttons (forward, back, left and right – not interpreted immediately after pushing) and a GO button which runs a sequence of instructions given before. **ScratchJr** [4, 15] is an introductory programming language based on Scratch simplified and redesigned to be developmentally appropriate for 5–7 years old children. Comparing with Scratch the set

K. Kori and M. Laanpere (Eds.): ISSEP 2020, LNCS 12518, pp. 197–208, 2020.
https://doi.org/10.1007/978-3-030-63212-0_16

of programming blocks is smaller, and the program is built from left to right. Children can add sprites, change their image in a paint editor, program their behaviour, add voices and sounds, select a background and thus create interactive stories and games. **KIBO** [4] is a screen-free robot kit designed for 4–7 years old children. Children can build their own robot, use a variety of sensors and art supplies and program it – constructing physical computer programs by connecting interlocking wooden blocks. Each wooden block has a bar code that can be scanned by the robot's embedded scanner. After pressing a button robot executes the program.

We have looked at the space of opportunities of these three tools from the perspective of Kalas' three criteria [6]: *actor to control (physical or virtual), style of control (direct manipulation, direct drive, programming) and interaction (either controlling an isolated actor with restricted interaction, or controlling multiple interacting actors).* In mentioned three technologies:

- physical (Bee-Bot, KIBO) and virtual actors (Scratch sprites) are present,
- controlling of an isolated actor and multiple interacting actors are present,
- direct manipulation, direct drive and programming (or indirect control) are present.

In Slovakia we can notice an intense effort on supporting educational programming and building a systematic approach to the learning process in computational thinking across all learning stages. A complex intervention for Y3 and Y4 was developed in last years – Emil the Robot: programming environment with graduated units of tasks, workbooks for pupils and teacher materials (see [7, 8]). Emil is a virtual actor moving in a grid, with different levels of control (indirect manipulation, direct and indirect control). Two years before, closely collaborating with the members of Computing with Emil project, we started to think about a microworld appropriate for pre-primary stage, that would be a natural predecessor of Emil concerning computational concepts, procedures and level of control.

2 At the Beginning

At the very beginning (before designing the first prototype) we had decided to have *one virtual actor* with the *direct drive* style of control. Direct control of an agent is obvious in many lower primary school programming environments in Slovakia described e.g. in [9]. We think that immediately executing of given instruction is an important step before indirect control (planning the future behaviour) of an agent. We also planned to include a functionality which automatically creates a *visual record of given instructions* – to make it possible to reflect on the previous steps, to explore and analyse the *sequence* of given instruction, *order* of instructions, etc. *Sequence* is in fact the main construct we wanted to develop by our tool.

When considering the figure of an agent we studied software applications used for lower primary programming [9]. Most of them use agents like bee, ant, ladybird, a robot or a magic-man. We would like an agent to be a character popular for children, which they can meet in a real word, which they can identify with or imitate. We have chosen a figure of a circus clown. We found the circus topic to be interesting for children and we also have some positive experience with circus background from Thomas the Clown application. In our application the agent lives in a circus stage where it practices and shows performances. It also has its own dressing room.

The actors in primary programming applications usually move in a grid (Emil, Bee-Bot), inside a map of roads (Thomas the Clown) or just free (Scratch) and in addition they collect, carry, draw or built something etc. Hence the basic instructions in these environments are the instructions for movement and rotation (like forward, backwards, left and right) and then other additional instructions for solving problems in appropriate application (e.g. collect, take, put,…). In *Circus* application we didn't want children to control the movement of an agent in the meaning of changing its position and direction. But still we wanted the instructions for an agent to be interesting, funny and representing some physical activity quite easy to be simulated by children themselves. Our first suggestions for instructions included clapping, jumping, blowing bubbles, drumming, inflating balloons, pulling subjects from a magic hat, doing handspring, riding monocycle, playing the trumpet and juggling.

The goal of our research was to find out, how the pre-school children would react to controlling this kind of agent and whether it is possible to use it to develop some pre-concepts of computational thinking. We also asked, what organization form is suitable for the work with this kind of tool in the real kindergarten class and whether we can support the learning with some unplugged activities and in what form.

3 Method

In our study we applied the design based research approach [10] and we were also inspired by former experience of our colleagues from development of a software for ECE education [11]. We have cooperated with three pre-school kindergartens classes from two different kindergartens: two classes in the first year, one class in the second year (approximately 20 children to a class).

We started the development of *Circus* two years before. The first year of our research was concentrated to designing prototypes of the software levels and activities for children to do with the software. Just a few unplugged activities were created in this year. We had six sessions with children (three with each class). In this year all the software interventions were conducted by one of the researchers.

In the second year the software went through big graphics changes, some user interface improvements, but almost no conceptual change. Most work in this iteration was devoted to improving the activities with the software and designing of related unplugged activities. We had three meetings in kindergarten this year. Interventions with the software were conducted by the pre-school teacher itself according to our methodology. Unplugged activities were moderated by one of the researchers.

In most our sessions two kindergarten teachers and three researchers were present. Researchers (those who weren't moderating the software or unplugged activities) were making observations, taking notes or doing photo or video-documentation. After each session we had a discussion with one of the present teachers. Outcomes from paper activities (if realised) were collected to be analysed.

4 Interventions

4.1 Organization and Structure of Interventions

Circus is meant to be used by children in front of an interactive whiteboard together with a teacher. The role of the teacher is to moderate the activity (learning process), by giving assignments, challenges, asking questions, not lecturing. It would not be possible to do this with the whole class. Being inspired by the experiences of our colleagues working with kindergarten children [12] we concluded that the best scenario for our interventions would be working with small groups of (4 to 6) children.

Most of Slovak kindergartens (including ours) have digital corners [13] with a computer or notebook connected to the interactive whiteboard in some of their classes, especially the classes of pre-schoolers. Thus, we were able to do interventions in children' natural environment – in the class. The disadvantage of this approach was the necessity of managing the whole class. We have used the scenario of distributing the children into groups doing independent activities in parallel. One group worked with the software, one group made unplugged activity (if prepared), and two other groups realized another two activities prepared by the class teacher. The groups have worked for 10 to 12 min on their activities and then they "rotated" (Fig. 1). Both our kindergarten classes have already some experiences with this kind of "distributed work" and with doing software activities on interactive whiteboard too.

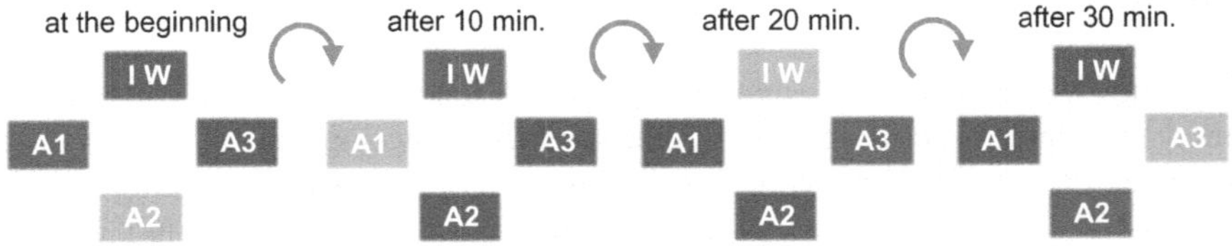

Fig. 1. Diagram of groups rotations. Groups are distinguished by colours. (IW = interactive whiteboard, A = activity)

Our sessions had the same structure every time, inspired by [14]. We started with a short discussion with all children sitting on the ground. Then the group work was realised. After all groups have finished all the activities there was a closing discussion with all children. The whole intervention took mostly about an hour.

4.2 The First Year of Interventions

Controlling One Agent. In the first session with children we used a prototype of *Circus* with a clown (agent) knowing six instructions: clap, jump, pull a subject from a magic hat, blow bubbles, drum and do handspring. In a *training stage* (see Fig. 2 on the left), children are training a clown (designing performance) – giving him instructions by clicking at buttons with action pictograms. Each *instruction is carried out immediately* and respective pictogram is added to a record panel. Thus, a visual re-cord of clown's training is created – which becomes a performance plan (a program) after switching to the *performance mode*. In the performance stage the clown cannot be controlled any more, he just executes the "program" instruction by instruction. The executed instruction on the record panel is highlighted.

In our first intervention we wanted to explore whether children would be able to create and understand a relationship between the actions carried out by the clown and the visual of record, read and interpret the record by themselves. We started by asking children what they think the clown can do. Each child has identified one of the action pictograms and then was asked to tell the clown to do it – children immediately tap on the appropriate button. This way the group trained the clown its first performance. Then we switched to a performance mode and watched the clown doing the show. While doing performance children spontaneously exercised with the clown – they clapped, jumped, simulated the magic hat, drumming and doing handsprings.

After the show we asked children *to name the actions the clown did*. We noticed two "ways" of answer: some children named the action by heart – sometimes not in right order, but as a group they were always able to name all of them, some children evidently looked at the whiteboard and read the record – they named all the actions in the right order. To support children of the first type, we asked questions more precisely: *What did the clown at first? What did it after that? What was the third action?*... Later, after designing other performances and before switching to performance mode, we asked a little bit differently – to motivate children not to remember the sequence but to read it from the record, e.g.: *What did the clown at first? What did it do at last? What did it do after clapping? What did it do before jumping? When did it drum?* ... We also asked them to simulate the performance personally.

We think that the basic principle of controlling the clown, designing a performance and its executing was understood and we confirmed that children discovered the meaning of the record, were able to read it and interpret it. We have identified some problems with GUI (switching mode buttons were not intuitive, the location of action buttons was not practical, etc.) and gain some ideas how to make the software funnier.

Controlling Two Agents. In the second prototype of *Circus* we added another level with *two clowns on the stage* (a boy and a girl) each one having its own record panel (see Fig. 2 on the right), *dressing room* for the clowns, some *new instructions* (playing trumpet, riding monocycle, ...). The graphics of the software changed a bit.

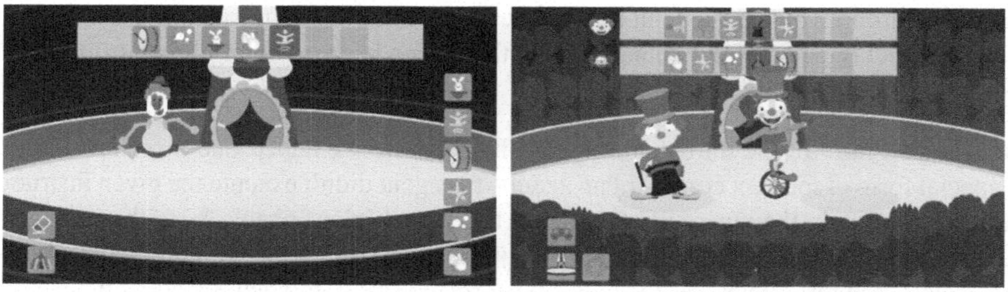

Fig. 2. Prototypes of *Circus*. A training stage in the first prototype on the left. A performance stage of the second prototype on the right – two clowns executing their own "programs".

We focused our intervention with children to controlling two agents – to develop a pre-construct of **parallelism**. We wanted them to realize we can have more agents which can do different actions independently but in the same time and to explore a relation between a concrete clown and its record.

First children were asked to design any performance for a boy and then any performance for a girl. After training a boy (who was active in default) they realized the need to "select" the clown, they want to control. Usually they tried to click at the clown itself, but some children also tried to click at the clown's icon in front of the record panel (both possibilities were implemented). After training performance for both boy and girl the group watched the show in performance mode and saw that both clowns do their actions in parallel. Like in the first intervention after executing performance or even before it (right after training) we gradually asked children:

- to name all boy's actions first and then the girl's actions: *What did the boy do at the beginning? What did he do then? What did he do as the third? ... What was the girl's first action? ...*
- to name boy's and girl's actions alternatively, but in the order: *What did the boy do as first? What was the girl's first action? What did the boy do as the second? ...*
- to name randomly boy's and girl's actions: *What did the boy do the end? What did the girl do as the first? What did she do after jumping? When did the boy clap?...*
- to argue: *Why do you think so? How do you know it?*
- to find out: *Did the clowns do the same action sometime? Which one and when?*

Answering the last groups of questions children often pointed at the record panels.

The second task in this intervention was to design any performance for the boy and the same performance for the girl. Some groups manage to do this task independently reading the first record sequentially and clicking the same action for the girl. In some groups we helped children a little bit by asking questions like *What did the boy do as first? Thus, what will do the girl do as first?...* Some groups made mistakes during solving the task, but they communicated with each other within the group and corrected it.

We can state that controlling two agents was not a problem for children and they also managed to orient in both record panels. Problems from the previous prototype were eliminated. We have found some new defects in software (not intuitive pictures) and in organization, too. Children were not distributed equally – we had one three members group which turned out to be uselessly small. The group ends up the software activity quickly but couldn't change for another group because other bigger groups still performed their activities.

Making a Plan. In the third prototype of the software we added one more level with a special form of indirect control of an agent – the agent didn't execute the given instructions immediately they were just written to the record (plan) panel. As in the previous level there were two clowns at the stage, but just the boy could be (indirectly) controlled. The role of the girl clown was to show a performance randomly generated by the application. The role of children was **to plan** the same performance for the boy – which in fact means **to make a record** of the girl's performance. Thus, the visual representation of the sequence of instructions in this level is **a record and a plan at the same time** – it is a record of the girl's show but a plan of the boy's one.

When we started working with this level children were confused. They clicked the instruction buttons, but any clown hasn't reacted. Just the pictogram of clicked action was "written" to the record. We encouraged children to switch to performance mode, where they could notice that the boy executed their instructions, but the girl didn't. Then we explained children what's the task – to watch the girl's show in the training mode and to prepare a plan for the same performance for the boy.

The way children solved the task could be denoted as "by heart". Children watched the whole girl's show and then they tried to recall what was the first, the second and the third girl's action and clicked the appropriate button. After making a plan for a boy, they switched to performance mode to see if both clowns would do the same (application didn't give them any other form of feedback). If not, they returned to the training mode, watched the girl's performance again and made a new plan.

As the girl's show was quite short at the beginning (just three actions), it was not so hard to remember and hence the children were very successful. Later when the number of girl's actions went up children as individuals were not able to remember the whole show but in cooperation, as a group, they always managed to prepare the right plan for the boy (although sometimes not at the first trial). In spite of becoming the task harder and harder (it is possible to choose from 3 up to 7 actions), children wanted to extend the girl's show – they took it as *a higher level of a game*.

None of the children tried to click at the instruction buttons during the girl's show, thus they didn't discover the possibility of creating the record/plan during the show.

4.3 The Second Year of Interventions

After the first year the software was completely graphically redesigned changed (see Fig. 3): the graphics of clowns, stage, dressing room, buttons, and action pictograms was. Some new clown's actions were added. In the level with the indirect control we changed the girl clown for a robot figure, so the girl clown would have the same role in the whole software.

Fig. 3. *Dressing room* and *Making a plan* level.

In our second year's meetings we used the same organization model as in the first one – children (not the same as in previous year) were working in four groups independently:

one group doing software activities using interactive whiteboard **moderated by the class teacher**, **one group working on our unplugged activities**, and two other groups working on other activities prepared by the class teacher. We had planned four meetings with children in the second year, but due to the Corona crises just three of them were realized.

The First Intervention with a Class Teacher. The teacher has prepared everything very carefully. She has divided children into four groups and explained all the groups all the activities they would do during next hour so that they could work relatively independently without managing them. Then she started to moderate the software activities which were similar to those presented in *Controlling one agent* part with the same questions asking. After being asked *How did you know the order of the instructions, clown did?* some children claimed that *they remember it*. But when designing next performance, we could clearly see that they looked at the record and choose the actions so that they would not repeat. We can conclude that children were able to control an agent and understand, read and interpret the record of the instructions.

Unplugged activities were oriented to *completing* and *creating sequences of two alternating pictures* – which was presented to children as designing a performance for the clown with two alternating actions. Children solved these tasks by gluing paper pictograms of actions to prepared paper cards with empty sequences. As the activity consists of three sub-tasks we have recorded their word descriptions with talking pegs (to simple recording and playing devices customized for children), so that children could hear them whenever they need, without the help of a teacher. But it was not a good idea because children took the pegs in wrong order, the voice from the pegs disturbed the other children and some children even overrecorded the assignment. We assured that the unplugged activities need to be managed by a teacher the whole time (not just at the beginning) – to explain assignments, answer questions, give feedback, etc. In fact, the unplugged activities are not necessary to be done in parallel with software activities. Thus, after this intervention we have specified the order of alternation of the software and unplugged activities in the methodology, so that they followed up didactically.

Children from the other two groups asked for some feedback too – they wanted to show the teacher their pictures, buildings or other outcomes. To be able to do this without disturbing the group by interactive whiteboard, an assistant teacher is needed. Another problem we noticed (if each group was doing and independent activity) was the rotation – some children were frustrated by interrupting their actual activity before gaining its goal (e.g. drawing some picture). We think it's a matter of training (in one kindergarten it functioned perfectly, because children were used to this organization model, and also in the second one the children got used to this method later) and types of the remaining two activities – they have to be chosen very carefully, so that they would not last more than 10–12 min and wouldn't have any specific goals.

Seeing these problems and knowing that in most Slovak kindergarten classes just one teacher is present (rarely two) we added another possible form of organizing the class work when doing *Circus* activities (see Fig. 4). All children do the same activity possibly such that needn't be managed (like building from cubes). Each 10 min different group of 4–6 children works with the teacher with the *Circus* software.

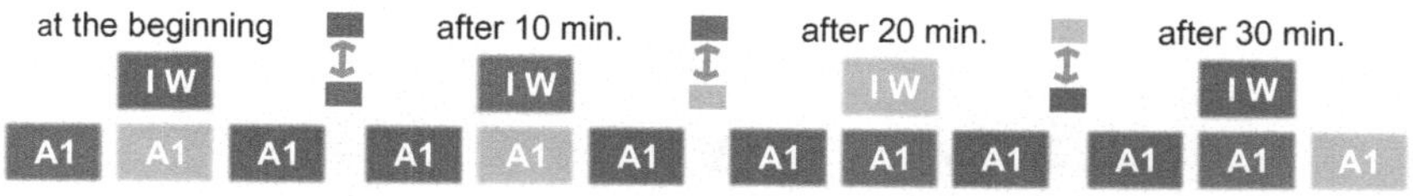

Fig. 4. Another type of changing the groups. Groups are distinguished by colours.

The Second Intervention with a Class Teacher. In the second session conducted by class teacher we prepared some new activities that were not presented in the first year. Children had to *design performances (for one clown) with some specific rules*: to use concrete action twice or three times, to do the same action one after another or not one after another. A bigger set of actions was used. While designing such performances children discovered various details of clown's behaviour, like:

- it doesn't do the same action in the same way (e.g. once it claps with hands down and once with hands up),
- when doing the same actions one after another it can "graduate" it (e.g. first juggling with three balls, later with four and then with five) or sometimes is not able to do it or it does it in a wrong way (e.g. loses a ball by juggling). We liked children's reasoning why the clown does it this way, e.g. *it is tired, it is being bored doing always the same, its hands or its legs hurt.*

Paper activities, presented on a paper worksheet (see Fig. 5 on the left), were also concentrated to *design performances with given rules*, e.g. design a performance where: the clown will juggle with plates, the clown will play some instrument, the clown will clap and run the monocycle, the clown will jump before blowing bubbles, the clown will play two different instruments. The tasks were ordered gradually according to their difficulty from our point of view. In each group at least one or two children didn't want to meet the given rules (they created a sequence they liked) or they placed the solution to the wrong line, although the teacher read just one assignment at the moment (e.g. they placed the solution of the second tasks to the fourth line, or they started at the bottom and finished at the top line). We agreed it would be better to have separate card for each task and introduce them to children step by step. After evaluating the worksheets, it turned out, that our estimation of tasks' difficulty was quite good - the succesfullness of the children' solutions was almost perfectly decreasing except of the last but one task, which turned to be the hardest.

The Third Intervention with a Class Teacher. The third intervention was concentrated to *controlling two clowns* – software activities were almost the same as described in the *Controlling two agents* part. As in the first year children were able to select which clown they want to control, distinguish between the boy's and the girl's record, read the records continuously and also in alternating way, use boy's record as a pattern for planning the girl's performance or vice versa. The most difficult was the task of designing a girl's performance with a reversed order of actions from the boy's one. But with appropriate helping questions from the teacher and cooperating with each other each group has managed to do it.

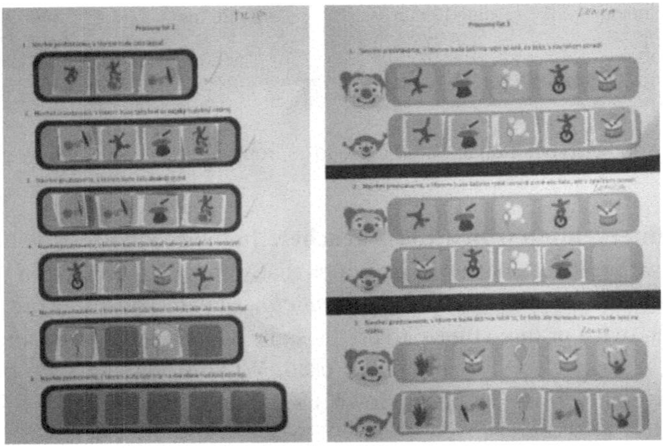

Fig. 5. Examples of worksheets for unplugged activities (with solutions).

Unplugged activities related to this session were concentrated to creating a sequence (girl's performance) based on some pattern sequence (boy's performance) but with given changes (Fig. 5 on the right). Changes were either in the order of the actions or in the replacement of action by another action. After our experience from the previous intervention we prepared each task on separate paper card and the moderator of this activity gave it to the children just after the previous one was solved.

After this intervention we has a discussion with the class teacher about the unplugged activities. Teacher liked the task we prepared but she didn't like their paper form and gluing. She found the paper sheets to be not ecological, just for one use, not practical for teachers (as the teacher would have to print it before the lesson) and not modifiable. As either children nor teachers do not need to save the tasks' solutions, she would appreciate such form that could be used repeatedly and without preparation – just take and use. We had several ideas:

- using magnetic cards with assignment (that means pattern sequences or just empty sequences to fill in) and magnetic pictograms of actions,
- using cards with assignment and pictograms from some (repeatedly) adhesive material, like some windows stickers,
- using paper-board pictograms that children will just lay (not glue) on the paper-board assignment cards.

We decided for the last – less expensive solution. We had prepared a set of pictogram pieces and a set of cards with the assignments – sequences (the description is not written on the card, just in the methodology). To be able to find the appropriate card very quickly we decided to mark the backside of the cards by different colours and numbers. Thus, teacher moderating the unplugged activities can tell just *Take the yellow card from the box and create a sequence such that …*

5 Conclusion

We have presented a two-years design-based research study conducted in three preschool classrooms. So far, we have iteratively developed the *Circus* application consisting of four levels and designed software activities scheduled to four meetings, eight related unplugged activities (consisting of 3 to 6 tasks), some supplement activities and methodology for teachers.

Children worked with the software without any familiarization – they intuitively figured out the meaning of instructions and were able to *directly control an agent*. They explored the *record* – a *sequence* of carried out instructions, discovered its meaning, were able to read it, interpret it, use it as a plan, or as a pattern *for planning another agent's behaviour*. They also managed to *control two agents independently*: they determined which one is active, observed, whether they can do the same or different actions, explored their records, read them, compared them, looked for differences or for the common actions.

Children participated on software activities with enthusiasm and joy. We consider the 4–6 children groups and the 10–12 min time for one group accurate for working with the software – children had the opportunity to cooperate and even it was enough space for everybody in the group to express itself.

Unplugged activities were concentrated to exploring sequence, as it was the main construct we wanted to develop by our interventions. Doing unplugged activities children were experiencing *the order* of instructions in a sequence, creating *patterns of alternating pictures, completing or creating sequences according to given rules* or *according to given patterns* with some defined changes. A few children showed interest in creating their own "sequence" tasks for their friends.

We have found that the unplugged activities shouldn't be realised in parallel with the software activities. They have to be moderated by a teacher, and the tasks should be given step by step on separate paper cards. We have also suggested a form of presentation of the activities' materials so that they would be reusable.

The *Circus* environment is open. It does not give any tasks and any explicit feedback. In fact, the mentioned software activities are not integrated in the software, they are just described in the methodology, thus the teacher can adjust them. Using the software and some unplugged activities' materials it is also possible to build links to other areas or topics of early child education e.g.: *dressing up*, *movement* (exploring the actions of the clowns, imitating them), *human body* (exploring in which actions does the clown uses mouth, hands, legs, in which both hands and legs, …), *counting* (designing performances with exactly three handsprings or counting how many juggling actions were in a given performance, …), *professions* (thinking about in which professions or occasions can we meet with jumping, with handsprings, with playing trumpet and so on).

Acknowledgements. We would like to thank our colleagues from research and developer team (especially to Andrej Blaho, Ivan Kalaš and Milan Moravčík), our design kindergartens, teachers that took part in our interventions, gave us feedback, comments and new ideas, to Indicia NPO for funding our design research process and to the project VEGA 1/0602/20, thanks to which the results of this research could be published.

References

1. Pekarova, J.: Using a programmable toy at preschool age: why and how? In: Workshop Proceedings of SIMPAR 2008, International Conference, pp. 112–121 (2008)
2. Palmér, H.: Programming in preschool –with a focus on learning mathematics. Early Child. Educ. **8**, 75–87 (2017)
3. Flannery, L.-P., Kazakoff, E.-R., Bontá, P., Silverman, B., Bers, M-U., Resnick, M.: Designing ScratchJr: support for early childhood learning through computer programming. In: Proceedings of the 12th International Conference on Interaction Design and Children, pp. 1–10. ACM, New York (2013)
4. Bers, M.U.: Coding, playgrounds and literacy in early childhood education: the development of KIBO robotics and ScratchJr. In: 2018 IEEE Global Engineering Education Conference (EDUCON), pp. 2094–2102 (2018)
5. Bers, M.U., Horn, M.S.: Tangible programming in early childhood: revisiting developmental assumptions through new technologies: childhood in a digital world (2009)
6. Kalas, I.: On the road to sustainable primary programming. In: Proceedings of the Constructionism in Action: Constructionism, pp. 184–191. Suksapattana Foundation, Bangkok (2016)
7. Kalas, I.: Programming in lower primary years: design principles and powerful ideas. In: Proceedings of Constructionism Computational Thinking and Educational Innovation, Vilnius, pp. 71–80 (2018)
8. Kalas, I., Blaho, A., Moravcik, M.: Exploring control in early computing education. In: Pozdniakov, S.N., Dagienė, V. (eds.) ISSEP 2018. LNCS, vol. 11169, pp. 3–16. Springer, Cham (2018). https://doi.org/10.1007/978-3-030-02750-6_1
9. Kabatova, M., Kalas, I., Tomcsanyiova, M.: Programming in slovak primary schools. Olympiads Inf. **10**, 125–159 (2016). https://doi.org/10.15388/ioi.2016.09. (2016)
10. Design-Based Research Collective: Design-based research: an emerging paradigm for educational inquiry. Educ. Res. **32**, 5–8 (2003)
11. Moravcik, M., Kalas, I.: Developing software for early childhood education. In: Addressing Educational Challenges: The Role of ICT. IFIP Working Conference, Manchester, 12 p. MMU (2012). [CD-ROM]
12. Moravcik, M., Pekarova, J., Kalas, I.: Digital technologies at preschool: class scenarios. In: Proceedings of 9th WCCE: IFIP World Conference on Computers in Education, Bento Goncalves, 10 p. (2009). [CD-ROM]
13. Kalas, I.: Recognizing the potential of ICT in early childhood education. In: Analytical Survey, 148 p. UNESCO IITE, Moscow (2010)
14. Ballonova, B., et al.: Škôlka hrou, Edulab (2010)
15. ScratchJr. https://www.scratchjr.org. Accessed 12 Jul 2020

ePortfolio Introduction: Designing a Support Process

Hege Annette Olstad(✉)

Department of Computer Science, Norwegian University of Science and Technology, Trondheim, Norway
hege.a.olstad@ntnu.no

Abstract. As a result of innovations within the computer field, educational content changes continuously. The constant change can make it challenging for some students to understand what competencies they have gained. Relevant literature indicates that ePortfolios can help students gain awareness of competencies they have achieved if given technological - and pedagogical support. The potential benefits of ePortfolios are the motivation behind the research questions: What types of support do students need when developing an ePortfolio for the first time, and how should the support be designed to make students independent when developing ePortfolios? Data is collected by observing four student assistants in computing education and their reflection on the experience of developing ePortfolios for the first time. The finding shows that the identified support process was appropriate but needs some adjustments to make students able to develop ePortfolios without further support from teachers or others. The support process identified and explored in this study will be customized based on the findings. Subsequent studies will try out the customized support among a larger group of students.

Keywords: ePortfolio · Competence · Implementation · Promotion · Support

1 Introduction

ePortfolios provides students with a place to collect examples of work experiences and reflecting on those examples and what they represent. The content in ePortfolios may include text, images, video, and sound. The artifacts and the associated reflections are evidence of achievement and demonstrate skills, competencies or learning acquired from education, training, or work experience [1]. Moreover, the opportunity to present this information in digital format makes the previously unseen visible to students and employers alike [2].

Several authors indicate that ePortfolios can be used as a tool to make competencies more visible for students because ePortfolios creates self-awareness [3–5], and demonstrate student development over time [6, 7]. However, ePortfolio implementation takes time and increases teachers' workload due to the support students need when first introduced to the tool. Most teachers do not have time to put in the necessary effort, and it is recommend that further empirical research on this topic incorporate approaches that

K. Kori and M. Laanpere (Eds.): ISSEP 2020, LNCS 12518, pp. 209–220, 2020.
https://doi.org/10.1007/978-3-030-63212-0_17

do not require as much time and effort from the teachers [8]. Lack of time to implement ePortfolios is one of the most significant barriers to the use of ePortfolios in classes [4]. Further, Pool et al. [9] point out that challenges to ePortfolio implementation need to be explored and addressed before effective integration can take place [9].

In this paper, we will explain and examines types of support students need when developing ePortfolios for the first time. The purpose is to identify what kind of support students need and develop a support process that may save teachers and university time when implementing ePortfolios. The methodology chosen for this research is an exploratory case study and is the first cycle in a broader action research. As this is an exploratory case study, a small group of students has participated in this study. Based on the study's findings described in this paper, the support will be customized and lanced in a whole class in proper courses in subsequent studies. Therefore, this research is in line with Poole et al.'s [9] recommendation, addressing challenges before the integration of ePortfolio.

2 Review of Literature

2.1 Technological Considerations

A survey conducted by Blevins and Brill [4] revealed that the ePortfolio technology system's design was the top barrier to ePortfolio use, and that that the students wanted more flexibility in the design of their ePortfolio then ePortfolios in Learning management systems (LMS) provides. The survey showed that students prefer to use tools such as Google and iWeb. Therefore, the university decided to use Google Apps in addition to LMS. All the students were given a Gmail account and had access to Google Docs. Besides, the university implemented a zero-credit class where students watched two video modules. The videos helped them create their Google Sites page and practice adding artifacts. In this class, they also tried to help students reflect on their experiences [4]. Class sessions seem to be a method often used when implementing ePortfolios for providing students technological instructions and training [1, 5, 8, 9].

A study done by Tosh et al. [10] on ePortfolio and challenges from the students' perspective reveals that the biggest technology-related problems for students included lack of control, lack of features, and lack of access or permission. In turn, such shortcomings can lead to students becoming less motivated to develop ePortfolios [10]. Shroff et al. [11] find that students get motivated when they perceive the ePortfolio system easy to use and nearly free of mental effort, which may also create a favorable attitude towards its usefulness. Whether the students perceive the ePortfolio as easy to use and nearly free of mental effort will depend a lot on how the support is designed and whether it is adequately addressed to the students' needs [11].

2.2 Pedagogical Considerations

The Learning Outcomes and Competence. Most ePortfolios are developed with a focus on learning outcomes and are described as developmental portfolios [1]. To address the intended learning outcomes teaching and learning activities and assessment tasks and criteria should be aligned to the learning outcomes [12]. The alignment is the fundamental idea of constructive alignment. Constructive alignment is a principle devised by Professor John Biggs [12] and used for devising teaching and learning activities and assessment tasks that directly address the intended learning outcomes. Higher education institutions in Europe develop lists with statements of intended learning outcomes for each course and program. The list is based on the quality of higher-education agreement called the Bologna Process. The agreement ensures comparability in the standards and quality of higher-education qualifications. Learning outcomes are statements of what a learner knows, understands, and is able to do on completion of a learning process, defined in terms of knowledge, skills, and competence [13].

Unfortunately, the term 'competence' is often used interchangeably with terms like skills and abilities, causing quite some confusion, according to Westera [14]. Kennedy et al. [15] point out that there is a need to avoid confusion when using the term competence by defining it for the context in which it is being used [15].

Frezza et al. [16], defines competence as an integrative function consisting of knowledge elements, a set of skill elements, and asset of disposition element. Disposition is described as the abilities to turn learning into action [16]. Cedefop [17] defines competence as "actually achieved learning outcomes, validated through the ability of the learner autonomously to apply knowledge and skills in practice, in society, and at work" [17, p. 30]. The definitions show that skills and abilities are part of the concept of competence for educational purpose together with knowledge. While knowledge represents facts, procedures, principles, and theories, skills are associated with the mental operations that process this knowledge. When considering abilities, we are somewhat in the sphere of intelligence [15]. Competence related to education is thus understood as applied skills and knowledge, and ePortfolios may make competencies achieved through learning more visible for the students.

Artifacts and Reflection. Reflections are central to raise awareness around what is learned [18]. One way of conceptually link reflection and learning is proposed in Kolb's [18] experimental learning theory. In the first stage, the students a concrete experience that they reflect upon in the second stage. The third stage is where experience and reflection are transformed, and the students build or modify their abstract conceptualizations. In other words, they learn from their experience. In the last stage, students use and apply these concepts in other situations and gain new experiences that starts the next learning cycle [18]. Reflection is the "heart" of ePortfolios [8], and according to Kolb [18], reflection is essential for learning. Further, Alexiou et al. [2] describe the process of reflection on artifacts involved in the development of ePortfolios as one that makes invisible learning visible.

In a study by Ring et al. [8], one of the findings is that students participating in ePortfolio instruction sessions with training and support are more capable of articulate what they know and how they know. In one-on-one sessions, students received instruction on ePortfolio technology and asked to complete a draft of their portfolios before participating in these sessions. For the draft, the students used their resumes, academic records, and extracurricular activities as a starting point, and wrote reflections on the potential artifacts to place in their ePortfolio.

For the reflection, Ring et al. [8] used a What? So what? Now what? model as instructions designed with guiding questions (see Table 1) to help the students to connect past experiences with present understanding and future use or action [8].The instruction was modeled after Kolb's [18] experiential learning theory. The questions cause the students to reflect on what they did and act in a cyclic process in response to the learning situation and what they learned.

Table 1. What, so what, now what with guiding questions [8]

Reflective category	Guiding questions
What?	What did I do? What was the assigned task?
So What?	What did I learn from this experience? What was the importance and/or significance of my discovered learning?
Now What?	How can I use the learning in the future? What am I prepared and equipped to do as a result of this learning experience?

Roberts and Maor [19] added the theoretical principle of the model in a gateway as an area of the ePortfolio [19]. The gateway may lead to less work for teachers than the method used by Ring et al. [8], but the results from the research show that the student did not engage in the gateway's content [19].

The What? So What? Now What? model is also very similar to a research method by Janosik and Frank [1]. In sessions, the students received copies of the program's learning outcome and were encouraged to develop an orientation toward reflection. The students were encouraged to reflect on their graduate experience, which led to achieving the learning outcomes. Here they should reflect on what they had learned and what they could do due to what they have learned. The students also got to see examples of evidence, based on expected achievements listed in the learning outcome [1].

Several authors also recommend to providing students with ePortfolio examples [19–22]. ePortfolio examples enable students to identify the areas they want to highlight in their ePortfolio [20, 22] and may motivate the students because they can explore the possibilities. Motivation is essential when implementing ePortfolios [10, 11, 23]. Lack of motivation may cause the students not to upload their learning material in the ePortfolio. These students often need to be forced through the course content to uploading the learning material because they do not feel that the ePortfolio has any value [23]. Together with motivation, promoting the ePortfolio to students is essential to succeed with ePortfolios. It is through the promotion that students' basic understanding of the value is created [19]. According to Tosh et al. [10], the effect of promoting the e-portfolio to students when introducing ePortfolio cannot be underestimated. Students need to know what an ePortfolio is, how to use one, and, most important, how it may benefit them [24].

3 Research Method

The methodology chosen for this research is an exploratory case study and is the first cycle in a broader action research. The principle in action research involves steps in an iterative, cyclical process of reflecting on practice, taking action, reflecting, and taking further action [25].

Four student assistants from the second year of an IT education at the Norwegian University of Science and Technology participated. Four students are a small group, but the study identifies only a first draft of necessary support. The goal was to identify what types of support students need when developing ePortfolios for the first time, and how the support should be designed to make students independent when developing ePortfolios.

Data were collected by observation and reflection notes written by the students after developing ePortfolios for the first time. The observation data were collected in a session that lasted for three hours, where four student assistants were to set up their ePortfolio. The observer took notes to identify challenges and had a participant role [26] where the students were free to ask questions and discuss with each other. In the following three weeks, the students continued working on their ePortfolio. After the three weeks, each student wrote a reflection on their experiences of developing ePortfolio using the support material described in the next chapter. The observation and the students' reflection sought to find answers to what worked and what did not work when it comes to the support and the students' overall impression of ePortfolios.

The qualitative data, observation notes, and students' reflections were imported into NVivo for coding and thematic analysis, observation notes, and interview transcripts are easily coded in NVivo. The identification of differences and similarities in the collected data, themes, and categories was completed using NVivo constant comparative. Observation notes and reflection notes were compared before clarifying the meaning of what worked when it comes to the given support and each challenge, identify sub-challenges, and describe potential links between them.

3.1 Case

At the university, the students attend, all the students use the learning management system (LMS) Blackboard, which also offers an integrated ePortfolio. However, when the students graduate, they lose access to Blackboard and their ePortfolio. In this study, we have selected Google sites ePortfolio solution to allow students to continue developing and using their ePortfolio after graduation.

Google Sites offer 10 GB storage for free, and this is far more than other solutions. The one closest to Google Sites is WordPress, which provides 3 GB for free. Google Sites has strong integration with Google Docs and YouTube and allows students to add all kinds of formats as artifacts that do not contribute to the storage limit. This possibility lacks for MyPortfolio, WordPress and FolioSpace. When it comes to ownership and lifelong access, Google Sites is the winner. The ePortfolio is owned by the learner indefinitely, thus encouraging lifelong learning and reflective practice. Google Sites is also easier to learn and use than WordPress. MyPortfolio and Foliospace. Ease of use is a favorable towards the usefulness of the system and, positively affects the acceptance of Google Sites [22]. Based on the benefits Google Sites holds as described above and the usability and ease of use [11], the ePortfolio solution offered through Google Sites is selected for this project.

The Support Processes. The session started with introducing the ePortfolio, focusing on promoting the ePortfolio and motivating the students to develop ePortfolio [19, 23, 24]. The students were informed what an ePortfolio is and why the ePortfolio could be of value for them [2, 6, 7, 10]. After the introduction, carried out by the researcher, the students were given a combination of three different types of support material. Figure 1 illustrates the support process and the combination of support material. The students had access to the support material throughout the session and the following three weeks. The introduction was followed up with a tutorial video that explained step-by-step how to set up an ePortfolio with Google Sites. Next, the students were given links to ePortfolio examples, which included one made for this purpose. The ePortfolio made for this purpose was created with Google Sites and contained artifacts and content relevant to IT-education. The ePortfolio consisted of two pages, were the first one introduced the owner, and the second one had a selection of artifacts with associated reflections. The other ePortfolio examples had the same setup but consisted of more than two pages and more detailed information as they were developed throughout a study program.

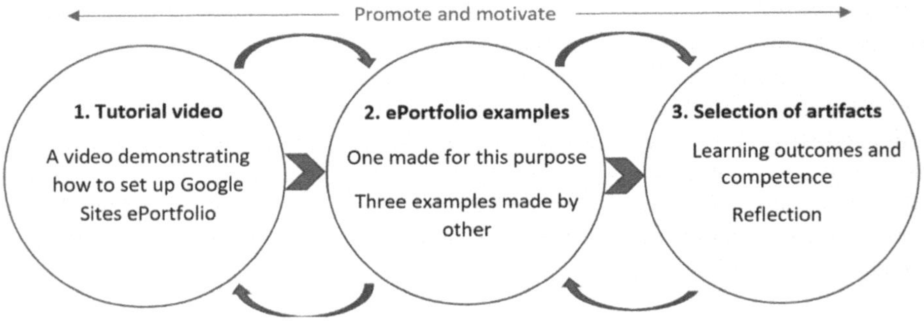

Fig. 1. Support process

Then the students started to build their ePortfolio, and for this, they watched the tutorial video and the ePortfolio examples. The students could design the page the way they wanted. However, a minimum requirement was that it should contain two pages. The first one should consist of a presentation of themselves, and on the second, the artifacts and the associated reflections.

For the selection of artifacts, the document explained how competence listed in the learning outcomes can be linked to the courses and how they can link the work they have done to the competence. This part of the document included three examples with different competencies from the learning outcomes in a course. The document also included the What? So What? Now What? model, described by Ring et al. [8], and an example of an artifact with a reflection.

4 Results

4.1 The Introduction

According to the students' reflection notes and the observation, the students were motivated to start developing ePortfolios for the first time. They actively participated with questions during the promotion and was eager to get started. One student asked an open question during the promotion, where the student wondered why they had not been informed about ePortfolio earlier during their university studies.

However, in one of the students' reflections, it appears that it is uncertain whether the student will continue to develop the ePortfolio:

"There are very few in the computer industry that uses e-portfolio today. If there is nothing a future employer is interested in, I am unsure if I will continue working on my ePortfolio." The other students, on the other hand, perceived the ePortfolio more useful to themselves and pointed out that they would continue develop their ePortfolio after this project. Some comments from the students' reflection notes:

> *"This is something that all students should be familiar with from the beginning of the education so that it is possible to collect experiences and competencies acquired during the study period continuously."*

> *"This was an amazing experience, the ePortfolio forced me to reflect on what I have done. I have not thought that is useful, but it is and especially when I look for a job after graduation.*"

ePortfolio Technology. The observation revealed that the students actively used the tutorial video and the ePortfolio examples while setting up their ePortfolios They went back to the tutorial video several times and the ePortfolio examples while setting up their ePortfolios. The usefulness of the tutorial video and the ePortfolio examples and the fact that they had access to this simultaneously as they developed the ePortfolios were also mentioned in one of the students' reflections:

" The tutorial video and the examples helped me a lot at the beginning, and it was useful to have it available so that I could go back and look when I needed to. All in all, I think it is an ingenious and easy-to-manage tool for creating an ePortfolio. The layout is excellent, and it was easy to add new elements to the page."

One challenge occurred when students were to add artifacts. They managed to organize them in a folder in Google Docs, but the artifacts were not visible in the ePortfolio when they signed out of Google. Those who visit the ePortfolio will thus not be able to see the artifacts. No support material addressed this challenge, but the students managed to solve the problem together by discussing and trying out different ways. The observation shows that although the students eventually solved the challenge, it required time and effort. The students' time and effort to solve this challenge were also mentioned in their reflection, and one of the students wrote:

"When we managed to solve it, we found out that it was easy, but it would have saved us time if this was explained in the video or in any of the other supporting material we received in the session."

Competence and Artifacts. The students find the document *Selection of artifacts* to be useful when it comes to writing a reflection. Still, the students found it challenging to find work done throughout the education linked to competencies without further support. The students 'reflections and the observation show that it is challenging for them to select appropriate artifacts. In particular, it was challenging without an understanding of the meaning of the term competence. One student pointed out in the reflection that they have many theoretical subjects and that theoretical subjects do not result in any competencies. The observation revealed that the students spent much time discussing what was meant by competence when trying to select artifacts evidencing achieved competencies. Eventually there was a need to explain what was meant by competence so that they would not spend more time of the session to understand the concept of competence. When they finally understood what was meant with competence, the process of selecting artifacts became somewhat easier. All the students argued in the reflections why it was difficult for them to select artifacts. Example from one of the students' reflection:

"*I did not understand what was meant by competence, and therefore it became difficult for me to select work that proved my competencies. It became easier when explained what was meant by competence. Without having it explained, I think it would have been challenging for us.*"

The students did not face any challenges when writing reflections based on the guidance in the document. On the other hand, it is evident from the observation that the students initially did not understand the reflection's purpose. After they had written it, they understood the purpose, and at this point, the student also started to see the value of developing an ePortfolio. As one of the students said: "*I don't think the reflection would have had the same effect if I were to reflect on previous work without putting it together as we did in the ePortfolio.*"

5 Discussion and Implications

This study investigates types of support students need when developing ePortfolios for the first time and how the support should be designed to make students independent when developing ePortfolios. The challenge the students faced, the shortcomings of the support the students received and how this may be addressed are discussed in this chapter.

5.1 The Promotion

In our study, the students' reflection revealed that ePortfolio promotion has an essential role when it comes to the students' decisions whether to continue developing their ePortfolio through their education. The observation revealed that the students were motivated to start developing their ePortfolio. However, one student's reflection revealed that not all the students were motivated to continue working on the ePortfolio. The ePortfolio was evaluated against potential employers' interest, and not one's own value, hence the lack of motivation to continue developing the ePortfolio. There may be several reasons why employers do not ask to see a job seeker's ePortfolio, such as not knowing this opportunity for students to show what they can. ePortfolio can be shown to a potential employer without being asked for, for example when those who apply for a job are asked about competence or how they have solved challenges. As Alexiou et al. [2] point out, an ePortfolio can make the previously unseen visible to employers. It might be that the explanation in the introduction was to general, making distinction between own value and the ePortfolio as a showcase vague. This may indicate that there should be a clear distinction between the own value of developing an ePortfolio and that own value should be given more focus than how the ePortfolio can be used as a showcase. It is through the promotion that students' basic understanding of value can be created according Roberts and Maor [19]. In our study, it has been found that motivation arises when the students understand the value. However, it will be essential that all the students understand the value when implementing ePortfolio.

5.2 Technological and Pedagogical Challenges

The students frequently looked at the tutorial video and the ePortfolio examples while setting up their ePorfolios and managed to set them up without further support. Compared to the sessions used by, e.g., Ring et al. [8] with the same goal, the tutorial video, and the ePortfolio examples may lead to less workload for teachers when introducing ePortfolios. The students found the ePortfolio examples useful, and mostly they looked at the one developed for this purpose. When it comes to the tutorial video, the students also found this very useful when setting up the ePortfolio. However, the video did not provide any support when it comes to making artifacts in the ePortfolio visible to visitors. It may be appropriate to add a document in the supporting material that considers the technological challenge. Alexiou et al. [2] recommend that support is guided by both technological and pedagogical considerations. The document *Selection of artifacts* is more of a pedagogical nature. Providing students with two documents, one with pedagogical support and the other with technological support, may create a clear and positive distance between those two. Maybe it can also be an advantage considering the length of the document if operating with one document. Not all students may experience the same challenges. Suppose some students do not meet any technological challenges but find it challenging to select artifacts. In that case, they will not have to read a document that also supports technological challenges and vice versa.

One challenge of a more pedagogical nature occurred when it was time for the students to select artifacts that demonstrated their competencies. Both the observation and the students' reflection revealed that the students did not understand what was meant by the term competence. There may be several reasons for this (e.g. different terms are used in their everyday language), but it became essential to explain for the students the definition of competence. Findings in the study described in this paper demonstrate the importance of defining competence for the context in which it is used, as recommended by Kennedy et al. [15]. The students need to understand what is meant by competence, especially against the student's expectations related to the learning outcome. When they understood what was meant by competencies, it became less challenging for them to select artifacts among their previous work assignments.

The document *Selection of artifacts* support the students well with the writing of reflections. It can be argued that reflection alone with the use of the What? So what? Now what? model towards work carried out in education will lead to the same result as ePortfolios. Our study points to the combination of selecting artifacts, reflecting on them, and putting them together in an ePortfolio as essential. The students who participated in this research point out that this process was what made the invisible visible. This may indicate that the ePortfolios itself supports Kolb's experiential learning theory [18] and takes the theory a step further because of the ability to put experiences and reflections together in a more practical direction.

However, different results may be obtained by a different sample from another field. The students in this research have high experience using computers and using different kinds of digital technology, systems, and applications. This may be a limitation in the research. Students who lack this experience possibly face other challenges than the students in our research. Another limitation may be that the students in this research are student assistants. They are interested in this kind of work and are getting paid for it. One can assume that the enthusiasm these students show is higher than for students who do not receive such incentives. On the other hand, this research is mainly about identifying appropriate support for beginners, and none of the student assistants have previous ePortfolio experience. Finally, a small group of students participated. Therefore, it is essential not to make strong conclusions, whether the results are positive or not. Instead, data from this research should be used to design more extensive confirmatory studies.

6 Conclusion

The goal of this research was to find answers to what types of support students need when developing ePortfolio for the first time, and how to design the support to make students independent when developing ePortfolios.

Three types of support material were identified through relevant literature as essential: tutorial videos, ePortfolio examples and descriptive documents. Even though the student received such support material, they still encountered some challenges. Three main challenges were identified as not adequately addressed: students' value of developing ePortfolio, an explanation of what is meant by competence in an educational context, and how to make artifacts visible.

In addition, the support was identified as a process with the goal of promoting ePortfolio in a way that motivates students to develop ePortfolios and to continue to develop them through education. The promotion is complex and requires the presence of a teacher or another who is engaged in ePortfolios. This research indicate that students may be capable of developing ePortfolio without support from teachers or others engaged in ePortfolios. However, the promotion cannot be left to the support material.

Another conclusion drawn from this research is that challenges may vary from challenges identified in other similar studies, as this study shows when it comes to students' understanding of competence. The conclusions driven from this research are not strong conclusions, but rather a way of identifying what kind of support students need as a starting point before trying out the support among a larger group of students.

Acknowledgements. Birgit Rognebakke Krogstie provided valuable comments on draft versions of the paper.

References

1. Janosik, S.M., Frank, T.E.: Using ePortfolios to measure student learning in a graduate preparation program in higher education. Int. J. ePortfolio **3**(1), 13–20 (2013)
2. Alexiou, A., Paraskeva, F.: Inspiring key competencies through the implementation of an ePortfolio for undergraduate students. Procedia Soc. Behav. Sci. **197**, 2435–2442 (2015). https://doi.org/10.1016/j.sbspro.2015.07.307
3. Okoro, E.A., Washington, M.C., Cardon, P.W.: Eportfolios in business communication courses as tools for employment. Bus. Commun. Quart. **74**(3), 347–351 (2011). https://doi.org/10.1177/1080569911414554
4. Blevins, S., Brill, J.: Enabling systemic change: creating an ePortfolio implementation framework through design and development research for use by higher education professionals. Int. J. Teach. Learn. High. Educ. **29**(2), 216–232 (2017)
5. Johnsen, H.: Making learning visible with ePortfolios: coupling the right pedagogy with the right technology. Int. J. ePortfolio **2**(2), 139–148 (2012)
6. Chang, C.-C., Liang, C., Liao, Y.-M.: Using e-portfolio for learning goal setting to facilitate self-regulated learning of high school students. Behav. Inf. Technol. **37**(12), 1237–1251 (2018). https://doi.org/10.1080/0144929X.2018.1496275
7. Donnelly, R., OKeeffe, M.: Exploration of ePortfolios for adding value and deepening student learning in contemporary higher education. Int. J. ePortfolio **3**(1), 1–11 (2013)
8. Ring, G., Waugaman, C., Brackett, B.: The value of career ePortfolios on job applicant performance: using data to determine effectiveness. Int. J. ePortfolio **2**(1), 225–236 (2017)
9. Poole, P., et al.: Challenges and supports towards the integration of ePortfolios in education. Heliyon **4**(11), e00899 (2018). Lessons to be learned from Ireland
10. Tosh, D., et al.: Engagement with electronic portfolios: challenges from the student perspective. Can. J. Learn. Technol./La revue canadienne de l'apprentissage et de la technologie **31**(3), 1–17 (2005). https://doi.org/10.21432/T23W31
11. Shroff, R.H., Deneen, C.C., Ng, E.M.: Analysis of the technology acceptance model in examining students' behavioural intention to use an e-portfolio system. Australas. J. Educ. Technol. **27**(4), 600–661 (2011). https://doi.org/10.14742/ajet.940
12. Biggs, J.: Aligning Teaching for Constructing Learning, vol. 32, pp. 347–364. Higher Education Academy, New York (1996). https://doi.org/10.1007/BF00138871
13. European Commission/EACEA/Eurydice: The European Higher Education Area in 2018: Bologna Process Implementation. Publications Office of the European Union, Luxembourg (2018)
14. Westera, W.: Competences in education: a confusion of tongues. J. Curriculum Stud. **33**(1), 75–78 (2001). https://doi.org/10.1080/00220270120625
15. Kennedy, D., Hyland, A., Ryan, N.: Learning outcomes and competencies. In: Best of the Bologna Handbook, vol. 33, pp. 59–76. DUZ International, Berlin, German (2009)
16. Frezza, S., et al.: Modelling competencies for computing education beyond 2020: a research based approach to defining competencies in the computing disciplines. In: Proceedings Companion of the 23rd Annual ACM Conference on Innovation and Technology in Computer Science Education, New York, NY, USA, pp. 148–174 (2018). https://dl.acm.org/doi/10.1145/3293881.3295782

17. Cedefop: Defining, writing and applying learning outcome: a European Handbook, Publications Office of the European Union, Luxembourg (2017). https://www.cedefop.europa.eu/en/publications-and-resources/publications/4156
18. Kolb, D.A.: Experiential Learning Experience as the Source of Learning and Development. 2nd edn. Pearson Education, Inc, New Jersey (1984)
19. Roberts, P., Maor, D.: ePortfolios to scaffold the development of reflective practice in bachelor of education Students. In: World conference on E-Learning in Corporate, Government, Healthcare, and Higher Education (ELEARN), Montreal, Canada, pp. 1274—1279 (2012)
20. Parkes, K.A., Dredger, S., Hicks, D.: ePortfolio as a measure of reflective practice. Int. J. ePortfolio **3**(2), 99–115 (2013)
21. Ring, G., Ramirez, B.: Implementing ePortfolios for the assessment of general education competencies. Int. J. ePortfolio **2**(1), 87–97 (2012)
22. Ciesielkiewicz, M.: The use of e-portfolios in higher education: from the students' perspective. Issues Educ. Res. **29**(3), 649–667 (2019)
23. Hanum, S.R., et al.: ePortfolio: a descriptive survey for contents and challenges. Int. J. Emerg. Technol. Learn. (iJET) **11**(01), 4–10 (2016). http://dx.doi.org/10.3991/ijet.v11i01.4900
24. St Jorre, T., Oliver, B.: Want students to engage? Contextualise graduate learning outcomes and assess for employability. High. Educ. Res. Dev. **37**(1), 44–57 (2018). https://doi.org/10.1080/07294360.2017.1339183
25. Cohen, L., ManionL, L., Morrison, K.: Research methods in education, 8th edn. Routledge, New York (2018)
26. Cotton, D.R., Stokes, A., Cotton, P.A.: Using observational methods to research the student experience. J. Geogr. High. Educ. **34**(3), 463–473 (2010). https://doi.org/10.1080/03098265.2010.501541

Student-Centered Graduate STEM Education Integrated by Computing: An Insight into the Experiences and Expectations of Doctoral Students

Vladimiras Dolgopolovas(✉), Valentina Dagienė, and Tatjana Jevsikova

Vilnius University Institute of Educational Sciences, Universiteto Street 9, 01513 Vilnius, Lithuania
{vladimiras.dolgopolovas,valentina.dagiene, tatjana.jevsikova}@mif.vu.lt

Abstract. Graduate education system is in the process of ongoing changes driven by the employers' requirements, ongoing demographic changes, changes in students' career expectations and the new vision of a wider scientific enterprise. There is a need to refocus graduate educational system from the needs of the academic institution and related research towards student-centered paradigm. The purpose of this research is to analyze the practice of STEM doctoral studies from the student-centered perspective by examining a case practice from a doctoral educational event. The paper deals with the questions whether the aims and expectations of graduate students are consistent with the goals and requirements of academics (researchers and teaching staff of higher education) and to what extent; what aspects of academic policy and pedagogical approaches correspond to the needs and requirements of the non-academic and innovative industries; and how the students understand their career prospects in terms of innovation, future job requirements, and knowledge-based entrepreneurship requests. In order to address this problem, a case study was conducted in four dimensions: academia, pedagogy, industry and entrepreneurship. As a result, a qualitative study provided several implications for organizations preparing future researchers and employees. The results show which students' needs, challenges and problems and relevant requirements for academic institutions are related to the prospects of STEM education with an emphasis on computing (computer science) and software engineering as an integrating part.

Keywords: Student-centered education · Doctoral education · STEM education

1 Introduction

STEM (Science, Technology, Engineering, and Mathematics) movement has been transforming education on different levels: from early pre-school years to graduate education. This transformation is driven towards the holistic view on educational subjects in combination with project-based and student-centered teaching and learning methodology.

K. Kori and M. Laanpere (Eds.): ISSEP 2020, LNCS 12518, pp. 221–232, 2020.
https://doi.org/10.1007/978-3-030-63212-0_18

While computer science and software engineering education is usually seen as a part of Engineering education, it can be considered as an interconnecting, integrating part of all the STEM components [1–3].

Successful STEM education in schools depends on the processes in research, industry and other areas and, accordingly, on preparation of students at all educational levels. In this paper, we discuss the need of change in doctoral studies (also called graduate or post-graduate studies) in STEM subjects. Graduate studies are usually classified into one main research area, however, the application of research may cover more fields that correspond to the STEM idea.

Graduate educational system is in the process of ongoing transformation driven by the changes in employers' requirements, ongoing demographic changes, changes in students' career expectations and a new vision of a wider scientific enterprise. As stated in the report on STEM education in the U.S., "many graduate programs do not adequately prepare students to translate their knowledge into impact in multiple careers" [4]. There is a need to refocus graduate educational system from the needs of the academic institutions and related research towards a student-focused paradigm [5]. This includes opportunities for students to communicate their work and understand its broader impacts, encouraging them to create their own project-based learning opportunities, giving students time to explore diverse career options, and helping them identify advisors and mentors who can best support their academic careers development [4, 6].

Are there any strategical goals for graduate education other than promoting students' careers in academia? (In this paper, the term "academia" is used as "the environment or community, usually university, concerned with the pursuit of research, education, and scholarship"). We advocate a shift for graduate STEM education to pay the major attention on students' needs and expectations by (i) providing opportunities for wide communication and sharing research results within academic institutions as well as with broader communities and industry, (ii) understanding the impact of students' research on local community and society, (iii) inspiring students with their own learning style and project-based learning opportunities, (iv) introducing various career options and (v) support students with the best suited advising and mentoring opportunities.

Such rearrangement should be based on a holistic vision of academic educational system and its impact. Furthermore, the rearrangement should include refocusing of academic policy, educational and pedagogical approaches at understanding the landscape of the future technological changes, innovations and working places, providing requirements for future career and entrepreneurship opportunities. Current learners should comply with the new digital society requirements, such as self-fulfillment, societal needs [7], creativity, collaboration and communication [8] in pursuance to stay competitive in market and guarantee employability. At the same time, the focus on entrepreneurship carrier opportunities provide requirements for related major competences such as ability to be creative, innovative, generate knowledge, and share with other STEM professionals and organizations – by having a clear strategic approach toward technology change, faster adoption of technology and business changes.

It is still a challenge to reduce the gap between industry and academia. To this end, multiple solutions have been proposed, such as new teaching approaches implementations, policy changes, societal needs analysis, an educational reform movement, such as

STEM [9]. STEM is also considered as an educational approach that consists of Science, Technology, Engineering and Mathematics disciplines and enhances students' inquiry skills, problem solving skills, computational thinking, and creative thinking [10].

The rest of the paper is organized as follows. We continue the discussion of the problem in the next section based on the literature review and describe methodology of our study. Then we present the results of a case study: an initiative of annual International Doctoral Consortium on Informatics Education and Educational Software Engineering Research as education activity for STEM graduate education and results of interviews with doctoral students. Finally, we discuss the results, draw conclusions and provide limitations and directions for future research.

2 Problem Statement and Methodology

Traditional measures of research productivity are the number of academic researchers being produced and the number of research papers published, but place much less emphasis on the quality of teaching and mentorship that students receive [5].

There is a vision/hypothesis that many students after doctoral/PhD graduation pursue non-academic careers, a vision which is not always supported inside the academia. Furthermore, graduate students are often treated as inexpensive skilled labor – researchers and undergraduates' teachers [4]. The reason of this is mostly due to non-conformity of industry and academia goals. Another question to study and hypothesis to test is the doctoral students' understanding of the requirements for future and non-academic professions in terms of innovations [11], innovations focused social [12, 13], knowledge-based [14, 15], digital [16, 17] and academic entrepreneurship [18–21], and prospective requirements for working places [22, 23]: is such knowledge and understanding relevant and properly supported in academia?

The **aim** of this research is to analyze the practice of STEM doctoral education from the student-centered perspective. The **questions** we address are the following. Do aims and expectations of doctoral students correspond to goals and requirements of academics and to what extent? Which aspects of academia policy and pedagogical approaches correspond to the needs and requirements in a non-academic and innovative industry sectors? How do students understand their career prospects in terms of innovations, future work-places requirements, and requests for knowledge based entrepreneurship?

Based on the synthesis of insights and reasoning presented in [5, 14, 24, 25] the problem of our study is analyzed in four dimensions:

1. **Academia:** Current policies focused on student-centered educational needs, support from within and outside of academia.
2. **Pedagogy:** Student-centered approaches and graduate students as individuals with diverse needs and challenges from educational perspective.
3. **Industry:** Students' career perspectives and understanding through creativity, expertise and innovation.
4. **Entrepreneurship:** Opportunities, awareness, and motivation for knowledge-based entrepreneurship.

In order to analyze the conformity of industry and academia experiences and expectations on STEM doctoral graduates' career ambitions and current situation (what academic offers, what industry needs), a case study research on international level is performed. At this stage, seven doctoral students from three countries (Hungary, Ukraine, Austria), participants of the International Doctoral Consortium on Informatics Education and Educational Software Engineering Research presented in the next section, have been interviewed using structural interview methodology.

3 Research Context: An Initiative of the International Doctoral Consortium

The International Doctoral Consortium on Informatics Education and Educational Software Engineering Research is an annual event, organized since 2010 by the Vilnius University Institute of Data Science and Digital Technologies and Institute of Educational Sciences in cooperation with Lithuanian Computer Society. The Doctoral Consortium provides an opportunity for doctoral students to explore and develop their research interests in a workshop under the guidance of distinguished senior researchers. The Doctoral Consortium is designed primarily for students who are being enrolled in any stage of doctoral studies with a focus on informatics (computer science)/software engineering/computing education research. Every year, and especially in 2019, the Consortium turns to be a non-formal STEM graduate studies event, as topics of participating doctoral students go beyond solely computer science or software engineering, and integrate several STEM (or, more precisely, STEAM, as "education" can stand for "Arts") disciplines (see Table 1 for students' dissertation field distribution).

Table 1. Research fields of the surveyed doctoral students.

Student no.	Primary research field	Secondary research field
1	Software engineering	Education
2	Software engineering	Education
3	Mathematics	Physics
4	Software engineering	Physics, mathematics
5	Mathematics	Physics
6	Computer science	Education
7	Computer science	Mathematics

The Consortium is designed as a student-centered event and offers:

- Friendly forum for doctoral students to discuss their research topics, research questions and design in the field of their research;

- Supportive setting for feedback on students' current research and guidance on future research directions;
- Comments and fresh perspectives for each student on his/her work from researchers and students outside their own institution, as well as help with choosing suitable methodology and strategies for research;
- Support networking with other researchers in the informatics engineering education research field, and promote the development of a supportive community of scholars and a spirit of collaborative research;
- Support a new generation of researchers with information and advice on research and academic career paths.

This event is attended annually by 12–18 doctoral students, and at least 6 senior researchers representing several countries who give lectures and work with small doctoral student groups. The methodology used in the Doctoral Consortium is project-based: going through methodological stages, students develop posters of their research project; and share and discuss their project with the Consortium's community.

4 Results

In this section we present results of interview with seven participants of the Doctoral Consortium held during December 2019 in Druskininkai, Lithuania.

The classification of STEM research topics of surveyed participants is presented in Table 1 (as the classification of research fields differ in various countries and universities, we classified the doctoral topic according to its actual research problem).

The responses are classified according to the four dimensions we mentioned in the previous sections.

4.1 Academia Dimension

Academia dimension explores current policies focused on student-centered educational need with support from within and outside of academia. Hypotheses (propositions) and interview questions are presented in Table 2.

A summary of the findings: (1) In terms of university activities (jobs), not related to doctoral thesis, most of the respondents indicated that they take part in such activities. These activities for some students are implemented on a voluntary basis and include: project work, cultural activities of the university, lecturing and engineering. Students, whose doctoral thesis topic is related with education (see Table 1), give part-time lectures for the university they study at; (2) Current occupation and future career question showed that doctoral students mostly work (in addition to their doctoral studies) in industry, e.g. as software developers, and see their future career in industry as well; (3) Possible application of the doctoral research area in industry is clearly perceived by most of respondents; (4) The goal of pursuing doctoral level studies vary between the countries. Some believe it will positively affect their future career in industry while some indicated it as the obligatory criteria for possible work in academic environment.

Table 2. Hypotheses and questions of the structured interview for Academia dimension.

No.	Hypothesis/proposition	Interview questions
1	Graduate students are still too often seen as being primarily sources of inexpensive skilled labor	Do you take part in any activity of the university that is not directly related to the topic of your doctoral dissertation? What type (teaching, research, etc.)? What amount of time (hours per week)? Is it formal? If so, why you take part in it? Are you satisfied with this additional activity?
2	Most students now pursue non-academic careers	What is your main occupation at the moment? Do you have formal employment contract, if so, in what area? What is your vision for your future career (teaching/research/industry/public sector/self-employed/etc./do not know)?
3	Many graduate programs are not preparing students adequately to succeed in a variety of careers: employers are finding many recent graduates overly naïve about research and development activities in government and industry	What types of industry/public sectors related to your research topic you know? Do you know about research/innovation activities they conduct? Do you think your research area/topic could be relevant or interested to apply in that industry/public institutions?

4.2 Pedagogy Dimension

The second dimension, Pedagogy, focuses on student-centered approaches and graduate students as individuals with diverse needs and challenges from an educational perspective (hypotheses and questions asked are presented in Table 3).

A summary of the findings: (1) The current doctoral curriculum evaluation in terms of personal respondents' development is quite positive with the positive impact of curriculum providing opportunities for professional skills development, such as, programming, making presentations, foreign language. However, the improvement could be made in curriculum by covering society aspects and soft skills, as it mostly focuses on engineering and science relationship aspects; (2) Only some respondents pointed out that science should have social value besides the scientific one and that research should benefit the society; (3) Regarding commercial value and value for doctoral education on the whole, the experience on participating in seminars on career perspectives from industries and organizations was indicated as valuable for professional development by respondents but not highly important; (4) Most of the students think that valuable and important experience is mentoring or advising others as it allows to improve communication and management skills, is good experience and practice, and allows to feel satisfaction on personal achievements, such as self-efficiency on being a good mentor and teacher.

Table 3. Hypotheses and questions of the structured interview for Pedagogy dimension.

No.	Hypothesis/proposition	Interview questions
1	There is a shift from the current system that focuses primarily on the needs of institutions of higher education to one that is student-centered, placing focus on graduate students as individuals with diverse needs and challenges	How can you evaluate your current doctoral curriculum in terms of your personal development? Does your institution provide you an opportunity to adjust the curriculum to suit your personal preferences?
2	Students encounter a variety of points of view about the nature, scope, and substance of the scientific enterprise and about the relationships between science, engineering, and society, and they would be encouraged to understand and grapple with differences of opinion, experiences, and ideas as part of their graduate education and training	How can you evaluate your current doctoral curriculum in terms of covering relationships between science, engineering, and society? Do you think these aspects are important/relevant for the curriculum?
3	Students have opportunities to communicate the results of their work and to understand the broader impacts of their research. This includes the ability to present their work and have exposure to audiences outside of their department, ranging from peers in other departments to the broader scientific community and nontechnical audiences. Students also understand and learn to consider ethical and cultural issues surrounding their work, as well as the broader needs of society	What is your experience about communication with your colleagues/mates/community outside of your department? Do you think these aspects are important/relevant for the curriculum? Do you think your colleagues/peers/community members who are not directly related to your research topic could help improve your current research/future career prospects?
4	Students are encouraged to create their own project-based learning opportunities—ideally as a member of a team—as a means of developing transferable professional skills such as communication, collaboration, management, and entrepreneurship. Experiences where students "learn by doing," rather than simply learn by lecturing and coursework, would be the norm	Does your curriculum include professional skills training such as communication, collaboration and management skills? What are your expectations regarding the commercial value of your research?

4.3 Industry Dimension

The third dimension, Industry, explores students career perspectives and understanding through creativity, expertise and innovation (Table 4). One of the aims was to identify the understanding of the relation of creativity and innovation to the research that the respondents are doing.

Table 4. Hypotheses and questions of the structured interview for Industry dimension.

No.	Hypothesis/proposition	Interview questions
1	Both innovation workers and knowledge workers adhere to the idea that only a postgraduate education, such as a Master's or a doctorate, can ensure a good job in the future, i.e., they believe such an education is necessary in order to be successful	Why you decided to continue your education on a doctoral level? Do you think that doctorate will support your future? If so, in what sense? What are your career perspectives? What is your vision of success?
2	One of the results of globalization is that companies have realized that creativity, expertise and innovation are the new competitive parameters. Profit relies heavily on businesses being able to bring creativity and innovation to the market (including long tail marketing strategy)	Do you think creativity is important? How do you understand the meaning of being creative? Do you think creativity is related to innovations and in what sense?
3	Education in the global economy has become a commodity in line with other commodities. Thus, in the future, the quality, brand and reputation of educational institutions will be given greater emphasis. This will result in an increased emphasis on the ranking of educational institutions – that is to say, students from the best universities will be given more opportunities in their working lives	Do you know the ranking of your educational institution (country/world)? What is opinion about the importance of the ranking for the educational institution on the whole? What was the importance of ranking while selecting your institution (did you choose your study program because of university rankings or the relevance of the study program, etc.)?
4	A characteristic of the innovation worker is that he or she is extremely connected in social networks. In the global knowledge economy, the office of the innovation worker and the knowledge worker will be wherever they happen to have access to their digital technology	What is your attitude to the practice of a social networking? What is your social networking experience? Do you think social networking will help you with your career prospects?

A summary of the findings: (1) Respondents think that innovations require creativity. The aim of their research is innovation in the form of: new solutions and combinations of approaches, gaining new results, and technology applications in new context. They believe that (1) Research in general is innovation based and is supported by a creative idea or by applying technology in a new context and way; (2) The most important factor is the ability to implement ideas in practice; (3) The importance of education institution ranking was indicated only by two respondents; others stated that the ranking had no influence on institution selection; the majority of respondents stated that the reputation of institution made no impact on former graduate students' careers according to the former students'; (4) Some of the respondents indicated that entrepreneurship is an important experience and has some role in innovation development. The direct research application in emerging technologies was noticed by more than a half of the respondents. They see the connection to 5G Mobile technology, artificial intelligence, machine learning, augmented reality, autonomous cars, nanotechnologies, and block chains. These new technologies provide various opportunities for improvement research and incorporating various forms of innovations-based entrepreneurship; (5) Only some of respondents were familiar with entrepreneurial management and three were familiar with risk management topic (which is related with the fourth dimension). One respondent noted the importance of harnessing the abilities of entrepreneurial and risk management, as without them, most start-up cases fail; (6) Analysis of responses showed that doctoral students mostly work (in addition to their educational activities) at industry and see their future career in industry as well. Some respondents indicated that they try to combine their research or teaching activities and work in industry. Most respondents highlighted that even when their working activities are not related to their doctoral topic, they consider them as important, as their involvement into these activities develops generic competencies, such as teamwork, communication and collaboration. Mostly, the current assessment criteria of respondents' educational results are the number of publications in peer-reviewed scientific journals. The doctoral curriculum was rated as moderate by a number of respondents. Some respondents stated the problem that the curriculum does not include an internship, as it could help keeping an open mind and making new connections inside and also outside the research area. Moreover, the procedure on some changes (e.g. the topic change) are not well regulated; (7) Respondents also agree that doctoral curriculum is covering relationships between science and engineering, but there is a lack or no focus on society, and this is a problem as the overall goal of research is to provide some benefit for the society. Respondents indicated that there is a need for collaboration between academics working on different fields as it could lead to many improvements in both research and work. One of the challenges is a lack of management skills training which is important for the promotion of research results; (8) In terms of doctoral degree for career perspectives, the respondents' opinions split into two directions: doctorate supports future career also in industry, and doctorate supports future career only in academia. Most of the students believe that creativity is related to innovation and is a very important skill in science and needs to be improved and used throughout life. They believe that research in general is innovation based and is supported by a creative idea or by applying technology in a new context and way. Moreover, the most important factor is the ability to implement ideas in practice. Some of the respondents indicated that entrepreneurship is an important experience, and has some role in innovation development.

4.4 Entrepreneurship Dimension

Career and Entrepreneurship dimension explores the opportunities, awareness, and motivation for knowledge-based entrepreneurship. Hypotheses and interview questions presented in Table 5.

A summary of the findings: (1) In terms of doctoral level for career perspectives the respondents' opinions splits into two directions: doctorate supports future career also in industry, and doctorate supports future career only in academia. Additionally, they were asked to define the vision of success. The answers vary but the focus was on the being able to do the things you want and realize your own ideas which makes you

Table 5. Hypotheses and questions of the structured interview for Entrepreneurship dimension.

No.	Hypothesis/proposition	Interview questions
1	In this connected world, for organizations and individuals to stay competitive, they must speed up the process of creating value-added knowledge and share it at a rapid pace. Our ability to be creative, innovative and generate knowledge, and share with others have amplified many fold owing to the Internet with numerous repositories and information platforms	How do you understand creativity in relation to your topic/occupation? What does creativity mean to you? Could you describe your research/research results as innovative? In what aspects? Do you plan to share your research results? If so, how practically are you going to do this? Do your research/ research results have a direct/indirect impact, related or will apply in emerging technologies?
2	Knowledge economy will continue to evolve societies and bring economic prosperity in decades to come. It means for individuals having a focus on continuous education, understand, learn and embrace technologies, and cultivate entrepreneurial mind set and approach toward new opportunities that knowledge-economy brings	How do you understand the importance and role of entrepreneurship? Do you have any business experience? Have you entered/plan to enter any business/entrepreneurial courses/training programs? Do you think your research results have any commercial value? If so, do you have any plans/expectations/opportunities regarding the commercialization of the results of your research?

feel happy. One student stated that success is the ability to combine different aspects, such as professional grow, emotions, personal life success. Most of the doctoral students believe that creativity is related to innovation and is a very important skill in science and needs to be improved and used throughout life; (2) For communication with graduates and researchers, the respondents use social networks. They believe social networking is useful for career and connections maintenance. Thus, most of the respondents regularly improve and enlarge their networks; (3) In terms of level of connections, the responses showed that relationship with academia staff and colleagues are good in most cases as well as attitude to team work.

5 Discussion and Conclusion

This research provides insights into STEM graduate education adaptation to students' needs in concern with industry needs and evolution, not only of academia. The Doctoral Consortium on Informatics Education and Educational Software Engineering Research as one of the activities for student-centered educational events has been presented. The presented qualitative study provided several implications for organizations preparing future researchers and employees, as they showed which students' needs, challenges and problems, as well as relevant requirements for academic institutions, are related to the prospects of STEM 4.0 education, defined here as a student-centered STEM focusing on an industry 4.0 strategy and the corresponding requirements for STEM education. It could be concluded that:

1. Most of the doctoral students already pursue part-time careers in industry. Only a few are planning to combine their future work with research.
2. In order to stay as competitive individuals, the development of abilities to communicate, adapt innovations and implement creative ideas practically for the benefit of the society are crucial.
3. In parallel to the research for their doctoral degree, the students wish to intend to focus on development of soft skills and entrepreneurial skills. To respond to this wish, the academic community should focus on developing students' soft skills, consulting and mentoring students in terms of personal development, managerial and entrepreneurial skills.
4. Professional networking was indicated as important. Universities should provide extended support for students' networking and professional communication at the local and international levels.
5. There is a need for extended support from professional audience and further improvements in aspects related to graduate students' future professional careers.
6. Despite the fact that the innovation focus aspect is partly supported by the academic community, there is a need to further improve the educational programs of doctoral studies with a focus on entrepreneurial management, risk management and entrepreneurial practice in line with the requirements of modern industry.

The research presented in this paper provides a first step towards deeper STEM improvement research for graduate studies. A limitation of this study is the limited group of respondents associated with a doctoral event. In addition, a comparative study of students' expectations and attitudes of academia representatives towards directions of doctoral studies is positioned as future research.

Acknowledgements. This research was funded by Vilnius University, Lithuania. Project funding agreement No. MSF-LMT-7.

References

1. Štuikys, V., Burbaitė, R.: Smart STEM-driven computer science education (2018)
2. Dolgopolovas, V., Dagienė, V., Jevsikova, T.: Methodological guidelines for the design and integration of software learning objects for scientific programming education. Sci. Program. **2020**, 6807515 (2020). https://doi.org/10.1155/2020/6807515
3. Pears, A., Barendsen, E., Dagienė, V., Dolgopolovas, V., Jasutė, E.: Holistic STEAM education through computational thinking: a perspective on training future teachers. In: Pozdniakov, S.N., Dagienė, V. (eds.) ISSEP 2019. LNCS, vol. 11913, pp. 41–52. Springer, Cham (2019). https://doi.org/10.1007/978-3-030-33759-9_4
4. Leshner, A., Scherer, L.: National Academies, N.A. of S., National Academies, N.A. of E., National Academies, N.A. of M.: Graduate STEM Education for the 21st Century. Consensus Study Report (2018)
5. Leshner, A.I.: Student-centered, modernized graduate STEM education. Science **80**, 969–970 (2018). https://doi.org/10.1126/science.aau0590
6. How, J.P.: New STEM and engineering education paradigms [From the Editor]. IEEE Control Syst. Mag. **38**, 3–4 (2018)

7. Digital society index (DSI): human needs in a digital world (2019). https://www.oxfordeconomics.com/recent-releases/digital-society-index-2019-human-needs-in-a-digital-world
8. The future of jobs: employment, skills and workforce strategy for the fourth industrial revolution. In: Global challenge insight report. World Economic Forum, Geneva (2016)
9. Wells, J.G.: STEM education: the potential of technology education. In: The Mississippi Valley Conference in the 21 st Century : Fifteen Years of Influence on Thought and Practice (2019)
10. Psycharis, S.: STEAM in education: a literature review on the role of computational thinking, engineering epistemology and computational science. computational steam pedagogy (CSP). Sci. Cult. **4**, 51–72 (2018)
11. Fowosire, R.A., Idris, O.Y., Elijah, O.: Technopreneurship: a view of technology, innovations and entrepreneurship. Glob. J. Res. Eng. **17** (2017)
12. Agrawal, A., Kumar, P.: Social entrepreneurship and sustainable business models: the case of India (2018)
13. Portales, L., et al.: Social Innovation and Social Entrepreneurship. Fundamentals, Concepts, and Tools. Palgrave Macmillan, Cham (2019)
14. Kabir, M.N.: Knowledge-based social entrepreneurship (2019)
15. Cagica Carvalho, L., Rego, C., Lucas, M.R., Sánchez-Hernández, M.I., Viana, A.B.N. (eds.): New Paths of Entrepreneurship Development: The Role of Education, Smart Cities, and Social Factors. SESCID. Springer, Cham (2019). https://doi.org/10.1007/978-3-319-96032-6
16. Kraus, S., Palmer, C., Kailer, N., Kallinger, F.L., Spitzer, J.: Digital entrepreneurship: a research agenda on new business models for the twenty-first century (2019)
17. Sahut, J.M., Iandoli, L., Teulon, F.: The age of digital entrepreneurship. Small Bus. Econ. (2019). https://doi.org/10.1007/s11187-019-00260-8
18. Siegel, D.S., Wright, M.: Academic entrepreneurship: time for a rethink? Br. J. Manag. (2015). https://doi.org/10.1111/1467-8551.12116
19. Wright, M., Clarysse, B., Mustar, P., Lockett, A.: Academic entrepreneurship in Europe (2007)
20. Peris-Ortiz, M., Gómez, J.A., Merigó-Lindahl, J.M., Rueda-Armengot, C. (eds.): Entrepreneurial Universities: Exploring the Academic and Innovative Dimensions of Entrepreneurship in Higher Education. ITKM. Springer, Cham (2017). https://doi.org/10.1007/978-3-319-47949-1
21. Shepherd, D.A.: The aspiring entrepreneurship scholar: strategies and advice for a successful academic career (2016)
22. Lasi, H., Fettke, P., Kemper, H.-G., Feld, T., Hoffmann, M.: Industry 4.0. Bus. Inf. Syst. Eng. **6**(4), 239–242 (2014). https://doi.org/10.1007/s12599-014-0334-4
23. Lele, A.: Industry 4.0. In: Smart Innovation, Systems and Technologies (2019)
24. Johannessen, J.A.: The workplace of the future: the fourth industrial revolution, the precariat and the death of hierarchies (2018)
25. Sharples, M.: Practical Pedagogy: 40 New Ways to Teach and Learn. Routledge, Abingdon (2019)

Author Index

The manufacturer's authorised representative in the EU is Springer Nature Customer Service Centre GmbH, Europaplatz 3, 69115 Heidelberg, Germany. If you have any concerns regarding our products, please contact ProductSafety@springernature.com

Printed and bound by CPI Group (UK) Ltd, Croydon, CR0 4YY
30/09/2026
02225439-0016